The Fall of
Brad Hawley

The Fall of Brad Hawley

AL BLANTON

ISBN: 0692790349
ISBN 13: 9780692790342
Library of Congress Control Number: 2016916882
White Lab Media, Jasper, AL

This book is dedicated to Alton Lee Blanton

*Some names and identifying details have been changed
to protect the privacy of individuals*

The First Thought

Identity is the hub of our belief system. What we believe about ourselves, who we believe we are, dictates our core beliefs. If we believe we are hopeless wanderers, we will always find ourselves hopelessly wandering. If we believe we are without fault, that we are good without God, we find no need for grace. If we believe we are unforgivable, that our prodigal journey has taken us too far down the perdition road to ever turn back, we will remain lost. If our identity is found in the trappings of the world, its shifting and spoiling will devastate us. If our identity is in Christ, however, we find rest. For unlike imposters vying for our lives, Christ will never leave us. Yet, coming to Christ requires something of us. It requires a humbling.

Part I

*Pride goeth before destruction, and an
haughty spirit before a fall.*

—*PROVERBS 16:18*

*According to Christian teachers, the essential vice, the utmost
evil, is Pride. Unchastity, anger, greed, drunkenness, and
all that, are mere flea bites in comparison: it was through
Pride that the devil became the devil: Pride leads to every
other vice: it is the complete anti-God state of mind...
it is Pride which has been the chief cause of misery in
every nation and every family since the world began.*

—*C. S. LEWIS, MERE CHRISTIANITY*

THE LAST DAY

I once knew Brad Hawley.

That morning he stood in his living room, staring out through the big french doors of his home, his face pressed close to the glass. As he scanned his backyard, there were no children playing, no tromp of bare feet across the freshly sodded lawn, no yardmen performing curlicues with their fat mowers. Alone in his house, his mind roamed in the absolute silence.

He didn't yet miss his wife, who was somewhere in the hard blue above him, on a plane nosing its way through the clouds to Charlotte. His two kids were tucked away at day care, and he thought this time alone was rare and precious.

At the time, his wife, Ellen, was a sales rep for a furniture company, and from time to time, work took her away. Truthfully, the marriage wasn't going well, and Brad wondered if they would make it, or if he cared whether it would survive at all. Things had changed over five years, so Brad thought, and those settling years had eroded the newness, the spontaneity. He was no longer in love, but in work. Every day was a battle. The marriage was like an old house that Brad seemed to be growing out of, growing too big for, a desperate inconvenience holding him back from the man he was becoming.

He walked over to the kitchen and snatched a blueberry protein bar from the shelf. He skinned back the wrapper and tore off a bite. He sat down on the couch and slumped back in it. The flat-screen was turned to ESPN, the volume muted. Toys were strewed like random pebbles across the floor.

He crunched the last bite of the bar, crumpled the wrapper, and flung it onto the coffee table. He opened his laptop. Three new messages.

He sent out a few conciliatory e-mails (though his mind wasn't really on work at all), closed the cover, and checked his watch.

Eleven fourteen.

Hour and a minute.

He walked back to the kitchen and dropped the wrapper into the trash bin and walked down the hall into the bedroom in his socked feet. He noticed the hardwood in the hallway floor juxtaposed against the carpet in the bedroom. He grabbed his favorite New Balance Minimus shoes off the top closet shelf, sat down on the side of his bed, and slipped them on.

When he walked into his large, two-sink bathroom, he stood for a long while at the mirror, studying himself. He liked what stared back at him. He saw himself as an athlete, primarily if not wholly. He was part of a rare, elite phylum of the human race, convinced that Steel Company Fitness, his newfound workout regimen, defined his manhood. As a consequence, his identity, the thing that glared back at him, the lens through which he viewed the world, was not husband, father, or Christian. It was warrior.

As he negotiated the mirror, he observed the changes in his body since he started his new workout routine. Because of Steel Company, he had become artfully built, sculpted like marble-work of the Italian masters. It had been a blood-, sweat-, and tears-type affair, the most physically exerting workout of his life. Not only had Steel Company written its signature on Brad's body, it had also lifted him out of an emotional quandary. It was the poultice that soothed his wounds, the daily antidote to the numbness of midlife, and the resounding answer to the thing he feared most: a glum and uninspired life.

Brad looked forward to his workout at Steel Company more than he looked forward to spending time with Ellen and the kids. Steel Company was the most important part of his day. In his universe, the axis.

He leaned over the bathroom counter and pressed down on his wrists, gaining a closer look. He plucked a lone gray strand from a forest of blond hair. He turned the water up hot. A cloud of steam dusted the mirror. He swatted his face with a washcloth. Wrung it out. Folded it.

The Fall of Brad Hawley

He walked over and pressed a dry towel against his face.

Then he went out the door.

That would be the last time Brad Hawley ever saw himself. The heavy hand of death came down on him later that day.

He was thirty-four years old.

Brad Hawley was a man with a restless spirit, always reaching for a bar. Slavish to exhilaration and thrill seeking, Brad found worth in physical risks and the benchmarks that came as an accompaniment. For a while, he had a good run. That untamable spirit—greedy for adventure, greedy for thrill— carried him through one terrific life. His remarkable portfolio included snow-boarding, catching high ollies in midair flights on the double-black slopes of Breckenridge. Kayaking through snaking white-water rapids. Mountain biking. Training for triathlons. Skydiving the Swiss Alps. Quarterbacking his flag-football team on the White House lawn. Running with the bulls in Spain. Scuba diving. Bungee jumping off bridges. Swimming with sharks. Hang gliding in Rio.

He couldn't get enough. He believed life was truly lived on these ledges and edges, where untrammeled freedom would sweep him away from the geography of boredom, monotony. But it was only a mirage, hiding a desert place of thirst. Behind the façade, something was terribly wrong.

He was masquerading as someone else.

Neurotic about his image, Brad was on a journey to build the white-picket-fence life, his version of Paradise. This vision of success and worth rested in the staples of the American dream. The attractive wife. The right neighborhood. The right house. Perfect, well-scrubbed children. SUVs boasting vacation-spot stickers on the rear window. Clothes with the right label. The family dog. The gadgets. The country club.

But Paradise was not found in these indulgences.

Because he felt he always had something to prove, every effort, every move, was meticulously calculated to project strength, money, success, and stability. He captained his life in such a way, and in late summer of 2012, he almost had his perfect life assembled.

Brad had substantial validations. He and Ellen had just moved into their newly renovated house in one of the nicest neighborhoods in Birmingham, Alabama. They had two beautiful kids, Webb and Marlen. They had a German Shepherd kept in an invisible fence. They were invited to parties and mingled with the in-crowd. They were members of Vestavia Country Club, and Brad was president of the Phoenix Club—a group self-dubbed as the "hundred best twenty-six-to-thirty-six-year-olds in town." He had a great job working in the patent industry, making gobs of money. Physically, he was in the best shape of his life, working out at the premier gym in Birmingham, killing it, reveling in the oily approbation he received daily from other members, many of whom considered themselves elite athletes. He was living the American dream. His dream. He had a firm grip on the throat of his life, had total control, all the pieces interlocking into one incredible gallery.

But the cosmos offered no relief. For no matter how fierce the straining, he could not find peace. Once he conquered one obstacle, another one appeared. It seemed as if he was always reaching for a perpetual bar that kept going up, out of reach. The next adventure, the newest gadget, the latest skill. Unwittingly, he sought activities to fill a void, a deep scar of the soul.

What Brad didn't comprehend was that he was constructing a solid narcissist along the way, a man whose chief infatuation was self. His was a Brad-centric world where the fulcrum of all humanity swung. Feeding the wolf of the flesh, his spiritual life suffered. If asked, he would have called himself a Christian, but a nominal one at that. He had little interest in following Christ or walking in the dust of the rabbi carpenter from Nazareth. The whole of weeklong faith activity had been reduced to his Sunday morning obligation—a brief yielding of will to a higher authority—and his Christian life embodied little more than Nicene Creed recitation of belief. There was no walk. No pursuit. He didn't think deeply about Christian concepts, as the lessons of Sunday spoiled quickly. Prayer was notably absent. Holiness and godliness were notions unworthy of attempting. Faith had more to do with rigid conformity to rules than closeness of relationship. Except for one hour per week, he was virtually indistinguishable from the rest of the world. The most frightening thing was that he was lost and didn't know it.

The Fall of Brad Hawley

On August 27, 2012, the bar proved to be too high. Not a physical height, for it was only seven feet from the ground.

You see, the bar was me. Brad Hawley himself.

I grabbed my workout shake out of the refrigerator, walked down the stairs to the basement, cranked my Jeep, and thumbed the garage-door opener. I flipped on iTunes, backed out of my drive, and drove to the place of my death.

I had become an imposter in my own life, a wax figure of my true self. I had built a caricature of manhood, believed in it, sought it. I shaped and polished him and he emerged glossy and pristine. But he was rotting within. My fifteen year old self would not have recognized the man I became at thirty-four.

I often wonder what happened to me.

I spend many hours replaying the events of August 27, but more important is my understanding of the stimulus for the manic, subterranean force that set me adrift, the fuel for the bitterness and rage that filled the chapters of my young adulthood, and the root factor of my flesh inking the dotted line to conspire with the world. I was not a warrior in the purest sense. I was a poser who duped himself into thinking he was strong, a disordered gamer attempting to order his life using the wrong pieces, the wrong board.

My conclusion is that I had to die.

Now, I can tell you these things. I look back at my life from this place I'm in. Here, I've shed the graveclothes I once wore so cravenly and tossed on a new tunic. Somehow, I have rematerialized out of the pitiful fog of my life, part-timorous and wrecked—but strong. I see much more clearly. I have learned not to count on myself.

So do not feel sorry for me. The blinders have been removed, and I am at rest.

And if I could go back in time and prevent all of this from happening, avert the things leading up to the natural course of my death, I wouldn't stop it.

The Fall

The clock in the bell tower in Crestline Village overlooks the city of Mountain Brook, Alabama, and stands like a sentinel. There are no skyscrapers here, few five-star restaurants, no museums, yet Mountain Brook is considered the most prestigious patch of turf in all of Alabama. Some might say it has a certain air about it. Take that as you will. Others say it reeks with class. Perhaps the truth is somewhere in the middle.

Mountain Brook is a place where summers have a particularly delicious pulse. Arranged into three villages forming a triangle—Mountain Brook Village, Crestline Village, and English Village—this neat municipality is accentuated by half-timbered Tudor-style buildings with vibrant, street-level shops. It is a place where big-bagged shoppers stroll and squint at diamond wares displayed in large cases, on bony fingers. A place where patrons sit at outside tables at bakery coffee shops, the smell of bread and beans wafting in the air. A place where mothers cave in to begging children, who, from the counter at Gilchrist, victoriously slurp grape limeades out of Styrofoam cups, climbing knee-first on stools to summit the long straw. A place where Land Rovers and Mercedes sedans, shiny and peerless, glide down avenues past creameries and open-door boutiques. A place where kicky salons are chocked with cross-legged housewives thumbing through magazines. A place that exudes money.

Though this is not a gated community, the societal threads that bind Mountain Brook are always pulled taut, forming an invisible barrier that keeps the riffraff out, as well as the rubes. So on August 27, 2012, when

The Fall of Brad Hawley

Brad Hawley fell and shattered his skull, needless to say ripples went through this protective community.

At 11:58 a.m., a Jeep hurtled through the green mouth of the woods, taking slopes and curves, breaching speed limits. Brad Hawley was driving to his 12:15 p.m. workout class at Steel Company Fitness in Crestline Village as the whirr of the AC wiped away the grimace of summer. His Maui Jim sunglasses tinting brown the sky, Brad gripped the steering wheel contemplatively, feeling the leather, its texture. Inside his mind, he was having a conversation beyond the drowned-out rhymes of rapper Wiz Khalifa that belted through the speakers:

> It's your anniversary, isn't it,
> And your man ain't acting right.
> So you packin' your Domiar luggage up callin' my cell phone;
> Try and catch a flight.

Passing by the country club, Brad ran his eyes across the manicured fairways that directed golfers to purple-and-white flags wagging from exceptionally cared-for greens. Now, to his left, a long, road-hugging hill rose up and was punctuated by a series of mansions with steep driveways and stirring porticos. To his right was a leaf-speckled trail, appearing and re-appearing haphazardly and adorned with an occasional jogger. This was his bucolic scenery as he drove to his workout every day.

As was ritual, Brad polished off the last soury remnants of a preworkout drink called Buzz-Saw. Downing it, he screwed on the top and pitched it on the passenger seat. The blond-headed rock-star Steel Companyer hoped that his morning priming for the midday workout—the diet, the shakes, and the "second breakfast" consisting of grilled chicken, vegetables, and sweet potatoes—would crescendo at quarter past twelve.

Up ahead was the dreaded WOD, the "workout of the day" as it was known in Steel Company lingo. Sun Tzu–like in his mental preparation, Brad knew that the battle is won *before* it is fought, a lesson he learned as a high-school track star. Indeed, the blood and guts that had carried him all the way to the state finals in the four-hundred-meter run would carry him today. So he coaxed those competitive spirits and banished any thought of failure to a faraway sanctum. Because on this day, he would not compete against other athletes. This battle was a risky, soul-level game fought within.

Six weeks earlier, Steel Company threw down the gauntlet, issuing a "40-Day Fitness Challenge." The athletes endured the initial savagery, times and weights were measured and noted, and a retesting would determine if there was improvement in forty days. For Brad, August 27 was the date of his retest, and he was stoked to shatter his PRs (personal records), especially on the ever-grueling exercise known as *toes to bar*.

Over the last year, Brad's gym metrics had been tattooed on his mind as if they were dates to memorize for a high-school American-history quiz. And even if he tried, his coaches wouldn't let him forget them. Records and record holders created a certain hierarchy at Steel Company. For Brad, they became his personal measuring stick, the litmus test for the once-retired athlete, and the measure of manhood.

At Steel Company, the mere names of the exercises struck fear into the hearts of athletes, carrying a near-papal reverence. So when Brad drove to the gym that day, these four horsemen stood snorting at him from inside the walls of the gym:

Box jumps
Max seated rows
Handstand push-ups
Toes to bar

That might not mean anything to most people, but it meant everything to Brad Hawley. Brad wasn't just going to the gym to work out, to push around a little weight, chat it up with the regulars, and make repeat trips to the water fountain. This was a lifestyle. This was religion.

The Fall of Brad Hawley

While most of the Birmingham working community would be spending the noontime hour at lunch—fubsy men in starched JoS. A. Bank shirts gorging on $9.99 all-you-can-eat buffets—Brad was überloyal to his 12:15 p.m. class, taking great pride in his testosterone-filled hour. After the workout, Brad and several of the members would ease over to Taco Mama for a plate of nutritious Mexican fare that fell squarely in line with their Paleo diet. The meal, created specifically for the group, was named "Nod to the Company," per Brad's suggestion.

And so, that day, as he made his usual drive through the beautiful Mountain Brook woodlands, he pondered these things. He didn't think about Ellen, or her day, or whether or not the sales meeting in North Carolina was going well. He didn't think about whether or not she would impress the president of her company. He didn't think about his relationship with God or about moving the needle of his Christian life forward. He thought about breaking his own records.

Nowhere in the portals of his mind had he considered that today he might shatter his skull and that blood would soon be pooling up inside his brain.

THE JEEP PASSED THE ERODING STONE WALLS patched with moss, the regal steeple of a Methodist church, the happy houses, the tennis courts fronting the junior high school, and the high spire and many-windowed façade of the Baptist church before turning onto Montevallo Road. Brad made a quick left and as the Jeep deposited him into the village, he felt its thump, his heart quickening a beat. He was here.

Making a right at the narrow, one-way street beside Vogue Cleaners, the Jeep dived into the back parking lot of Steel Company Fitness. The tires crunched across the gravel—trading their shine for a white ring of dust—and the truck came to a rest as Wiz still reverberated from its interior. The cocksure, Adonis-like, 155-pound athlete with 6 percent body fat hopped out into the stifling August weather and strutted through the glass garage door of the gym.

Brad was wearing his Lululemon shorts and his favorite T-shirt, which touted "CROSSFIT ON THE PLAINS" across the chest. It reminded him of his days at Auburn University—"the Plains"—and furnished a bit of impunity from old(er) age. But although things were different now, the years had produced a handsomer relic of the once-well-known college student. His hair was now cropped more closely than the fraternity swoosh he once wore proudly. A pair of crow's feet crinkled up like an accordion beside his maturity-filtered brown eyes. God had carved his baby face out with age and brushed it with a darker, healthier hue. Stubble made an appearance in greater frequency, shadowing his face when he didn't feel like a morning shave.

In terms of physical dimensions, Brad was not a man of tremendous size, but he was packaged in a wiry, explosive five foot nine. He was athletic, fast, and deceptively strong, with cut-up muscles and abs like plantation shutters. His legs, slightly bowed, were well developed and statuesque. When he walked, he sauntered with hubris. When he shook your hand, he looked you dead in the eyes, piercing into you with a hard, visceral stare.

Brad felt the chill as he hurled open the door to the box, as the gym was called. Frills such as AC, nonexistent at similar gyms, were one luxury at Steel Company. He did not notice the lingering, dank musk, for his olfactory senses had adjusted to the varying aromas of the warehouse gym. Brutal equipment, smacking of sweat and work, awaited the grip of powdered hands on bars and the stab of feet on boxes. On the wall, a timer was blank, reading, –:–.

Writing boards, with the ghostly remnants of Expo markers in various handwritings and colors, displayed times and reps drafted by hands trembling from exhaustion. Medicine balls were stacked against the walls in a large chute with a circular mouth at the bottom that spit them out, one by one, like a PEZ dispenser. Sturdy chin-up rigs, caked white with chalk, stretched down the length of one-half of the gym. Kettlebells resembling helmeted soldiers were assembled in the corner. Rings and ropes were suspended from the ceiling, as motionless rowers, mats, rubber plates, and PVC pipes were pushed neatly against the walls. Barbells were snagged like prized marlin on wall hooks, and a series of haphazard boxes dotted the floor.

Brad, a hair early, threw a wave at Coach Mark before popping down immediately into his stretching routine. Brad had been sick that Friday, so the coach allowed him to postpone his retest until Monday. While the class was in session, Brad and Mark would be working one-on-one.

A small hive of members began to trickle in, sporting their cultish togs, greeting one another with small talk, workout talk. They spat lingo out as if they were in a foreign-language class. In Steel Companyspeak, they were fluent.

Mark didn't have to hold Brad's hand through warm-ups—that was already ingrained in him from being under the Steel Company curtain. In fact, according to his panel of peers, Brad was one of the best athletes at Steel Company, now a multi-gym affair with four gyms stretching across Birmingham and opening their doors to all brands of athletes. To be the best of the best among a great many people across four campuses, one had to be in tip-top shape.

Brad hunted for a space to stretch, the first drip of sweat cascading down his brow. Mark walked over.

"Big day today," Mark said, though Brad needed no reminder.

"I know, man," Brad said, stretching, his legs wide. He then leaned forward, closing his body like a clam. Center. Right leg.

I gotta beat my old record, Brad thought to himself.

Left leg.

"You remember your last PR on toes to bar?" Mark said.

"Yeah, I think so. Was it thirty?"

Mark checked his clipboard, paper curled up at the corners. "Yessir. Thirty. Easy. Piece of cake."

Mark scanned the gym seriously, taking inventory of today's attendees as music hummed low in the background.

"Hey, Mark!" shouted Jimmy from the other side of the gym. "What we listenin' to today?"

"Heck, I don't care. Up to you. Bee Gees?" Mark said, tossing Brad a smirk. "Just kidding. Um, what about Beastie Boys?"

"That works."

"Dude, I'm feelin' pretty good today," Brad offered, assenting to the functionality of his bloodstream, his overall swag and confidence. "I feel forty coming on."

"Forty? Wow, I didn't know you were that old," Mark said wryly.

"Oh, you're hilarious dude." Brad chuckled.

"Just messin' with you, man," Mark said. "Forty. I don't know. You have been killing it lately."

Brad smiled and turned away. By now, the other Alphas in the box had completed their stretching and warm-up routines, and the WOD was underway. Once the clock started, the box morphed into a mosh pit of activity.

"OK. You 'bout ready to hit it?" Mark asked.

Brad rubbed the Ace bandages cuffing his wrists, like a hitter's mindless at-bat routine. And though he wouldn't technically need them in the first exercise, box jumps, Brad believed the bandages provided a mental edge, superstitious as it might have been.

"Here we go."

A serious theme enveloped Brad's face. He shook out the stiffness in his legs and arms and drew a circle with his head to kill rigidity in his neck. A twenty-four-inch box rested in the center of the floor, directly in front of him. He pounced up and down, underscoring the gravitas of the moment.

With a remote control, Mark flicked the timer on the wall—2:00— and crouched down, snapping his stare back at his athlete. Brad rocked back and forth until the clock reached five seconds, when he steeled himself.

Three, two, one.

"Go!"

Brad leaped up with fists clinched, fluid as a skier, onto the flat ceiling of the box, his beaten New Balance sneakers landing with a soft thud. He clicked back off the box, down the same arc from which he had arrived, a reverse pantomime of the first jump. Perfect execution.

"One."

Mark stood up, counting now, jacking Brad up with the fire and mechanics of his voice.

Brad leaped up, then down. Up, then down. Ten, fifteen, twenty.

"Back up. Thirty. Up. Thirty-one—keep pushing. Thirty-three— come on, man! Thirty-four."

Mark prodded seriously, matter-of-factly—"Come on, Brad"— as the athlete set into a Pavlovian rhythm, pumping his arms forward, inhaling a lungful of air, using his lean frame, his terrifically conditioned body, his long-worked quads. Harnessing this force, he was fierce in his attack on the box.

"Fifty—come on, dude!" Mark implored hotly. "Forty-seven seconds left. You're not tired. Come on, Brad! Fifty-one!"

The clock pulsed down—00:39, 00:38, 00:37—as the slower tides of Brad's leaps increased Mark's desperation.

"Sixty-two. Let's go—fifteen seconds! Let's get seventy!"

Brad was near exhaustion. The fusillade of effort was now like embers waning to their eventual death. His body was writhing with pain. Sweat flecking his shirt, legs misted over. A tribute to his excess.

"Five more!" yelled Mark. "Five more! Sixty-nine! Ten seconds! Seventy! Get three more!"

Brad exhaled, paused for a half-second, and hopped back up. Back down.

"Time!"

As the clock expired, Brad landed back on the rubber floor, completing his seventy-third rep. It was a new personal record.

"All right! Seventy-three!" Mark said. "You OK, man?"

Doubled over, Brad stood up now, clasping his hands together, the backs of them against his forehead. Gasping, he began to stagger in unintended routes across the room, hoping that new venues would find better air. Brad went for the water fountain in the corner of the gym and uncaringly let a few errant drops tumble onto his chest, his shirt. He mopped his mouth with the back of his hand and walked back into the arena.

"What's…next?" he asked between gulps.

"That would be handstand push-ups," Mark said, almost sardonically.

I felt as if I was in a safe environment. Everybody in the gym was close. We all went at it hard together. We had bonded. Mark had been training me for months, and he was aware of my limitations. Mark was a very good coach—he knew his stuff. He looked the part. Had a shaved head. Shaved arms. He was very confident in himself, and perhaps I was too confident in him.

I got caught in the allure of it. My life began to revolve around that 12:15 p.m. class. My morning was spent gearing up for the workout. Everything was a build-up to the moment I stepped into the gym. My routines. My diet. It had become my idol and my master. Of course, I loved my kids and wife, but for some reason, I was forgetting that. I had become a glutton for punishment. The workout was the best part of my day. But that would soon change.

I reached my max on handstand push-ups and beat my PR at Squat Cleans—225 pounds. Mark suggested that I try 235, and I did, but I couldn't get it up. It was evident that today he was going to push me harder than I'd ever been pushed in my life. I knew that toes to bar was coming up, and I was trying my best to pace myself. My goal was to go all out.

Brad slowly paced over to the chin-up rig and looked skyward, the long bar paralleling the ceiling. Mark was to his left, sweating, vigilant, clipboard ready.

Brad blew out a hard breath, leaped up, and gripped the bar with both hands. He became aware of the layers of bandages coiling his wrists, his dead weight heavy on the rig.

He began to sway his body back and forth in a kipping motion: as his shoulders moved forward, his legs swung back, forming a human *C*;

then, as his shoulders pushed backward, his legs swung forward, forming a crude *V.* He built horizontal momentum by unlocking the shoulder joint, and in a severe, violent yaw, he elevated his hips, swinging his legs upward until his toes pecked the cold iron rig between his hands.

One.

The first twenty were easy. No sweat. Licking the last ten would be the hard part, the severest test, the only thing standing between failure and achieving a personal vendetta with himself. Steel Company had trained their acolyte to push through the pain. Progress is mental. When thoughts ramble, a battle is waged between the inner voice that speaks sedition against the soul and the voice that begs us to press forward. It's what separates the average from the best, and Brad found himself at that mental juncture as he approached thirty.

Mark continued to spit challenges, his howls even more urgent than before, near bestial. But his words arrived in low, indiscernible white noise. A silent orchestra of chants occurring outside the realm of real mental war.

Like an old car trying hard to crank, Brad caterwauled with each pull. He was on the verge of becoming fully unhinged, hands aching and slipping with each rep. Once he reached twenty-five, he began to decelerate. His form was poor, his mechanics now a ruined ritual. Thirty-one reps appeared to be a cruel joke contrived in some distant, primal fantasy world. That had been the risk when he started Steel Company, and every day.

Today, he might not be better than before.

I thought, "Am I even going to get back to thirty?" I started to do two at a time and then one at a time. At thirty, I reached a dead hang. My fingers were cramping with pain. The nerve endings. The bones. An overpowering ache. One more was all I needed. So I twisted my hands to regain my grip. I shot out a breath and began to kip.

My wife, by now, had landed in North Carolina. My children were at the day care, running around with other sweet and unruly children. The only thought in my mind was taking care of this last rep. I would take care of work later this afternoon. Once I got done with this. My dog, Rocky, was probably napping, safely tucked away within his invisible fence. But, like dog fences, I have learned there are invisible fences in life. Like the kind of fence I tried to create. I had this perfect little world I was working on. Brad's world. It looked the way I had always imagined it in my dreams. But ultimately what it gave was a false sense of security. I didn't want to just keep up with the Joneses—I wanted to beat *the Joneses. It wasn't something I often stated aloud, but I sensed that its savage undercurrent was threatening to pull me under.*

He summoned his interior strength, that storehouse of ruthless testosterone, hauling with everything he had, thrusting his knees vertically and curling his feet at the bar.

But his fingers had simply had enough. It was too great a load to bear. He felt himself slipping off, finger by finger, losing his grip. He would not regain it. His hands gave way, and the zealous athlete, the obsessed pilgrim longing to climb the mountain of life, began to crash toward the earth. His shoulder was the first to smash the hard floor and then his head.

The last thing he remembered was the cloud of chalk coughing up into the air.

Then everything went black.

THE RUNNER

Royal Oak, Michigan, a suburb just west of Detroit, boasts a wide variety of watering holes, a zoo, an annual pop-up shrine for motorcyclists, and the Woodward Dream Cruise—a popular event where classic cars and hot rods parade the thoroughfare. Royal Oak was the setting for the famous sitcom *Home Improvement* and the movie *Gran Torino*, starring Clint Eastwood, and was once the home of Father Charles Coughlin, the Catholic priest who belted his messages from the tower of the Shrine of the Little Flower. In that same city, almost a half century after Coughlin issued his religious decrees from the art deco tower, Brad Hawley was born.

Before Brad came into this world, his mom, Sharon, was a looker and garnered the attention of many Detroiters. While working at the *The Detroit News*, Sharon turned heads, including a salesman, Bob Hawley, who worked in the same building. Once, while walking through downtown Detroit, Hawley remarked to a friend, "One day I will marry that woman."

Bob eventually snagged a date with the beauty from his building, but it was a non-exclusive relationship. Sharon became pregnant and Bob offered to marry her. Sharon agreed. The couple greeted a son, Bradley William Morris, on December 30, 1977. After Sharon and Bob were married, Bob officially adopted Brad and changed his last name to Hawley.

Bob chased job offers and the family moved frequently. Each stop took them farther and farther south, the last move emptying them deep into Dixie.

When Brad was five, the family lived in Ohio, though memories from his time in the Buckeye state remained few and remote. The Hawleys moved to Bristol, Virginia, when Brad was in the third grade, and it was there that Brad first encountered the thrill and ferocity of sports and had his first foray into the unique and perplexing world of romance.

Although Brad was a smallish boy, Sharon encouraged her son to get involved in a variety of endeavors, including football. The coaches of the High Point Yellow Jacket football team in Bristol pegged Brad, diminutive as he was, for a spot on the offensive line. All season long, the bigger, stockier young boys dominated him. But during the last game of the season, Brad was able to flip the script. On that immortal day, the defenseman to whom Brad was assigned was no match for an overzealous, amped-up offensive lineman who had been clobbered all year and had grown tired of being used as a tackling dummy. Over and over, Brad hit him, and every time, the boy crumbled. Brad was so anxious to "pop leather" that he could barely wait for the snap count, drawing false-start penalties in the process. Brad would later find himself blocking again, though of the emotional variety, not physical.

Brad also had success with girls, finding his first "steady" while in Virginia. Her name was Katie, and the innocent pair would express their adoration for each other with a kiss on the cheek. But the romance was short lived. Soon after the relationship commenced, Bob informed young Brad on a family fishing trip that the Hawleys would be moving to Alabama. Brad wasn't happy, arguing that a sudden move would sever his relationship with Katie.

"I'm not going," the eight-year-old offered simply and confidently—with no real options for room and board if his parents left him.

After a bit of prodding, Brad finally relented and agreed to move to Alabama. Of course, there were still the impending details of alerting the love of his life. How would Katie take it? Would she ever recover? The next school day, Brad, no more than three foot two in his white Reebok high-tops, walked somberly into Mrs. Sorah's class, where Katie was sitting in the third seat on the front row. As he passed her, he leaned down and whispered, "I'm moving to Alabama." Katie, crestfallen at the news, buried her head in her hands.

Cullman, Alabama, about as deep into Dixie as you can get, was the last and final stop on the Hawleys' tour of America. Cullman was like Hickville compared to the big city of Detroit, but nevertheless, Brad would assimilate nicely into this small Southern town. Much would happen to our subject as the years marched on, and Brad identified Cullman as the place where Sharon began to shield him from any activity she deemed dangerous.

As a young boy, Brad would sit Indian style on the floor, on the shag carpet in their Alabama home, watching television. The television was of the large eighties box-style that rested on a floor-level cabinet. As Brad sat, wearing his Spuds MacKenzie T-shirt, Duck Head shorts, and those trusty Reebok high-top tennis shoes, Sharon microwaved chocolate-fudge Pop-Tarts and served them up on a TV tray. This was standard breakfast, and it made Brad immeasurably happy.

Sharon was the louder and more active participant in Brad's life, whereas Bob was quiet and workmanlike. As a result, Sharon's influence rang in much higher decibels, both literally and metaphorically. In short, Sharon became Brad's whole world.

Bob's salary as a salesman was enough to provide for the whole family, and because Sharon didn't have to work, she used gaps of time to pour herself into the life of her only son. For instance, she volunteered as a teacher's assistant in Mrs. Weaver's eighth-grade English class. When a UPS truck hit the family cocker spaniel, Casey, the Hawleys buried their furry friend in Mrs. Weaver's backyard. Sharon seemed to take it the hardest when dogs died or even when Brad lost his gym shorts in seventh grade. She was always protecting him, sponging up all of his hurt while shielding him from any discomfort or embarrassment.

Brad rarely got in trouble, and missteps were minor in nature. Even still, reflecting on that era, Brad said that from time to time, Sharon would lose it, grab a belt, and wallop him. Minor infractions would trigger her, and Brad could sense these outbursts when he heard the familiar sound of the folding shutter doors creaking open (many generation Xers remember similar signs), whereby she would produce her chosen weapon of discipline, hunt Brad down, and swing like Jose Canseco for his behind. Brad remembered that the eruptions lacked consistency. There was no rhyme or reason, and the punishment didn't necessarily have to fit the crime. The corporal activity eventually subsided once Brad was old enough and elusive enough to avoid her. One cat-and-mouse game around a coffee table ended all pleasantries for good.

Since Brad had hit a growth spurt by the time he was in the seventh grade, naturally he tried out for the basketball team. As it turns out, Brad didn't just make the team. He made eighth-grade squad while he was only in the seventh grade. Quite a distinction. Brad thought that basketball might be a viable pursuit, but later found he had been cursed with an early sprouting: Brad stopped growing in the ninth grade while others kept growing. Sharon would not let him go out for football, a much rougher sport that included the heightened possibility of Brad getting hurt.

Sharon's active participation in Brad's life facilitated many interests, and it was because of Sharon that Brad was broadened. During his grammar and middle school years, Brad developed a fascination for the beatific, soothing instrument: the saxophone. In fifth grade, he was dubbed "outstanding beginner band student" and was ultimately named to the esteemed faction of musicians known as saxophone "section chair." As Brad approached the eighth grade, school whisperings alluded to Brad's running for drum major of the band. At this time, Brad felt torn between two magnetic forces—sports and band—both competing for his attention. This was an important pivot point in his development, where the road began to fork. On the one hand, he could choose the traditionally geekier of the two roads that diverged, band. On the other, he could choose the sexier fork, sports (right or wrong, these were the perceptions of many high schoolers across the country at that time). Brad eventually chose the latter.

The Fall of Brad Hawley

Sharon discovered she could not shield him from everything. In eighth grade, Brad got into his only fistfight, a donnybrook that occurred at the Cullman High School football stadium. After being incited by several meatheads thirsty for scrap, circling up like mouth-foaming hooligans, Brad and a young boy named Blake tussled at the top of the stairs during seventh-period PE. After the ceremonial prefight mouthing, Brad drew first blood by shoving Blake down the stadium steps. Flummoxed but able to recover, Blake got up and clocked Brad in the nose with a surprising haymaker, releasing a torrent of blood. That ended the festivities.

But the humiliation didn't end there. Every day, Brad would gather his saxophone from the band room on the way to meet his ride home. On the day of the fight, in his urgency to cower in the back of his mom's car, he forgot to make the quick stop in the band room to gather his brass. Around that same time, Sharon and her sister, known affectionately as Aunt Sandy, swung the car through the parking lot, unaware of the fisticuffs at the top of the stadium. Sharon gasped as Brad, nose smudged with blood, approached the car.

"Oh my goodness, Brad! What happened?"

"Nothing, Mom. Don't worry about it."

"Where's your saxophone?" Sharon asked in a panic.

"I forgot it."

Instead of forcing Brad to march in humiliation back to the scene of the action, Sharon went in and, serving as his agent, fetched the saxophone from the band room.

It was Brad's first experience with other young men questioning his manhood, and Brad had failed his first test. For the next twenty years, he would continue to try to prove himself worthy of taking up that mantle. In later life, Brad would umpire this childhood story as yet another example of Sharon's softening versus toughening. At the fuzzy line of parenting, Sharon erred on the side of affection and pampering, and her mollycoddling, while with good intentions, was not turning him into a man. In the parental dynamic, this is where Bob was supposed to come in. But because Bob was largely not present, Brad did not receive the consistent doses of tough love that every young boy needs from a father.

In terms of support, however, Sharon shone. Brad became interested in track his freshman year in high school, and Sharon slipped easily into the role of track mom. She was always present at meets, serving pizza and French fries and handing out T-shirts to children agog and standing on tiptoes at the concession stand. Regardless of whether or not Brad performed spectacularly, Sharon was always there with an encouraging word. "You did so well!" Many men who have suffered through the mental abuse of a dissatisfied father would have begged for such niceties, but the truth was that Brad needed at least some correction and challenge on the athletic fields.

Fortuitously, Coach Calvert, the track coach, stepped into Brad's life and became a model father figure. Brad even became his teacher's aide in class, and the two men gained such a level of closeness and trust that Coach Calvert would give Brad the keys to his house when he'd forgotten his lesson plans. Brad saw Coach Calvert as a man's man, someone whom he could look up to, emulate even. A target life.

Brad was placed on relay teams, where he learned the importance of group dynamics. The relay squad was a familial environment where accountability was crucial. You did not want to let your teammates down. Brad felt that, athletically, there was nothing he could do to disappoint Sharon. If he slipped and fell and finished last, he would still get the same praise as if he'd won the state finals. But the team created a sense of accountability that did not exist with Sharon. If he screwed up, it would be painfully obvious when Brad disappointed the team, and this thought worked on his psyche. He wanted to please the team. He wanted to *prove* he could compete. He didn't want to disappoint his brothers. When Brad needed something to hold him accountable, track provided it.

As time went on, Brad became the fastest member of the track team, clocking a 4.3 in the forty-yard dash and running a consistent sub-51-second four-hundred-meter dash. In addition to his skill as a speedster, Brad also displayed tremendous heart and determination. He possessed a true passion for running and treated his role as a member of the team with heightened seriousness. Coach Calvert took notice, installing him as the anchor on all relay events.

Feeling a certain duty and obligation to his teammates, Brad became the consummate team player, not seeking glory in his individual performances but focusing on helping the larger collective. If Brad did well, it helped the team.

Brad's dedication was apparent both on and off the track. On it, he would often collapse across the finish line from exhaustion. Off it, he demonstrated his allegiance in a variety of ways. One such example was the time he bought a gold baton and engraving tool from a local sporting goods store. Brad suggested that the members engrave quotes on the baton, marking it when they achieved a win and laying hands on it for pre-race prayers as if it were some consecrated object of Christendom. The baton became a symbol of unity among the squad, and Brad carried it with pride. After certain victories, the team smoked a celebratory cigar, and after one particularly stellar performance, they solidified the brotherhood by ashing out the cigar on their arms.

In Brad's sophomore year, the 5A Section 5 meet was held at Wallace State Community College, named after the famous Alabama governor and located fourteen miles south of Cullman in rustic Hanceville, Alabama. The rubber track circumnavigating the stadium became the arena for elite runners, jumpers, and throwers. Before the meet commenced, members of the Cullman team—without prompting—called a powwow in the locker room, shutting out the adult chiefs from the meeting. No one was joking around when the team emerged from the bowels of the stadium.

On the track, it was a tight meet. When the last event rolled around, the four-by-four-hundred-meter relay, Cullman was behind by one point to rival Bob Jones High. After a shotgun start on the relay, Bernard, the runner of the first leg, stretched Cullman out to a comfortable lead. Patrick fell behind on the second leg, and Jon, a freshman, ran the leg of his life on the third. Cullman was leading as the baton was shoved into the paw of its trusty anchor, Brad Hawley.

As he stood waiting on the baton, bracing, watching as Jon blistered the straightaway, face marked with superior agony, Brad reveled in the moment. This was his time. The Cullman faithful began to gather on the edges of the track, sensing victory, as Jon handed off the baton cleanly.

Brad's strategy was always the same: run the first two hundred wide open and hold on for dear life in the final two hundred. Halfway home, he was cruising, opening up a near-insurmountable lead. *It's over*, Brad thought. Yet rounding the final curve, the hustling athlete began to hear eerie footsteps and breathing. This was not ideal, as Brad was almost depleted from three hundred yards of grunt work. In front of him, Cullman's adoring fans were jumping up and down as if on pogo sticks, creating an archway of energy from one side of the track to the other. Howling in glee. When he had almost nothing left, Brad saw the runner, pulling up even, out of his periphery.

Brad continued to pump his arms and legs, but his body began to feel like he was running in the ocean. Steps were more deliberate now. He couldn't make his body move any faster, hard as he tried. But just when Brad thought he might be overtaken, he heard a most beautiful sound, perhaps more beautiful than the melodies he'd produced on his alto saxophone.

Clink, clink, clink.

The baton hitting the track.

Brad continued to run the straightaway, not looking back, baton tucked like a football. The other runner had dropped the baton inexplicably and left Brad to relish the triumph. It was over.

The other members of the Cullman track team had difficulty restraining themselves, holding one another back as Brad took the final step across the finish line. The moment Brad stepped over the line safely, he was mobbed. Cullman had won the meet by one point.

The Fall of Brad Hawley

Peace like a river washed over Brad. The joy. The glory. The pageantry.

Brad had been reaching for that moment his entire life. The elation he felt was like a drug.

He would reach for it again.

THE EXODUS

As Brad was growing up, he began to realize the wide gulf between his interests and the interests of Bob Hawley. Brad had been blessed with athleticism, and it seemed strange to him that Bob wasn't interested in athletics at all. He rarely attended any of Brad's sporting events.

Brad loved to watch his Michigan Wolverines, and he had also grown to love the Auburn Tigers. Bob, however, preferred *M*A*S*H* to any ball game. So when Bob showed up at Brad's basketball practice in his eleventh grade year, it seemed a bit unusual.

During a water break, Brad noticed Bob sitting in the bleachers and walked over to him.

"Dad, why are you here?"

"I can't talk about it right now, Son. But you and I need to talk."

Brad had never had a serious one-on-one conversation with his dad—much less one involving matters of the heart—and now Bob was showing up at practice needing to talk? An uncomforting thought hung in Brad's mind for the rest of practice. *This must be superserious,* Brad thought.

After practice, Bob led his son out to the car. Brad's sweat-sodden togs clinging to his skin. The portentous sting of an unkind winter.

"Let's go for a ride," Bob said.

The vehicle hummed down a dark corridor of Interstate 65, and the family dynamic—one that Brad had previously perceived as normal and intact—took a drastic shift as Bob revealed the ugly face of truth behind the mask.

The Fall of Brad Hawley

"Brad, your mother's leaving us," Bob said somberly from the driver's seat.

Brad sat voiceless, rubbing his thumbs together and noticing their texture. He contemplated how to respond to what he knew had to be the evilest form of misinformation. But the words cannonaded in Brad's mind, and he replayed them over and over like an old cassette tape.

Your mother is leaving (rewind).
YOUR mother (rewind).
Your MOTHER (rewind).
LEAVING US.

All his life, Brad had idolized Sharon—perhaps because of, not despite, the incessant cocooning him from all bedlam—whereas Bob resided at the colder frontiers of Brad's mind. Bob brought a sterner, rigid element to the household that offset Sharon's vitality. As a result, Brad was a dyed-in-the-wool mama's boy, hopelessly smitten by the bubbly, five-foot-four blonde who would secretly buy her son gifts, unbeknownst to Bob. Brad described Bob in stark contrast: remote, unaffectionate, aloof, seemingly numb to life, not inflamed with passions or burdened with overblown reactions to life events. From what Brad could tell, he was not intimately involved in his son's life, as was Sharon. Sharon had through the years built pyramiding trust, such that at this point in their relationship, Brad couldn't imagine Sharon doing anything to hurt him, much less destroy the family. But that would soon change as the atmosphere in the vehicle took on a more sinister air.

"Your mother's leaving us"—it made no sense. To Brad, it was a surreal notion that would have crossed his mind only on some obscure planet, not this earth. Sharon had never done anything to cause Brad emotional distress. Now, if this were true, she was purposefully knifing open a wound that might never heal.

Bob broke the silence.

"Your mother is not who I thought she was," he said contemptuously.

Nothing. The car continued to chew up the road. Bob leaned in farther.

"Do you understand what I'm saying, Brad?"

Brad's eyes veered to the dashing-by roadside, to the uncut weeds flanking the highway, to the staccato trash that emerged as the headlights routed the night. His mind veered to nothing at all. Several seconds ticked away in bizarre stillness. Minutes. Time was swift. Escaping. The lights of the car continued to scream at the Southern darkness. The radio clipped.

Awakening, Brad became conscious of the heat gusting from the vent. The sweat desiccated on his body. The flaking, pressed-on graphics of his jersey. Covering his hands was the black dust from manipulating basketballs across the parquet floor. Now impending was the joy-stolen moment Bob Hawley appeared in the bleachers and interrupted his life. This was too much for a sixteen-year-old to take in. It felt like swallowing the world.

"Brad?" Bob said, breaking the silence again.

"Mom wouldn't do that," Brad said.

He tried to salvage hope.

"Brad, I'm not lying to you," said Bob, more desperately. "Why in the world would I make something like that up? She's back at the house as we speak, packing her things."

"Packing her things? I thought everything was fine. What'd you do?"

"I didn't do anything," Bob pleaded. "Anything at all."

"Where's she going?"

"Michigan."

"*Michi*gan?"

"Yes, she's going back to Michigan."

Sharon's decision was a guillotine against the throat of an intact family, sixteen years of accord. As he was processing the information, his future passing through his mind like cars in a funeral procession, Brad realized that not only were his parents severing their marriage but he was also no longer going to see his mom. Divorce from Bob also meant divorce from Brad, because Brad wasn't going anywhere. Anchored soundly in Alabama, he wasn't about to pack up and leave Cullman in his junior year in high school.

Brad thought about life alone with Bob. He thought about his dad, the man with whom, over the next several months, he would be forced to grow more intimate. In review, Bob had taught Brad to tie a tie and had administered more discipline than Sharon. But he hadn't been *present*, either physically or emotionally. Bob never attended track meets or basketball games. He was not as heavily involved in Brad's life as Sharon, taking on the role of mind-averted family manager of sorts. Perhaps Brad mistook this aloofness for uncaring. Nevertheless, it affected him profoundly.

Now the distant disciplinarian was telling Brad that the most influential person in his life had compromised their trust. It was a rancid pill to swallow, an assertion that, if true, would clatter through the years, like a noisy can being kicked around by a strong wind. It was imponderable to Brad that the person whom he thought he knew so intimately would do such a shameful thing, would stoop to such a low, but he knew, in the dark places of his soul, that this car ride, that Sharon's eventual leaving, were images that would not be blotted out. At least, anytime soon.

He knew what Bob was saying was the truth.

Wrath began to ferment in Brad's mind, so that when the car pulled up to the home that would soon be radically shaken, Brad flung open the door and stormed into the house uncontrollably. He was up the stairs of the split-level home before he even knew what was happening. He tried to remain calm, but when he saw his mother, padding a travel bag with toiletries in the bathroom, he could not contain his emotion.

"Mom, what's going on?"

"Back already?" Sharon said, remaining busy. "Basketball practice must've—"

"Yeah," Brad interrupted. "Dad said that you're moving out. What the hell is going on?"

"Yes, I'm moving out."

"*What?*"

"I'm moving out, Son. I'm going to Michigan. It's complicated. But you and Bob are going to be fine," Sharon said beneath tears. She was still trying to shelter him from hurt, but this time she could not buffer him from the destruction, nor mitigate the severity of her offense. The woman who had done everything in her power to protect Brad through the formidable years of adolescence, who had tried to create a perfect snow globe of Brad's life, was now shaking it. Sharon tried to cushion the blow once more, but her words rolled out ungallantly: "You guys are going to be OK."

At that moment, Brad entered adulthood.

Sharon began to walk down the hall, but Brad stopped her impolitely, his anger mercurial. Fists clinched by his side, he was boiling with rage. While he wanted to cause physical harm, something in him prevented him from doing so. He went for a wall instead, slamming his right fist through the hollow wood paneling directly in front of her face. Perhaps he grazed her nose with the violent punch. Perhaps he *hoped* he grazed her nose. If nothing else, the act would at least scare her and serve notice that Brad could be strong without her. That he was going to win this encounter.

"How could you do this?" Brad asked, screaming.

Sharon tried to approach him, reaching for her only son. But Brad pulled away.

"Get away from me!" he yelled. "I cannot believe you are doing this to me! Get out. Get out now!"

Brad motioned for the front door, but Sharon walked down the hall to her bedroom. For some time, Sharon had been sleeping in the guest room and was sharing a bathroom with Brad, evidence that the marriage was on the rocks. She began to fold clothes, brushing tears from her eyes as she folded each garment. But Brad was not letting her off the hook. He chased after her and, filling up the doorway with his coiled-up frame and rage, continued the verbal assault.

"Get out. Get your stuff."

"Brad, I'm very, very sorry. I'll explain it one day."

"I don't want an explanation. I want you to get out of the house!" Brad yelled venomously. "Get out now!"

It was a violent hour. Sharon then went over to the nightstand, picked up the phone, and called the police.

THE PATROLMAN RAPPED ON THE DOOR OF THE HOUSE. Arriving shortly after Sharon's call was a D.A.R.E. officer whom Brad recognized from high school. As the policeman stepped into the Hawleys' home, Brad slipped out behind him. Not to elude arrest but rather to elude humiliation. Brad had nowhere to go, but he felt he had to leave. As he stepped into the middle of the street, he looked around incredulously, hopelessly. Trying to devise a plan. Not knowing what to do, he resorted to the one thing in his life that had been consistent. Running.

Inside, the officer chatted with Bob and Sharon. Later, pulling Bob aside, realizing that Sharon was in emotional distress, the officer suggested that Bob sleep at a local motel.

On the road, Brad figured that if anyone would be able to absorb his hurt, it was his girlfriend, Kelly. It must have been ten or eleven o'clock at night when he ran to her house. When Brad arrived, he rang the doorbell anxiously, desperate to tell her what had happened.

Kelly arrived at the door with her protective father in tow. Investigating the commotion. Brad broke down in her arms.

"My parents are getting a divorce," Brad sobbed. "I just found out."

Kelly tried to console him, but her father, unhappy with Brad's untimely arrival, seized control of the moment, offering quasisympathetically, "I am sorry to hear that, Brad." But he ended with the caveat, "but you can't be here at this hour. You have to leave."

Expecting an outcome different from being discarded at the door, Brad about-faced and began walking again. Back to his isolated nadir. After a while, he came upon a house that was under construction and climbed on top of the roof. He wasn't thinking about suicide but that if he jumped off and hurt himself badly enough, it might bring his family back together. Maybe if he broke his leg, it would save his family.

He stood for a long while on that roof, the montage of life images running through his head. These were files that he cherished, and it was as if a button had been pushed and his mind, bombarded with confused thoughts, was downloading them all at once. Things he hadn't thought of were coming back, mental snapshots of his mother. Pain inundated his body. Pain so intense that it bled over into temptation to jump. End it. Break something.

That night, Brad did not jump. Instead, he climbed down off the roof and trekked back to the home that was now eternally broken. Upon arrival, Brad noticed that his mom was on the phone. Because of her severe misdeed, he felt his mother no longer had the right to use their phone, so he picked up another receiver in the house.

"*Hello?* Who's this?" Brad asked. The other party on the line remained silent.

Brad began a seething monologue, alerting the silent party to Sharon's transgressions. Brad was now administering discipline, not Sharon. He wanted to punish her.

But nothing was stopping the exodus. The next day, Sharon was gone, and Brad was left to live out his high-school days with the traveling salesman who left twenty dollars on the kitchen counter on Monday with a note that said, "See you on Friday." Sharon had gone back to live in Michigan, and now the woman who had meant everything to Brad was viewed as the devil—or worse. Severing all lines of communication with his mother, Brad began to rely on Bob for everything.

Brad suffered in the wake of Trial by Mother. His grades dipped during his senior year. He was cut from the varsity basketball team. His track performance declined. He became listless and despondent. He wasn't excelling, as he'd done before. He was eking by. These were the initial consequences of a ruined boy.

Brad graduated unremarkably at Cullman High in the spring of 1996. What was supposed to be a welcome culmination was instead anticlimactic. That summer, all Brad could think about was getting away, putting Cullman in his rearview. He would spend his fall as a student at Auburn University, and he hoped that this might be just the fresh start he needed.

He didn't have anything else.

Seventh Street Baptist

There was no foundation. Brad Hawley did not grow up in the church. There was no luxury of Vacation Bible School, no artsy books with stories of men in flowing robes and tunics. Moses, Noah, and Jesus. No sweeping view of how God created the heavens and the earth, how the human race got here, or why he was here. There were no pastel-swathed Easter celebrations, no parables, no Old Testament stories to pique the imagination of a curious child. It was a childhood devoid of arks and whales and palm branches and lions' dens. There was no customary explanation to him of the plan of salvation, no confirmation class, no Bible drill, and no "Jesus Loves Me" sung by a choir of boisterous children.

Until the seventh grade, Brad had little exposure to the Christian church. Brad and his mom would attend occasionally, but there appeared to be no pressing need to lug her only son into the sanctuary every Sunday. It was an anomalous mind-set in the Deep South, where faith and church attendance were societal expectations. The Hawleys' lives were, for the most part, secular. Family, school, and sports were important to Brad, but for a while, nothing sacred entered their lives.

Beginning in middle school, as Brad slowly gained more interest in girls, he quickly discovered that church was an adequate venue for social interaction. His friends were there. Girls were there. Church, though possessing a more serious, eternal element, could be fun. Girls—not the Gospel—were the initial allure.

The Fall of Brad Hawley

So he went. Seventh Street Baptist Church in Cullman. A boxy brick edifice with a stained-glass window on the front facade that patrolled the city like an immovable eye. Branded as the Friendly Church, Seventh Street sat in the quiet middle of downtown Cullman, its green double doors providing a pathway to large doses of God and Gospel and a cavalcade of fun for youngsters. Brad attended on Sundays and Wednesdays, and a trip to Pasquale's Pizza with friends Matt, Mark, Jason, Josh, the other Jason, Laura, Rochelle, Leah, and Etta, always followed the Sunday night service.

Brad was finding his first group. The sociological effect was critical to Brad's development, as it added a certain balance to his only-child isolation. He realized he did not have to live on an island and that others could welcome him into the fold. He became popular with the kids. They liked him. The girls liked him. In youth group, he was drawn to the availability of friends, and though the youth ministers were careful to inject a scriptural basis to church lock-ins, road trips, and Wednesday-night meetings, the message of Christ often came in distant second in the minds of callow youth. The sociology of Seventh Street was probably not much different from many other Southern Baptist churches across the South. Most kids were there to interact with one another, some found Jesus. The church leaders hoped, at the very least, they were receiving spiritual milk. They hoped they were planting seeds that would one day sprout, trusting their efforts were not in vain.

Anyone familiar with church life in Brad's part of the country will tell you that Southern Baptist Life 101 encourages youth to attend a conference known as Centrifuge, held annually at cherry-picked venues across the country. When Brad was in seventh grade, he attended the famous youth extravaganza, that year hosted at Union University in Union, Tennessee. At Centrifuge, thousands of young eaglets migrated from all across the South to sing songs, share testimonies, and dive deep into the Bible, the overarching goal to grow stronger in Christ and trade their pedestrian faith for one that might soar. Perhaps the "centrifugal" force of the retreat would remove the underlying sediment of sin and, through displacement, purify believers so they could fly like eagles. Many came away with a spiritual high and were on fire for God.

The retreat was peppered with recreational activities that facilitated new friendships and, at times, budding romances. Brad went to the retreat more for the interaction with females than he did to learn the ways of Jesus, reserving at least part of his time for a little hanky-panky. As it turned out, he achieved both. Brad met a girl:

"A Centrifuge Tale"
Boy meets girl. Boy takes girl to the mall. Boy makes out with girl.
The End.

So we went to this mall. It was me, her, and maybe a couple of other friends. We were in this toy store, and when we were in there, we kissed for the first time. I remember after we kissed, she stepped back and said, "Cool beans." I thought, "How ridiculous is that?" That it was her response to our first kiss.

It was the first of many open-mouth kisses that week, so Brad recalled.

Even with the distractions, Brad found Jesus Christ. The retreat, ever-Baptisty, offered young children the opportunity to accept Jesus into their hearts. Many did so, and as the retreat was coming to a close, Brad began to feel, for the first time in his life, the swelling need to repent. To allow the washing effect of God's grace and forgiveness cleanse him of unrighteousness, the curse of all humanity since Adam took an unhappy bite out of the garden apple. Brad realized that he was a sinner and that because of the swift and fierce hand of eternal justice, someone had to pay for these transgressions. Therefore Jesus entered the world, lived a sinless life, died a horrific death at the hands of torturers, hung on a cross-topped hill in a corner of Jerusalem, served the sentence himself, and issued Man a pardon. Brad realized that Jesus had died for him. And on the last day of Centrifuge, Brad Hawley accepted Jesus Christ as his Savior and Lord.

The Fall of Brad Hawley

This impassioned moment of justification in the life of the believer made hell no longer a consideration. Brad could rest easy, eternity secure, and nothing could ever pluck him away from the indefatigable grip of Christ.

I went to Centrifuge for the girls, although the emotional part of salvation—I got that at Centrifuge. Was I repentant? Reflectively, yes. I came back to Alabama wanting to vocalize my faith. Vocalize this transformation.

Brad did experience the spiritual high, and he carried New Testament–filled ether back to Cullman. That mountaintop experience at church camp would slowly erode, however, as the new believer found it difficult to maintain a heightened level of spiritual equivalence. Brad discovered that the walking it out part was the more challenging endeavor, and God was not a magician who was on-call 24/7 to wave His eternal wand when Brad needed fixing. This descending effect eventually left Brad confused and disdainful, even though safety nets, erected by the church as a soft place to fall, encouraged discipleship. Once home from utopia, the world was waiting, roaring like a lion. "Normal life" and its petty annoyances threatened ecclesiastical zeal, and soldiering on with the same fervor of faith proved difficult in a fallen, secular world.

But for Brad, the carryover high lasted for at least a little while. One night, Brad and some of the youth had gathered for the Sunday-night adult service in the sanctuary, where something extraordinary happened. During the service, Brad boldly leaped to his feet and yelled, "Jesus is Lord!" Oddly enough, the reaction did not come in the form of crickets or gruff looks.

I sat down thinking, "All right, that may have happened in a silo." But instead, I started this chain reaction. I bet thirty people stood up and repeated me. Adults stood up too. It made me feel warm. I cried. I had actually felt compelled to say it. I didn't sit there and marinate on it before it happened. I just did it. It was pretty neat. I can picture my feelings. I remember feeling that I thought that God was present in that room. It was very emotional.

As time went on, Brad began to experience spiritual atrophy—not in abrupt changes, but rather through a series of small compromises. In ninth grade, he went on a youth mission trip to the beach. Like Centrifuge, the needle of the trip was to tilt more toward the spiritual and transformative than the recreational, but this did little to dissuade mischief in the Florida panhandle. Brad and some friends, no more than fifteen years old, procured a case of beer, smuggled it into the resort, and hid it in the bushes. The boys thought they had gotten away unscathed and looked forward to imbibing on their "bush" beer. But the caper was quickly thwarted when the youth ministers discovered the contraband and parents were phoned, including Brad's.

Brad recalled that his parents "weren't too concerned" that he and others had got into trouble at the youth retreat. After all, boys will be boys, right? But something much more sinister was developing. Brad and his friends were becoming the "wild" kids of the youth group, straddling the fence that bisected the secular world on the one side, the sacred on the other.

I didn't make church a priority like I did when I was younger. But I guess I could have been in a back alley somewhere, smoking pot. But I wasn't. I was in church. There were worse places to be.

One incident left a particularly sour taste in Brad's mouth and would affect the way he viewed Seventh Street, the Baptist church, and, through association, Christianity itself. As a by-product of being a world-marveling young boy, curiosity about sex came to the forefront of thought during his teenage years. Brad soon realized that the "birds and the bees" had a wider connotation than the mere perpetuation of the human species. Sex could be utilized for enjoyment and pleasure as well. Brad had reached that awkward phase where innocent kissing leads to awkward fumbling on living room couches, and curiosity with your own body often leads to spiraling, vivid fantasies. To provide remedy for the lust of the eyes and the bottled-up boyhood frustrations, church leaders counseled Brad and a group of his friends, both individually and collectively, on the wiles and snares of sex. Brad remembered that one particular man, instead of stressing purity and pursuing God when temptation arrived, suggested masturbation as a viable and natural option for the lust-plagued youth.

The church leader pulled us aside and suggested that we masturbate when we experienced lust. As a young kid, that was very disturbing. A little creepy. It made me not want to go back to church or be in a room alone with him. Did it have an effect on my faith? Back then, my perception of Christianity was so shallow. Here was this older man of God telling me this, and it just made me feel icky. It changed my perception of church leadership, to the core. It started eroding my view of the church.

Disconcerting as it was, Brad stayed involved. He was somehow able to look past the peculiar suggestion and continue his affiliation with the church, for there was enough of a foundation and rapport with his friends to continue his involvement. Brad even participated in a church performance known as *The Judgment.* In this portrayal, audience members walked through different rooms of the church to experience the feeling of heaven and hell, and Brad happily joined in the festivities. He later became interested in theater and used his church experiences as a springboard into the high-school drama club. In eleventh grade, he was named a "regional thespian" for his portrayal of a character that was cast to hell from purgatory. The character's name was Shad.

The value Brad found in youth group had more to do with human relationships than spiritual ones. Person-to-person interaction supplanted the metaphysical, and the people with whom he made fast friends trumped the seemingly one-way conversation with the Trinity. In other words, Brad could hear his friends' voices audibly, whereas he felt he was lobbing conversation to the heavens with little or no response. Further, Brad's view of "home" was built, not by brick and mortar, but by groups that embraced him.

All my family was in Michigan. My mother was close to me, and my father was not. I was living in Alabama with no family. I found family at Seventh Street Baptist. It was my family outlet. Sunday nights. Wednesday nights. Two times a week, I was there.

Because of Brad's mistaken view of Christianity as a religion of compulsion and obligation, the Good News didn't take. Brad saw the Gospel as a set of dos and don'ts, the Bible a mega rulebook, and God a statistician marking off missteps in his eternal ledger. Somehow the goodness of Christ and the availability of a personal relationship with Christ escaped him, and Brad settled for a life barren of grace.

Youth group was an inlet, but nonetheless an important inlet, that was part of a much larger sea of Seventh Street. At Seventh Street, the youth assimilated into the greater congregation nicely, and Brad felt at ease among the adults. Given the reputation of some Baptist churches as "hard graders" in terms of the Christian walk, Brad said he felt no real sense of condemnation at Seventh Street, even after the heinous beer incident.

Youth group was very powerful. We were known. We were important. My friends were the core, and the younger guys in youth group seemed to look up to us.

Still forming an opinion of Christianity, Brad went to Seventh Street sporadically through twelfth grade, while other interests warred for his attention. A new girlfriend and the track team stole time, and slowly he began to feel as if he didn't need youth group anymore. Brad could get interaction anywhere. He didn't have to go to the church. And because his faith lacked an abiding element, he began to drift from that salvific moment at Centrifuge when he invited Christ to reign in his life as Lord and Savior. Brad would later place blame—at least in part—for his fall-ing away on the failure of the church to employ enough "scholarly" at-tention to the faith. In other words, no organized study or program was instituted for young people that might usher him down the road of dis-cipleship. Perhaps the church concentrated too much on getting people saved as opposed to the actual walking out of faith. Thus he saw little use for church or biblical concepts, no inherent need for application to his life. Besides, one's youth was not the time to think critically about serious matters, so Brad thought. It was time to be a boy, have fun, and chase chicks. Conversely, the serious Christian, Brad believed, lived a life that was mundane and boring, the rigidity of rules zapping the life out of its adherents.

Yet Brad failed to understand that moving out church and youth group created a void in his soul. He would try for years to fill it with the pleasures of life, but only found emptiness. He would get sucked into the vortex of fraternity life. He would walk away from Cullman and never come back. He found a new life as a college man, became an es-capee of small-town life with its small-town whisperings. He was able to construct a new Brad. He was free to do whatever he wanted, without the perceived chains of Christianity enslaving him to obedience. His life didn't have to be interrupted anymore with the constraints of the Bible. He could be free to do what he wanted, live by impulse, and feed the de-sires of the flesh. Besides, college wasn't *real* life—right?—and Brad was eager to sample from a buffet of pursuits. His secular uncoiling centered on the vertical pronoun, "I," and biblical thoughts evaporated. Leaving Cullman marked the beginning of his odyssey into the world.

Brad's path to his own perdition seemed peaceable. C. S. Lewis once wrote, "Indeed the safest road to Hell is the gradual one—the gentle slope, soft underfoot, without sudden turnings, without milestones, without signposts." To be sure, nothing tipped Brad off as he was inching closer to the cliff. Nothing alerted him to the slow and covert degrada-tion to which he was lured. There were no flashing signs, no heralds to announce the coming of destruction. The cruel authors of the godless narratives in his mind came maliciously and anonymously as he was presented the choices of life. They didn't alert him to their twisting and spinning, their malevolent tweaking of the truth, as Brad reveled in that blessed commodity that God bestowed upon the human race: free will.

So when he did fall, it was a shocking revelation.

When he did fall, he wondered how in the world he had come so close to the edge without realizing it.

Auburn

Auburn was a wonderland. On the campus of this homey Southern university, the clock tower atop orange-bricked Samford Hall stood guard over a series of strong oaks scattered prettily throughout the plains and a sign that read, "AUBURN UNIVERSITY, Established 1856." Students flashed across the angular paths of campus, between the soaring porticos, wearing backpacks and blue jeans, extending courtesies to their fellow Plainsmen and Plainswomen. The clannish Auburn community produced few strangers, and Brad hoped that a change of scenery, the embrace of new friends, and distance from Cullman would be the best cocktail for the life that ailed him. In Auburn, Brad would find the family he desired.

Brad found much to explore in this quaint town, and he was ecstatic to drink from the chalice of a world without adults. Instead of getting back to center with his Christian walk, Brad discovered that the secular pull of American college life was initially too strong a temptation. The motherless, lovelorn nineteen-year-old retreated into the bottles of the night: cheap Natty Light beer consumed in apartments with antiseptic walls and thrift-store couches. The former athlete who had once been in tip-top shape began to smoke cigarettes and party to excess, hitting a strip of grungy bars on nights that seemed to never end. Brad even smoked a little pot from time to time.

In his first year at Auburn, Brad became the average college student, meaning he wasn't excelling at much of anything, except being average.

He bought in to the secular college experience, this sort of otherworldly domain outside of real life, thrusting himself into its severe clutches. He bought into the lie that "this is what you're *supposed* to do in college." Meaning party, hook-up, and get hammered. He viewed Auburn as an escape from reality, college life a sanctuary for rebellion. In his first quarter, his grades plummeted. He scored a paltry 2.13 GPA, barely eligible to remain on campus. A member of the Auburn intelligentsia, Brad was not.

Brad did keep in touch with Bob, but the two could muster no more than a phone-length relationship. There was very little depth or discussion. The relationship was affectionless. Sharon was totally out of the picture.

Brad's main purpose at this crossroads of life was to construct a new identity. Let's see…what could he be? The slovenly, tie-dye-wearing dope smoker? The medieval weirdo, engaging in swordplay and hardcore LARPing on the grassy quad? The bratty fraternity guy wearing loafers with no socks and sloshing cheap bourbon in tumblers? As Brad circulated campus, he found that Auburn life offered an array of packs, and this critical choice of a friend group would have a profound impact on what Brad would become.

For Brad, new identity making involved shutting out the person of his past. There was a current at Auburn, an electricity that fed to his baser passions that Cullman particularly lacked. He rarely thought about his former life. He no longer wanted to be the boy of his youth, but stronger. Initially, he thought that if he became callous and uncaring, it would help him to achieve an identity of strength, but he quickly realized that chasing the average life was empty. Ease had a trade-off. You lose purpose. Lose respect. Mediocrity's opportunity cost was a bad trade.

A turning point occurred in his sophomore year. Inexplicably, Brad decided to participate in fraternity rush and was accepted into one of the premier Greek organizations on campus, Phi Gamma Delta. Fiji, as it is known nationally, consistently ranked in the top three of Greek academics and athletics, and Brad was happy to become a member of this brotherhood. The fraternity took on a role similar to what the track team had provided years before. Served as the accountability that he otherwise lacked. Again, Brad did not want to disappoint his newfound band of brothers.

Since Brad had grown up as an only child, his associations with friends, both inside and outside of fraternity life, took on grand importance. He viewed his friends as brothers and sisters, siblings he had never had, and believed that water could be just as thick as blood. He became known as a hugger, as he did not first reach for a hand but instead offered an embrace as a token of affection.

What Brad truly wanted was to stand out, and his mind-set on manhood was based largely on performance. He took an assessment of his life and realized that he could not rise up fraternity or campus ranks if he became the John Belushi of *Animal House*, or if he simply got lost in the crowd. He wanted to be a leader, not a clown. He surmised that the first order of business was to drop the binge drinking and the smoking. Done. Then he focused on becoming a leader in his pledge class. Done. Once he was initiated, his natural leadership abilities made him an influential active member, and he eventually segued these experiences campus-wide. Brad applied for orientation counselor for incoming freshman students and for the position of student recruiter, and he was one of the many applicants to be tapped for these revered organizations. His career on the campus at Auburn continuing to develop, he was soon named to the elite Plainsmen. Twelve impressive young men donning orange sport coats and serving as the official "hosts" of Auburn University.

Brad had officially become a disciple of Auburn.

It took a little convincing, but at the insistence of friends, Brad ran in a campus election for the position of student government treasurer. Announced as the winner at the school amphitheater with over a thousand students in attendance, he attributed his victory to his catchy slogan emblazoned on T-shirts and billboards across campus, which read, "MONEY." Then came the ultimate honor for an Auburn student. Spade Honor Society. This group was and is defined as the ten most prominent and influential students on campus. To add another feather in his cap, he began dating Miss Auburn. In a matter of years, Brad had risen from average, unassuming Auburn student to Big Man on Campus.

Given Brad's checkered background, it is unexplainable why everything began to fall into place at Auburn. Perhaps it was because of the groups through which he moved, ensembles he silently treated as familial units. Perhaps these groups took on the role of parent in helping Brad mature. Perhaps Brad, wounded by his past, possessed an indomitable spirit that would not be denied.

With accolades piling up, he was learning to be self-reliant. Success was finding him without God, without family. *Why did he need those things?* He could do it himself. He hadn't considered that God might have had a hand in manufacturing these achievements.

Brad's uprising against childhood, against the feeble, easily wounded mama's boy, was realized by his ascension to Auburn heights. In his mind, this should have been enough to cure the lesions of his history. Yet title and influence, the masks he wore, could not satisfy the inner workings of the heart. It was all a pretty image, the campus image he created, the awards and accolades. But it betrayed the bog of agony in his interior.

While all seemed to be trending in the right direction at Auburn, his home life was dreadful. When he was in Auburn, he could put his family life on a shelf. On holidays he had to face a broken family. Had to replay it. He hated visiting Cullman. The severed home. The awkward conversations. The gossip. For all the benefits of living in Small Town, America, the nosy nature of it was particularly disgusting to Brad, especially when your family wears a letter the hue of scarlet.

But the ache grew. After years of operating without a mother, Brad slowly began to desire a relationship with the woman who had been the most prominent part of his youth. Though they were physically distant, Brad was still emotionally invested in Sharon. For all the pain Sharon had caused, the need to have her in his life outweighed the agony of not having her at all when Brad applied the scales of justice to his situation.

The Fall of Brad Hawley

After all, she had brought him into this world, hauled him around in her womb for the equivalent of a major league baseball season, doted on him, fed him, clothed him, loved him, and nurtured him for the first seventeen years of his life.

During his senior year in high school, news from Michigan revealed that one of Sharon's old suitors, a man named Tom, had emerged from the mist of the past. Brad didn't know anything about Tom, but he would soon learn of a long-standing relationship, once dormant but now active. Sharon married Tom later that year.

Enough time had ticked away, Brad surmised, to drown a regiment of demons from the army that raided his relationship with his mother. So he sucked it up, pulled up his bootstraps, and called her.

The initial conversations ending the two-year estrangement were very terse, very brusque. As the dialogue softened, Brad was able to admit he wanted to see his mother and, potentially, meet Tom. He could try to forgive, though forgetting the ordeal Brad believed to be an impossibility.

Thus the meeting of The Big Three—Brad, Tom, and Sharon—was scheduled for Thanksgiving weekend in Nashville. Nashville was chosen because of its location. It was halfway between Michigan and Auburn. Brad drove up, Sharon and Tom drove down. The family stayed in the Opryland Hotel, and Brad insisted that Tom and Sharon provide him his own room. Perhaps the fee could serve as reparations.

Awkward as it was, the meeting went surprisingly well. Tom obviously cared enough about Sharon to make nice with her son, though Brad stiff-armed him when Tom made affectionate advances. It was clear that Brad wanted to wrest control of the situation and keep Sharon a safe distance away emotionally. A place where he could manage her. Given the breach of trust, this was understandable.

In the coming months, Sharon was in and out of Brad's life at Brad's discretion. Like an allowance, Brad gave her time as he felt she needed it. The relationship had shifted from mother-son to debtor-creditor. One of the few instances of mercy occurred when Sharon and Tom attended Parents' Weekend at Auburn. The relationship was mending, but there was something bothering Brad. Someone at Parents' Weekend had casually mentioned how much Brad "looked like Tom," and that thought began to torment him.

Several months later, Sharon and Tom were driving through Auburn to their winter home in Florida. Sharon and Tom were snowbirds, living half the time in Michigan and half in Florida. When the pair arrived in town, Brad asked if he could see his mother and speak to her alone. Brad then suggested they go for a drive.

They pulled the car over near some railroad tracks, and Brad asked her the question that had been haunting him.

"I gotta hear you say no, 'cause I can't get this outta my head," Brad said.

Fidgeting, Brad looked toward the tracks and boldly asked his estranged-and-now-back-again mother the truth of a twenty-year-old event: "Is Tom my real dad?"

Because of Brad's development into a student leader at Auburn, he had gained a considerable amount of chutzpah that had been somewhat absent as a high-school student. His involvement on campus had further helped him to grow up, and instead of waiting on life to come at him, he seized life by the throat. He realized that he could captain his own ship and do it admirably. As a result, Brad's upstart maturity made him particularly curt with Sharon.

Astonished, Sharon broke into tears as she rummaged her mind for the right words.

"It's complicated," she replied.

"Mom, no—it's not. It's not complicated at all. Just answer the question. Is Tom my dad?"

Sharon paused and looked up tearfully into Brad's brown eyes. Then she dropped bomb number two: "Yes, he is."

The three-word explosive fell, and the seamless continuum of ancestral truth was thwarted by one riveting statement. Brad gathered himself, considering the entirety of the implications. He thought about Bob. *Did he know the truth?*

The Fall of Brad Hawley

Two months after Brad received the news about his biological father, Brad officially broke the news to Bob that he had suspected for years. Bob, whom Brad had referred to as "Dad" for the entirety of his life, was now sent into a paternal abyss, the world of a stranger, an imposter who had unknowingly posed as his biological father for two decades.

The day Brad told him was the first time the two men had cried together.

His own family in total disarray, it is not surprising that Brad sought out familial outlets as he marched along this lone adult highway. By his senior year, Brad had already begun poaching campus for the future Mrs. Hawley. He wanted a family of his own.

At Southern universities at the time, there existed an inherent undercurrent to marry, and many co-eds operated as if college graduation were an impending cliff to a lonely life of singleness. When daydreaming of his own family, he kept an image of a fortress in his mind. He came from a fractured middle-class family, one that, ultimately, did not provide a great deal of emotional stability. He wanted his new fortress to be impressive. Like everything else in his life, success was within his grip.

As he credentialed several candidates for marriage, he made sure they were of solid stock. Trustworthy. Dependable. Loyal. Wouldn't bolt if things got testy. Because of Sharon's protectionism and incessant shielding of him from the truth, Brad desired someone who instead cherished the truth and wasn't afraid to tell him what he didn't want to hear. He looked back at the dysfunctional makeup of his own family, the porous, insincere nature of it, and purposed to have a successful family of his own. Once he had the chance, he would be dogged in his desire to make it work. His and his eventual partner's collective honesty and transparency would avoid the familial fatalism that had ruined his own family. Unfortunately, the scars from his youth would pose the greatest threat to him down the road.

Future plans were threatened, however, when Miss Auburn moved to Boston, the wedge of distance creating an uneasy dynamic. When

Brad visited her on the weekends, the couple often attended Saturday night Mass. Brad had always held an appreciation for the Catholic Church, its history and ritual, but now he began to develop a greater interest as he sat idle during the Eucharist, as any good Protestant would do. While an onlooker to the sacrament, Brad pondered the Catholic belief in transubstantiation—that the consecrated bread and wine transformed into the *actual* body and blood of Christ—and, genuinely moved by the ritual, felt that Christ was indeed present in that room.

When he returned to Alabama that Monday, he investigated further. He phoned a local parish and inquired about RCIA (Rites of Christian Initiation for Adults) and the requirements to become Catholic. Coincidentally, RCIA started the following week, and Brad saw this as a sign. The next Monday, Brad was sitting in a chair at Saint Mark's Catholic Church, commencing the six-month program. A sponsor was required for Brad's conversion, and God placed a man in Brad's life named Walt, whom Brad grew to highly respect. Brad and Walt shared moments together and pored over the academic side of Catholicism. He learned about the early church. He learned about Catholic doctrine regarding Mary, confession, and purgatory. In addition, Brad shared stories of his journey and what he believed God was teaching him in the midst of his experiences. Though Brad did not feel obliged to join the church or to be confirmed, as Easter of that year approached, the date when all the catechumens are confirmed, Brad felt a calling. He had been saved in the Protestant church and was now a practicing Catholic.

Brad and Miss Auburn would eventually break up, and even though he had achieved a great college experience, Brad yet again felt the urge to get away, start a new life. After graduation, he spent a summer in Costa Rica before moving to Washington, DC, to find gainful post-college employment.

Escapism proved to be expensive for Brad. Moving to DC almost penniless, he was soon baptized into the cruel waters of job life in the nation's capital. Luckily, he found a job as a marketer with an outfit called the Corporate Executive Board, a global firm specializing in corporate performance. The running/escape/brotherhood theme continued in DC. There, his work associates would become like brothers.

Later, Brad would get the opportunity to hurl himself into the breach of marriage. He thought that creating a family of his own would somehow abolish the baggage of childhood. But neither change in geography nor construction of his own clan could erase the untoward feelings he had for Sharon. He had let her back into his life, but he hadn't forgiven her.

At Auburn, Brad had begun to believe in himself again. He had found a second family, a second life. What he didn't realize was that the devil was up to some old tricks. As the old saying goes, "Ships don't sink because of the water around them; ships sink because of the water that gets in them."

THE DEATH OF BRAD HAWLEY

Brad Hawley always had a premonition he was going to die early. He never saw himself as an old man, sitting on the couch watching *The Price Is Right*. Because of this, he had always lived adventurously. Taking it to the line, toeing it, leaning over, testing it. For thirty-four years of his life, he lived life from this ledge.

Since Sharon walked out when Brad was sixteen, Brad had no problem taking risks, the sense of invincibility and egoism men feel in their twenties bleeding over into his time in Washington, DC. Into married life. It never occurred to him that people were relying on him, counting on him. So he'd just go for it.

For Brad, the real cream of life was found in the ecstasy of hairpin turns, butterflies-in-the-gut falls, steep slopes, dizzying altitudes, raging rapids, heavier weight, the Pilgrim's Progress up the mountainside, conquered skies, the guts to try it. Life from the ledge. Since Brad didn't think he'd make fifty, he crammed as much adventure into his life as his money allowed. It was his Mickey Mantle syndrome, a feeling that he was going to die young. Perhaps subconsciously, Brad didn't care if he lived or died. Or, perhaps, vanity clouded his logic.

Brad had never been conscious of physical risks, and he had never been injured at all until Ellen came into his life. Now it seemed that every passing year brought another injury. Eight years straight. One year, he broke his wrist. Another, he blew out his knee. Then there was the venomous snakebite. Then there was the year he got hit by a car. He was riding his bike when a car struck him, knocking him unconscious. His helmet was impaled, and he sustained a minor vertebral fracture. A week later, he was back on the bike.

Brad failed to realize that these shakings, increasing in severity, were a warning for him to tamper it down.

At 12:45 p.m., Brad Hawley was dying on the floor of the gym. Although Brad's life was in peril, there seemed to be a peculiar calm among the other gym members, who, showing little sense of panic, seemed undisturbed by the grim event. Perhaps no one working out that day comprehended the severity of the fall. Perhaps the obsession and preoccupation with finishing the WOD took prime importance. Perhaps the athletes had been programmed to take cues from their coaches, and trusted them to handle the situation. Or—and this is the most cynical of the "perhapses"—perhaps few really cared.

When Brad involuntarily dismounted from the bar into a dangerous aerial dance, his right shoulder blade hit the floor first. Then, in a violent motion, his head whiplashed backward and pummeled the hard surface.

It was an eerily low thump.

It didn't sound as if anything had shattered.

The weight of his legs came down hard on top of him, scrunching and arcing his vertebrae, like a plow pose in yoga. He flipped over.

Coach Mark jumped up incredulously. Gathering himself, he crouched in terror at his pupil lying supine on the floor, thrashing, legs flailing as if kicking invisible objects. Witnessing this type of scene was a coach's worst nightmare, something only dreamed of, hell.

A few of the other members slowly walked over to the grisly scene to investigate, standing over Brad with hands perched on hips, saturnine, stoic. One bent over to get a better angle of the disaster, like a miner squatting to look through a tunnel. Others seemed indifferent. One man marked his time on the board and walked over to take a swallow from the water fountain, glancing at the calamity out of the corner of his eye.

Did anyone call 911?

Two minutes.

Brad sat up with legs crossed, elbows on knees, holding his throbbing head inside cupped hands. He rolled over again, propping himself against the floor with one hand and rubbing the back of his head with the other.

He could not stay still.

His legs were convulsing as Mark stood over him.

Three and a half minutes.

By then, Mark was the only person standing next to Brad. Most others appeared focused on the exercises. Walking to and fro across the gym. Returning to their workouts. Getting water. Going about their normal routine as if the event was customary.

A female trainer crouched over Brad. Mark jotting on his clipboard.

As Brad writhed on the bloodless floor, a woman completed her handstand push-ups on a box, and two men chatted at the water fountain.

I cannot believe these people whom I had considered family left me lying there in the grip of death.

Six minutes.

Though no one could see it, the blood had begun. When Brad hit the ground, the force ruptured a blood vessel inside of his head. The blood wasn't visible to the other members because it wasn't pouring out of Brad's head. It was pouring into it.

Brad was moving and speaking, which was encouraging. Maybe he just had a bump on his noggin and he'll dust himself off and we'll all laugh about it later.

Unfortunately, this was not the case.

That's the scary thing about head injuries. One minute a person can seem all right. Three minutes later, he or she is dead.

Once in Charlotte, Ellen and her boss loaded up a rental car and drove to the town of Hickory, approximately an hour away. They arrived around lunch, just in time for the first training session with fifteen other sales reps.

"The founder of the company was speaking, so it was a big deal," Ellen recalled.

North Carolina is renowned for its furniture and Hickory, the epicenter of furniture country, formed a triangle with Charlotte to the southeast and Asheville to the west. Ellen's company specialized in high-end private office furniture, and one of the companies with which she was associated offered the following motto: "Great furniture does not live in a vacuum. Or a showroom. It lives in the real world of business."

Ellen, the kind of employee who took her job seriously, nestled into a chair, listening intently while scribbling notes. While she was sitting in the meeting, her phone rang. She checked the number and it was her next-door neighbor, Mary Katherine. Because Ellen didn't want to cause a disruption, she silenced her phone and put it back in her bag. Ellen and Brad had just moved into their home. They hadn't known Mary Katherine long and Ellen, thinking it odd that she was calling, focused back on the meeting and dismissed the call from her mind.

But Mary Katherine was not going to stop until she reached Ellen. From Alabama, Mary Katherine fired a text, which arrived in Hickory almost instantaneously: "Do you need me to pick up the kids?"

That's weird, Ellen thought.

"It was the middle of the day. Why would she be asking me if she needed to pick up the kids?" Ellen remembered. "A few minutes went by, and I couldn't stop thinking about it. So I excused myself from the meeting and stepped outside and called her."

Ellen would not find good news at the end of the call.

At 12:52 p.m., Brad's limp body lay prostrate on the floor as a carnival of exercise surrounded him. A man was against the wall doing handstand push-ups, kicking his legs like an upside-down frog swimming into deeper water.

Between breaths, Brad mentioned that he was about to vomit. As if in a relay race, Mark and Peter—a gym member and friend of Brad's— shot off in different directions, frantically looking for the nearest trash can. Two cans were simultaneously produced, and Mark's, arriving soonest, won. Brad sat up and tossed his left leg around the small rubber Walmart-like can, hugging it the way a parent would a small child in a beach portrait. He continued to squirm. He switched back to the more comfortable cross-legged position, reminiscent of his childhood, in front of the TV eating chocolate-fudge Pop-Tarts, alone on the floor.

Eight minutes.

The garbage can was moved. Brad stretched out, right leg behind him, forearm on the can's rim and head buried in forearm, like Christ at Gethsemane. No vomit was produced.

Now things were getting desperate. Brad was no longer making sense. His words were gibberish. He still had not gotten up off the floor. A small crowd began to gather around. Athletes. Trainers.

Eleven minutes.

It was becoming clear that something had to be done.

Had anyone called 911?

Brad was still contorting. He dropped to the floor again, on his side.

Thirteen minutes.

Mark squatted beside him and held the garbage can to his face.

Had safety response training prepared Mark for a situation this dire?

More working out around them.

A woman lifting a bar off the squat rack.

More handstand push-ups.

The gym should have stopped. The whole gym should have stopped.

Jimmy Brady, one of Brad's best friends at Steel Company, looks back on that day with retrospective grief, assessing the situation thusly:

The Fall of Brad Hawley

Everyone was a big fan of Brad. He was one of the better athletes in the gym. He knew everyone, and everyone knew who he was. He fit the mantra of what CrossFit is about. If you were struggling, he was there cheering you on.

When he fell, everyone else was doing their own workout. Part of the WOD was a two-hundred- and four-hundred-meter run, and he fell just as I ran into the gym. I did not see him fall.

This wasn't the first time someone had fallen at toes to bar. I had fallen in March or April and landed on my back. It also happened to Martin Brown. Although I was told that Brad had hit his head, there was nothing that gave me concern that this was really serious. He was talking to us. He was sitting up, carrying on a conversation. I coached Little League football, and I've learned a little bit about concussions. He wasn't knocked out. If anyone had thought Brad was really hurt, we would have been over there. At some point, he said, "My head really hurts" and "I think I'm going to be sick." He was getting nauseated. But the thought never crossed my mind that he had cracked his skull. If he had lost consciousness, he would have been knocked out. I even went over and started cleaning up my weights. If I had had any suspicion that it was serious, I would have been over there.

Jimmy was right. This wasn't a concussion. This was something much more threatening. Jimmy's assessment raises an important concern. With all the scuttlebutt surrounding football's new policies regarding head injuries, concussions particularly, has society been conditioned to think that being "knocked out" is the measuring stick for head-injury severity? With 1.7 million people sustaining traumatic brain injury (TBI) every year, society cannot afford to remain ignorant of the proper response when someone hits his or her head, especially without a helmet.

Brad began losing control of his limbs and motor function. He knocked the garbage can over like a clumsy child with a toy. A member came over to console him and prop up the can.

Sixteen minutes.

Cell phones were produced.

Paramedics in white shirts appeared.

The WOD was over.

Mark brought in a laptop computer and showed one of the paramedics something on the screen. Perhaps it was pedigree information on Brad. Perhaps it was security cam footage of the fall.

A stretcher was wheeled in, as Mark continued to consult with the paramedic, who retrieved the information he needed.

Time was running out.

Ellen didn't know.

Brad was lifted onto the gurney and taken away as the paramedics tended to him.

An archipelago of Brad's sweat was scattered ominously on the floor behind them.

The gym was attentive now.

"Take him to the nearest hospital," Jimmy urgently instructed the paramedics.

Brad Hawley was about to die.

THE MAKING OF A MAN

Death arrived on August 27. Brad Hawley, dead at thirty-four.
The cause? Head injury. Cranial trauma caused by an inflated obsession with defeating himself. The hysteria to push further. The need for one more rep. The unsatisfied machismo urge to win, achieve, overcome, prove. Perhaps a subtle snub of precaution, a cocky dismissal of hazard.

Screw it. Let's do this.

Place of death: Mountain Brook.

Mountain Brook. A gingerbread house of a community. A place where horrific events are not supposed to happen. Murders. Rapes. Traumatic head injuries.

Mountain Brook. A place of placid insularity. A place of rhythmic sameness. A place bent on upward mobility, where daddies pass hedge funds down bloodlines to their bow-tied scions and mothers push gurgling tykes, anchored in strollers, down its avenues.

Mountain Brook. A place where mansions, high on hills, emit an air of superiority, as passersby fantasize of becoming the resident kings and queens.

Yes, an event of this macabre nature was not supposed to happen here.

This was Utopia.

Living in Mountain Brook facilitated a dynamic that was an important vessel for Brad's demise, principally because "Brookies," as residents are called, are not content on being average. People live in Mountain Brook because they want to live exceptionally, and when Brad uttered the phrase, "I live in Mountain Brook," he found pleasure in the connotation. Though not a son of this city, though his was not a silver-spoon childhood, though his family had been middle-class, briefcase-fat Yankee transplants to the rural town of Cullman and he had married into the pleasant and protective Mountain Brook aristocracy when he found Ellen, he was nevertheless part of a cloister of success. Ellen's father, Milton Magnus, made a good living in the clothes hanger business, around which he continued a successful enterprise started by his grandfather. Bred to the bone in Mountain Brook and a wedding cake of a family, the Magnuses were well known throughout the town, well liked, and well thought of. Marrying into a family with the rich and scrupulous history of the Magnuses would further solidify Brad's fortress dream. This is not to say Brad married Ellen because of that fact, but ancestry certainly didn't hurt matters. Once he was in—meaning *in* the Mountain Brook conclave—there was no way he was going to be average, even by Mountain Brook standards.

Because of his past, Brad felt the need to show others that even though he came from a middle-class town and middle-class people, he was no rube. Perhaps if he could thrive, even though he was not indigenous to Mountain Brook, he could become naturalized and accepted into the citizenry.

In their first few years of marriage, Brad and Ellen lived in Homewood, another Over the Mountain town. Over the Mountain meaning over Red Mountain. A principally Birminghamesque term connoting prosperity. But the goal was Mountain Brook, for in the Hawleys' eyes, Homewood was a perfect place for the start of their marriage. Mountain Brook was the place where they would settle.

Brad and Ellen had been looking for ways to crack the shell, and when a fixer-upper came available, they pounced. True, its price tag and overall ambiance were on the low end of this phenomenal city, but they shared the same zip code with people who, long ago, built now-sprawling businesses and enjoyed the fruits of their labor while swallowing choice bourbon at the exclusive Birmingham Country Club. Now the thirty-somethings, in becoming happy denizens of Mountain Brook, could relax. There was a feeling that they'd made it.

But for Brad, there was no relaxing or rest. Echoing the performance-based mind-set that had germinated at Auburn, Brad focused on projecting an image of success and prosperity, the white-picket-fence life devoid of all toil, discomfort, and paucity. Brad had already achieved the American dream—house/car/wife—but he continued to long for a limitless more. Now it was all about accumulation, what he could gather and project. Every day became show-and-tell, and he would never be satisfied. As a pastor once said, "God doesn't mind you having stuff. He minds stuff having you."

It was at this precise locus where Satan pulled off his greatest charade on Brad Hawley. Buying into lies about true manhood, Brad was tempted into self-indulgence and self-identification through his possessions, performance, and body parts. In other words, Brad found his manhood, his identity, in the midst of his stuff, his scores, and his physique—this Alpha Male cluster. Brad would soon find that these were slippery and fickle indicators. The luster of cars waned. His performance wasn't always top notch. His body would experience atrophy. Someone always had a bigger house and nicer things. More money. Comparison became the thief that robbed him of joy.

Brad was hanging his hat on things that could easily be lost or taken away. Things that rot and spoil quickly. Scanning the neighborhoods, the residents, he looked at what he saw around him and began to covet. Square footage. Size of estates. Disposable income. Bigger and faster automobiles. Physical fitness. Expensive dogs wagging their tails in backyards. The feeling of importance in cigar-choked, green-carpeted rooms at the country club.

Mountain Brook made him burn to find extreme success. To matter.

Al Blanton

Because of this never-satisfied dynamic, Brad found only rare and evanescent joy, fleeting gratification. He was constantly trying to "show himself a man," but his idea of what manhood entailed became severely skewed, fitting the profile of worldly manhood rather than spiritual manhood. It was all about the material and the physical, and Brad found his identity in it. It would take a stark epiphany to change this mind-set. A fall, perhaps.

If there were such a term as "lost Christian," Brad would have fit the mold. He was so busy building his "fortress" that he'd forgotten his cardinal responsibility as a Christian father: to be the spiritual leader of the household and to love his wife as Christ loved the church. He was listening to the narrative of the world, concentrating more on what the world billboarded as hallmarks of manhood than measuring his manhood with the person of Christ. It mattered more what he was doing in the world than what Christ was doing in him.

One Saturday that August was particularly telling. A birthday party had been planned for the Hawleys' son, Webb. The party was supposed to begin at 10:00 a.m., but the night before and the morning after, Brad tried to convince Ellen that he had time for a quick 9:00 a.m. WOD before the party. Ellen assured Brad that it wouldn't be well received if he showed up late. And although Brad stayed at home that morning, it was clear that he wasn't able to think logically with respect to family matters. Worse, Brad even formulated a plan to show up casually late to the party, ensuring that the other parents who had arrived would *ooh* and *ah* at his sweaty shirt that clung to his well-constructed frame. Pecs with your cake, anyone?

He had gone Steel Company mad. Checked in to the Ritz-Carlton of pride. Myopic in how others perceived him, Brad was willing to trade what could have been a big day for a chance at a body show. A week later, he fell.

So as Brad was perishing on the floor of the gym, he didn't realize that people *were* counting on him. He didn't realize how greatly his absence might have affected his family. How his emotional absence *was* affecting his family. By not exercising caution, he was risking his and Ellen's future.

If something happened to Brad, Ellen would be left to take care of their family alone. It would be *Ellen* who would have to raise Webb and Marlen by herself.

It would be *Ellen* who would have to take on the duties left by an absent father.

It would be *Ellen* who would have to school their children and teach them The Way.

It would be *Ellen* who would be the sole authority on discipline.

It would be *Ellen* who alone would encourage them.

It would be Ellen who would have to pick up the baton that Brad fumbled.

See You on Tuesday

The Virginia Gold Cup Race is a yearly congregation of beautiful people. Held in Warrenton, Virginia, and known as the world's largest tailgate, this hoity-toity affair is a place where seersucker-swallowed men and their broad-hatted dates gather to watch ponies race through an obstacle course called a *steeplechase*. For many of these patrons, the race itself is really a sideshow, an excuse to throw one terrific party and dress up in clownish, magazine-worthy garb. The objective is to see and be seen, and the soused throngs promenading the grassy walkways in their sartorial splendor create an atmosphere that would cause one to think, upon viewing, that the pastel section of a paint store had been detonated or that a massive tryout for Peter Millar clothing is occurring. The myriad bow ties flash like fireflies. Elegant, suntanned arms and legs stretch out of expensive dresses. Vivid pocket squares poke their heads out of coats. Horse-bit loafers jingle. Sport jackets boast a variety of patterns: plaids, windowpanes, or solids. Pants are lime green, salmon, red, or madras. The general rule is the more pastel, the better. Per tradition, the bon vivants gulp mint juleps out of silver cups and namedrop to demonstrate their high social function and DC political connections. Through the gauze of bourbon and gin, they watch jockeys in vibrant uniforms guide the horses around the mile-and-a-quarter track. And it was there, among the many nations of color, among the haute spectacle, that Brad and Ellen first realized the chemical reactions between them.

The Fall of Brad Hawley

Ellen Magnus, the middle child of Milton and Gail Magnus, grew up in a strict Presbyterian household in Mountain Brook. She describes her mind-set of girlhood as an adherence to good. She was a rule follower who didn't drink, smoke, or curse. Major offenses in Southern culture. Like many girls in the Over the Mountain area, Ellen attended a Bible study called the Community Ministry for Girls, hosted by a strong Christian woman by the name of Donna Green. Ellen matriculated in the Mountain Brook school system and participated on the dance team. She loved to study the French language, taking a total of five years of that romantic, beautiful tongue in high school and later in college.

By the conclusion of high school, Ellen decided that she wanted to be an interior designer but began to feel claustrophobic in the pressurized Mountain Brook bubble. So after graduation, she plotted to get away and enrolled at Auburn in the fall of 1997. At Auburn, Ellen joined Alpha Delta Pi sorority and was elected as SGA senator in Human Sciences.

In the spring of 2001, she graduated in interior design with a minor in French, parlaying her studies into a post-graduation summer internship in Paris. Ellen moved to Washington, DC, in November of 2001 and worked as an interior designer for a commercial architecture firm. A little over a year later, Brad moved to DC.

In a cosmopolitan town, both Ellen and Brad would assimilate effortlessly. They had attractive personalities and made friends with ease. Since both of them reconnected with people with whom they'd had previous connections, who themselves ran in larger packs, the anonymity of big city life quickly dissipated. "DC was very transient," Ellen said. "This was during the Bush administration. I remember there were twelve people from my graduating class at Mountain Brook who were there and a bunch of different friends from college."

Ellen was drawn to the DC nightlife but, unlike others who drowned in its secular undertow, managed to stay relatively grounded in her faith. "It was a very social place," Ellen said. "We'd be out every night. I'd work till six or seven o'clock, go out, and get home around ten o'clock. It seemed like every night there was an event." Ellen continued to attend Presbyterian services, even after long nights in Georgetown or other bar-dotted boroughs.

Ellen and Brad never met at Auburn, even though their time in the small college town overlapped for three years. Like a needle in a haystack, doubtless it should have been more difficult to meet Brad in DC, a town of over a half million residents and millions more in the metro area. But indeed their lives were converging among the DC masses, and God was orchestrating their paths to cross at just the right moment, through the right friendships. "Brad and I met through mutual friends in 2003," Ellen said. "I feel like we kind of ran in similar circles, but we never dated."

It wasn't until the day of the Gold Cup in May when Brad and Ellen realized there might be feelings they needed to investigate. Brad was a part of a social club called the Capital Club, described by him as a "boozing, chick-getting club of guys from twenty-five to forty years of age." For the Gold Cup, the successful erudite capital boys chartered a bus, got dates, and smuggled in long-necked bottles of brown liquor. The race was a couple hours away, ample time to ingest some serious lubricant on the bus. Brad's roommate, Chris, asked a lovely interior designer and Auburn graduate originally hailing from Mountain Brook, Alabama, named Ellen Magnus to accompany him, and Brad had invited a swimmer named Hannah to come along on the spree.

After decamping from the bus and assimilating into the hordes of socialites, Brad and Ellen began to communicate via text message. Flirting sporadically throughout the afternoon. What seemed a bit innocuous during the day turned serious by nightfall. By then it was clear that Brad and Ellen were more interested in each other than in their dates.

Once the bus rolled back into the nation's capital, the kids were tired, hungry, and a little buzzed. A Mexican joint in Georgetown, Austin Grill, seemed like a good spot to unwind and conclude the long day. After dinner, the couples began to congregate on the corner of Wisconsin and Calvert Street, where other imbibed patrons swerved under streetlights.

The Fall of Brad Hawley

As the couples were talking and putting a bow on the day's pleasantries, Brad went to hug Ellen—his covert coconspirator on text messages—good-bye. When he did, she leaned in, pressed her lips close to his ear, and whispered, "I'll see you on Tuesday."

Brad could feel her breath. Perhaps the liquid inside her contributed to a bit more bravado than normal, for Ellen was typically a reserved Southern lady. Or perhaps she saw what she wanted and just went for it. Either way, Brad was taken aback by the remark, thinking, *Tuesday? What's Tuesday?*

Withdrawing in a confused stupor, he looked at her and repeated what was mirrored in his mind: "Tuesday? What's Tuesday?"

With a sly wink, Ellen whispered, "You and I are going to dinner on Tuesday."

Those words hit him like a thunderbolt. Brad thought Ellen's statement was the coolest thing a girl had ever done. Rockets and fireworks went off in his interior.

Yes, he would go home alone that night, but "See you on Tuesday" was enough to quench any semblance of loneliness. All he could think about was what Ellen had said. Not to let the evening get away, he texted her later that night.

Ellen's unparalleled bravura struck a spark inside Brad. No one had ever been so spontaneously sexy. Ellen had first captured Brad's attention because she was a dark-headed Southern beauty and an Auburn graduate. But to add further attraction, Ellen exuded class and possessed a very placid, welcoming demeanor. She was a churchgoing woman and possessed strong moral fiber. She was sweet and knew how to make others feel comfortable in her presence. She made everyone who came within her sphere of influence feel as if he or she mattered. It should be noted that those are all attractive qualities to the Southern male.

Riding a crest of exhilaration, Brad e-mailed Ellen about the date first thing Monday morning. Next, there were the necessary housekeeping details: breaking the news to his roommate, Chris, Ellen's date to the

Virginia Gold Cup. If ego got in the way, this could be an uncomfortable situation. But when Brad told Chris, Chris conceded that Ellen and Brad were a better match, graciously stepping aside without allowing vanity to sever the household.

Tuesday's locale was Clyde's restaurant in Georgetown, a *Cheers*-like venue with leather booths, wood-grain walls, and bartenders rubbing glasses clean with hand towels. Beneath the euphoria of a highly anticipated first date, the pair talked all night. Things seemed to just click. When they returned to Brad's house later that evening, Brad opened up even more, transparently sharing his life story.

If Brad saw something different in Ellen, Ellen saw something different in Brad, too. It wasn't that he was the complete man already. It was his *potential* that Ellen says shone the brightest. Alas, DC could be a fake place, a plastic place of superficiality, and she was duly impressed with Brad's transparency and realness. "When we went back to his town house, he told me his whole life story," Ellen recalls. "And everything that had happened in his life."

Continuing her bold narrative, Ellen later rewarded Brad with a kiss. "I remember when he walked me out to my car. I had kissed quite a few guys while I was in DC, but this time it felt different," Ellen said.

As Ellen's car drove away, Brad wanted to leap for joy but knew he had to play it cool. Rarely had he allowed someone to see inside so quickly. Usually, the open house tour of his life took weeks, months of trust building. If he allowed anyone in at all. The latent fears of his familial past had rendered him guarded, especially when it came to matters of the opposite sex. Turreted walls of defense had been erected, in the event someone developed the crazy idea of conquering Fort Hawley. But Ellen routed those fortifications on the first night. It was her soft allure that Brad particularly liked, trusted.

Brad and Ellen quickly sent the boats away, deep-sixing any potential suitors. Brad was very intentional with Ellen, and Ellen reciprocated his affection by being very intentional with him.

The Fall of Brad Hawley

After they had been dating for a few months and enjoying the revelry of Washington, DC, the relationship blossomed into something much more serious. That May, Ellen surprised Brad with a trip to Pinehurst, North Carolina. It was a weekend retreat at the chic Pinehurst Resort, where Brad golfed at Pinehurst No. 2 and unwound with Ellen in the luxurious spa. The moment when Brad and Ellen sat on the porch of the Carolina Inn at Pinehurst, scanning the bucolic, hill-happy vistas of Tar Heel country and drinking Arnold Palmers on rockers that creaked against the wood decking, Brad silently resolved in his mind that he was going to ask Ellen to marry him.

The North Carolina trip left an eternal patina. It was a trip of all trips. Brad had once lived in Costa Rica, Ellen in Paris, but these two picturesque venues paled in romanticism to that mythical North Carolina weekend amid the high pines and breezy air.

Brad was clearly in love, but he never let emotion or euphoria have authoritarian rule over his mind. Emotion and "feelings" certainly factored in, but God had given him a brain, and Brad used logic to conclude that Ellen was right for him and that it was a good "fit" after fourteen months on the threshing floor of dating.

The nuances of engagement were often difficult, so Brad discovered. For instance, it took six months to find the perfect ring. Brad finally settled on an online jeweler out of California, but there was a problem. He couldn't afford to pay for it until he got a fat commission check from his job. The moment the check hit his bank account, he logged on and bought the ring, setting, and diamond.

Brad decided to ask for Ellen's hand in marriage during a weekend in New York that coincided with her birthday. The month previous, Brad had secretly flown to Birmingham and asked Ellen's father, Milton, to lunch. Milton suggested that Brad meet him at his hanger company before lunching at the esteemed Shoal Creek Country Club. Milton drove his 2002 Corvette. Over lunch, Brad asked for Milton's permission to marry Ellen, and Milton responded with one condition. Brad now had to call him Milton instead of Mr. Magnus.

If all went according to schedule, the ring was to arrive UPS the day they were set to depart from DC to the Big Apple. Brad had booked an Amtrak train, which would rattle them just a few hours north, past terminals in Baltimore and Philadelphia, to the cynosure of humanity.

But UPS came and went that day, and there was no package to be found. Brad, growing concerned that his plans would be thwarted by the snafu, got on the phone with the ring dealer and discovered that the ring had been delivered to the company's home office, conveniently located in Fredericksburg, Maryland. So he hopped in the car and frantically headed for Fredericksburg, an hour's drive away from his townhouse in Georgetown. Once he got the ring, he drove back to DC to pick up Ellen. The couple then traveled to Union Station to board the train to New York.

Because of the debacle, Brad did not have time to insure the ring. He would have to watch it like a hawk the entire weekend as it passed from his luggage to Ellen's hand.

He encountered more strife along the way. Halfway to New York, the train broke down and all the passengers had to be unloaded. Brad had tucked the ring away in his luggage, and when a train attendant tried to grab his belongings, Brad, gripping it tightly, yelled, "Don't touch my bag!"

BRAD AND ELLEN WOKE UP to a warm October day in New York, the leaves not yet flaunting their autumnal hues of garnet, maize, and auburn. That morning, before they set out to explore the city, Brad slipped on jeans and a pair of cowboy boots. The weather was not conducive to such attire, but Brad surmised cunningly that the ring could be concealed inside his boot.

The first order of business was a Manhattan shopping excursion, a several-store, several-bag effort. Exercising uncharacteristic grace, Brad allowed Ellen to shop unabatedly throughout the morning. "He kept letting me go in stores and shop," said Ellen. "He kept saying, 'Go in and walk around!'" But Brad was digging deep to find patience as Ellen wove happily in and out of the stores and boutiques.

After a while, Brad suggested a walk in Central Park, adding a quixotic brushstroke to the near-perfect portrait of a day. While strolling—Brad *tenderly* strolling, with a "rock" in his shoe—through Central Park, Brad noticed a peaceful gazebo near a pond where paddleboats clawed the tranquil water. Jumpy and filled with nervousness, Brad suggested they take a break and sit down. At this charming place, he produced the ring from inside his boot, dropped down on one knee, and proposed marriage to Ellen. "As he got down on one knee, he said, 'I can't believe I'm about to do this.' Then I knew what was coming. He told me how much he loved me. I had no doubt in my mind when I said yes," Ellen reflected.

After she said yes, the elated couple exchanged a long embrace. They were so happy they flagged down the nearest person. A woman who happened to be passing by.

"Would you mind taking our picture?" Ellen said.

"Did you guys just get engaged?" asked the unnamed, makeshift photographer.

"Yes!" Brad and Ellen replied in unison, faces blazing with smiles.

Brad and Ellen decided to celebrate the knotting of two lovers at the Loeb Boathouse Central Park restaurant, branded as a "haven for romantics and nature lovers." The now-engaged couple walked in for brunch and celebratory champagne. It wasn't yet noon and the place was already packed.

"Two for Hawley," Brad submitted at the door. Brad had always relished moments like these, small moments when manhood was exhibited. This was one of the first of many manly acts as a fiancé. But he was soon stunned when the hostess wasn't immediately complicit.

"It's a two-hour wait," replied the hostess.

Brad shot a grin at Ellen that read, "I'll handle this."

"We just got engaged," Brad said expectantly. "Surely you can slide us in somewhere."

"It's a two-hour wait," echoed the hostess brazenly, uncaringly.

So much for Northern hospitality.

So THE DATE WAS SET. Mr. and Mrs. Milton Magnus requested the presence of two hundred people at the marriage of their daughter, Ellen, to Brad Hawley on May 27, 2007. The wedding was held at Community Presbyterian Church in Pinehurst, North Carolina. Nostalgically, it was a good decision, based on the couple's history with the place. And, geographically, it made sense as well. It was halfway between DC and Alabama.

All the pre-wedding cordialities were extended, and Brad carefully selected his committee of groomsmen from fellow Spades, fraternity brothers, and friends from DC. Ellen pared down her selections to a stable of seven glowing bridesmaids.

After a handsome ceremony, the reception followed at the Carolina Inn, where Brad crowd-surfed and flutes of champagne were hoisted. A band rocked away until late into the evening, when Brad presented his famous Michael Jackson "Billie Jean" performance, followed by a "dance off" with the handsomest groomsman, Jeb. The Jeb-and-Brad dance off had become a common occurrence in DC nightlife, with Jeb typically taking home the prize. But not this night. As the last beat of "Billie Jean" blared through the speakers, Brad rose from the dance floor to find that his patented knee slide had produced holes in his tuxedo pants. Blemishes he wore proudly the rest of the night as a badge of victory. Brad and the unruly DC professionals drove the whiskey-induced extravaganza, teaching the milder, more conservative Southerners a lesson on how a party is thrown.

Once the wedding was over, a marriage was to commence. Two months before the ceremony, Brad and Ellen decided to settle back in Birmingham instead of continuing their DC experience. After honeymooning in Hawaii, where they went scuba diving with sea turtles, snacked on lychees, and made love on the sandy beaches of the Na Pali

Coast, the Hawleys returned to DC before forging south to Heart of Dixie, whose long, jealous stare had finally lured them home.

As it turns out, patching together a life wasn't overly complicated. Step one was finding suitable living accommodations. Prior to their wedding in May, they scoured the Over the Mountain area of Birmingham, eventually settling on a house in Homewood. Check. Step two was finding suitable employment. Fortuitously, Brad got approved to continue his job as a virtual employee for an intellectual-property-management company, and Ellen would work as an interior designer. Check.

The couple decided to hold off on children for at least five years so they could explore the wanderlust of marriage. A couple intent on quality time. They wanted to travel, visit Europe, and enjoy each other exclusively, in all phases. Things were clicking along, and they were building the life in Birmingham they had always imagined and wanted.

But soon after Brad and Ellen were getting used to each other, they experienced their first major trial as a couple. One day Ellen's leg began hurting, the pain so excruciating that Brad had to cradle carry her to the bathroom. This mysterious ailment left Ellen and Brad scratching their heads in mystery. A day and a half went by, and her leg wasn't getting any better. Since Brad had been a drug rep early in his career, he had some knowledge of Ellen's symptoms, and as he thumbed through the old files in his mind—two days into the insufferable exercise—it clicked in a *Eureka!* moment. Ellen had a blood clot. Dr. Brad, diagnosing the issue, immediately rushed Ellen to the hospital, where doctors found two clots in her leg. Ellen was placed in intensive care while her concerned husband remained bedside. Though it was a frightening situation, Ellen was soon on the mend, and the couple had survived their first scare.

Ellen returned to work, and the couple maintained semi-independent lives. Brad's job was taking him back to DC frequently, and Ellen's job demanded long hours. Their lives did not converge every night, but satisfactorily for both parties. They enjoyed the fruits of marital bliss, including a healthy sex life. As a result, a surprise pregnancy occurred a year and a half into marriage. In August 2009, their first child was born, a boy named Webb. Eighteen months later the couple welcomed a baby girl, Marlen. While both children were born within the five-year window of childlessness the Hawleys had earmarked, the new members of the family were welcome additions.

After the babies were born, the first signs of discord began to surface. Brad was in and out at his discretion, mirroring the way he had conducted his familial affairs since Sharon had walked out when he was a junior in high school. This didn't always sit well with Ellen. "Brad still did his own thing, and he was very selfish," Ellen said. "I remember him saying, 'The kids are in our life. It's all about us. We don't need to adjust to them. They need to adjust to *us*.' And he believed that, strongly."

Before the pregnancies, money had been pouring into the household, and the Hawleys were blessed with a vast discretionary income. Brad often used this surplus to purchase a wide array of gifts. Custom suits from the world-renowned men's clothing store, Shaia's. Beautiful shoes. Thick silk ties with fat knots. Several-hundred-dollar shirts.

While Webb was playing with his first toys, Brad fed his own obsession with an array of much larger toys that certainly wouldn't be classified as jalopies or land yachts. "He had a brand-new car every year," Ellen remembers. "Explorer. Audi. He had two cars at one point. Seventy-seven Bronco with thirty-two-inch Bridgestone mud tires. Titan truck. Land Rover, Jeep Wrangler. Range Rover. I was furious with every single car he came home with. The cars were just the start. He bought a three-thousand-dollar bike, on which a car struck him. I was pregnant with Webb at the time. He came home with a concussion, stitches in his head, and a cracked vertebra. A week later, he brought home a ten-thousand-dollar bike."

"But it's Lance Armstrong's bike," Brad argued.

It seemed as though nothing was slowing Brad down. Feeding the material beast only left him hungry for more. His appetite for stuff. His longing to prove and re-prove. When his love for one gadget went stale, he would simply get another. He was smitten with newness. Everything had to have a feeling of freshness. Novelty. Driving a vehicle down to the nub wasn't a consideration. And why not? He had the money.

Brad came to measure his life in toys and numbers. Toys: the gadgets of life. Growling machines assembled in plants in the belly of Michigan by goggle-eyed laborers. Numbers: rising whiteboard integers at a gym in Mountain Brook, Alabama. Figures jotted with myriad-colored Expo markers by trembling, chalk-caked fingers.

Brad's longing to prove himself in the community and among his peers eventually became his identity. He defined himself through his gadgets and faced defiantly the aging process by refreshing everything in his life. One had to wonder when his marriage might grow stale, when his relationship with Ellen might be affected by his addiction to variety.

So when Steel Company leaned up and whispered in his ear, "See you on Tuesday," that was all it took.

A HOUSE IS NOT A HOME

"Of course, in a world estranged from God, even good things
must be handled with care, like explosives. We have lost
the untainted innocence of Eden, and every good harbors
risk as well, holding within the potential for abuse."

–PHILIP YANCEY

Steel Company seemed to satisfy it. Inside Brad Hawley, the five-foot-
nine-inch, 155-pound spitball, a fire had been raging for extreme
physical activity.

At first he tried cycling, after David, his neighbor, went on vacation
and tossed him the keys to a closet with a bike inside. This was David's
first insight into the identity and impulsiveness of Brad. David let Brad
borrow the bike, hoping that Brad might enjoy it enough to one day accompany him on a ride. By the time David had returned from his trip a
week later, Brad had bought his own.

His newfound obsession with road biking evolved into training for a
duathlon (run-bike-run), and the duathlon training naturally progressed
to training for a zenith of physical ardor: a half Ironman triathlon.

After a few years of living in Homewood next to David and his wife,
Cathy, Brad and Ellen bought a house in Mountain Brook that was in
grave disrepair. It was a 1950s ranch-style home with one barely working

bathroom and a family of fungus establishing tenancy in several of the rooms. Besides that, the doors wouldn't close. Nothing seemed to work. Instead of living in squalor, Brad and Ellen moved in with Ellen's parents while they hired a contractor to spruce up the place, an endeavor that would eventually end up taking four months longer than the original four-month projection.

At the Magnuses', the Hawley family plopped down mattresses and converted a basement and an office into makeshift bedrooms. Marlen didn't yet have an official crib and slept in a Pack 'n Play. The family was very unsettled. Boxes everywhere. This was by no means slumming it, but, measuring their situation against their previous environs, it was tantamount to a first-world living hell.

Ellen's father, Milton, was the successful president of M&B Hangers, the top wire clothes hanger producer in the United States. Milton, certainly not a man to be trifled with, enjoyed coming home from a long day at work to greet a glass of scotch. One night, Milton's blood was boiling from work, and Brad sensed that the overlong stay by the Hawley foursome did nothing but aggravate the situation. These weren't the olden days when frontier clans bundled up in the lone-room cabin with the matriarch and patriarch of the family, the burning logs shooting smoke through the chimney and into the night. This was 2012. Though Milton was happy to accommodate them, Brad saw through the obliging facade of Milton's eyes and the language of gritted teeth that he had had enough of the dillydallying. He read that it was time for them to go. But when Brad suggested that he and Ellen move into a rental house, hoping Milton would concede and make it easy for them, Milton refused to give his blessing. "It would be silly to spend your money. You—should—stay," Milton said graciously. Behind Milton's hard shell, he was a softy at heart.

Around the same time, his friend Warren, who suggested that the grueling workout was "right up your alley", introduced Brad to Steel Company. Warren was a friend from Auburn and one of Steel Company's Original Garage guys—an elite faction not dissimilar to a fraternity's founding fathers. Warren had high hopes for his five-star recruit, but Brad quickly quit his Steel Company pledgeship after only one workout. It wasn't that the exercise was too taxing, for Brad placed first in maximum-height box jumps. Oddly enough, it was the fee that dissuaded him. Yes, the fee. And it wasn't as if Brad was tight with money. He just didn't want to have to pay $250 to work out. Fair enough.

With Steel Company in his rearview, Brad commenced training for the half Ironman triathlon. He ran. He biked. He swam. Ellen, ever encouraging, continued in her support. Brad's plans were foiled when he tore his ACL while trying to play flag football with men ten years younger. He soon recovered and continued to crave workouts of the more intense variety.

In the meantime, he decided to go back to school to pursue his master's degree. While taking some classes to obtain his MBA, Brad bumped into a guy who introduced him to the swelling kingdom of CrossFit, to which, at the time, Steel Company was a cousin. Apparently, CrossFit had become *the* fitness craze, and, thinking it might be time to reinvestigate a more intense fitness regimen, Brad returned home from MBA residency week to take the Steel Company 101 introductory class. He was surprised to see how much Steel Company had grown in his year's absence and decided it was worth the $250-per-month fee.

Brad fell headlong into the sociology of group exercise. As he grew to know and like the people, he very much thought of Steel Company Fitness as a family, and they reciprocated by gladly welcoming him into the fold as a fellow Steel Companyer.

Because Steel Company was structured in a class format, Brad reveled in the fellowship and the newfound friends who seemed to truly care about him. Historically, once Brad felt welcomed, felt that he belonged, felt that he had a certain stake in the success of something, he would dedicate himself to giving it every ounce of energy he had. Whether a community service organization or exercise routine, he went at it with gusto, foot to the floor, all in. So once Brad tendered his $250 to become a member of this *corps d'elite*, he had no intentions of going halfway.

The Fall of Brad Hawley

At first, Ellen was perfectly fine with Steel Company because Brad wasn't gone from home as long. That ferocious triathlon training could chew up the better part of a Saturday afternoon, whereas with Steel Company, Brad was back home within an hour, hour and a half, even after a killer WOD.

Brad even persuaded Ellen, who had been trying to shave some baby fat after having two children, to join Steel Company. He was so kind as to buy her a membership to Steel Company as a present for Valentine's Day. Clothed as a sweet gesture, the membership was perhaps a little hint that she needed to drop a few, and one could imagine how well that must have gone over.

When you broke Steel Company down, it was like a family. I got very close to people. I have a need for close relationships, and Steel Company pulled in a small group of people and walled up friends. There were people on whom I could depend. I was a full-timer, but Ellen was only coming about two times a week. My workout times soon approached the top of the list, and I think that brought me into the family more tightly. As Steel Company became more important, my wife and my kids suffered. The axis of my day rotated around a workout. But it was there that I found family. It was at the gym that I found love. Results. Not that I didn't feel it from Ellen and the kids. But my competitive spirit was driving me more toward the workout and away from my family. I had an addictive personality, and Steel Company fed that.

Within the walls of Steel Company, Brad forged friendships with guys like Caine Hill and Jimmy Brady. Caine and Jimmy were both in their thirties and, like Brad, seemed to be seeking more out of life. Many of the members, former athletes who had become doctors, lawyers, and financiers working long hours at stressful jobs, found in Steel Company both a physical challenge and a scrapheap to dump the mounting stress that didn't involve a bar and bottle. Steel Company provided not only the physical rigor they desired but also mental and emotional strength as well. Brad saw this as a group who wanted to live exceptionally, iron sharpening iron, and if he could rise in the ranks this would certainly garner a measure of prestige.

What separated Steel Company from other gyms was that growth was not just seen, it was measured. Steel Company provided an apparatus so members could measure their weekly progress, providing tangible results as stats soared on whiteboards. For example, when Brad started Steel Company, his personal record on dead lift was 195 pounds. Working hard to improve that number, Brad maxed out at 265, then 295, and finally, 300. As personal record after personal record was broken, the members cheering him on the entire way, his confidence continued to swell. In Brad's mind, Steel Company was the best vehicle around to measure development. In the past, spiritual and personal growth had seemed somewhat amorphous and difficult to ascertain. Now Brad could see results firsthand and receive the praise he desired.

The basic beginner program for the Steel Company athlete was Steel Company 101. This introductory course allowed each athlete to wade into the waters before plunging into deeper seas of elite fitness. During this class, Brad was often partnered with Chris Rives, who became a friend and fellow competitor. The pair hit it off immediately, enjoying a friendly banter that masked the interior rage to defeat each other. During workouts, Brad was conscious of where he stood on the leaderboard and also looked for Chris. It should be noted that Brad did feel compassion for Chris. He cheered him on and always hoped that he finished a close second. The competitive nature and family atmosphere were the gym's biggest selling points for Brad, and by the end of 101, Steel Company had sunk its hooks into him.

Steel Company would push Brad as he had never been pushed before. Once he graduated from the 101 class and was accepted as a regular Steel Company member, he was taken aback by the difficulty of the workouts. Steel Company 101 proved to be child's play compared to the daily grind of the class, his whole body aching with pain by the end of the WOD. Steel Company was structured after the CrossFit model, and most members faced a steep learning curve until exercise form was perfected. Many, if not most, had never performed exercises as were performed in this gym. In one of the early workouts, the members were tasked with performing an exercise called "cleans." Susan Beason, Warren's wife and who was seven months pregnant at the time, took one look at Brad's sloppy form and huffed, "Brad, your cleans need some work." This window into Steel Company's severity—especially coming from a pregnant woman—was a real question of Brad's manhood.

So they collected there, every day at 12:15 p.m., the twenty men and women of Mountain Brook's Steel Company Fitness. Friends suffering together through the daily WOD. Brad's daily goal became not to simply finish the workout. His goal was to be the best in the citywide gym. "Brad had a very competitive personality," says Ellen. "At the gym, it became very important how each athlete scored each day. The Rx was posted on the board so everyone could see it. His life began to revolve around his diet and that 12:15 p.m. class. He wanted to be the best in the class and at the gym."

At Steel Company, Brad found bundles of exercises in an hour-long, punishing fitness routine. Brad liked Steel Company because of that structure, because it was different, painful, and exerting. Instead of walking into the gym and forming his own routine, Brad was at the mercy of the programmers. Typically, Steel Company's director of training devised the routine, a hard, varying affair which might be posted on social media, sent via e-mail, or leaked by spies: members who had performed the WOD in an earlier part of the day. An important standard for the Steel Company athlete was the "Rx," the recommended weight or "prescription" for each exercise. So a typical WOD might look like the following:

5 Rounds for Time:
12 thrusters (Rx 95, 135)
10 dead lifts (Rx 155, 225)
8 pull-ups

Brad soon became fluent in Steel Company vernacular, a unique lingo that almost required a Rosetta stone to understand. For instance, the gym was not referred to as the gym but, rather, the "box." Members were hastened to become familiar with movements such as kettlebell swings, clean and jerks, front squats, overhead lunges, handstand push-ups, wall balls, sumo dead lift high pulls (loincloth not required), thrusters, and everyone's favorite, burpees—believed by many to be the spawn of Satan. As it was a full-body routine, neglecting body parts such as, say, legs, wasn't possible with Steel Company. In other words, there were no top-heavy Steel Company athletes with spindly lower halves. Men covering up their insufficiencies with wind pants.

Development was radical. Loafers, previously mired in motionless, sofa-comfortable torpor, underwent a metamorphosis into fierce "warriors" and pepper pots. Pudgy, oafish men who rocked impressive Dad Bods transformed into swollen beefsteaks. Women with little musculature suddenly boasted a plumage of abundant gams. Because the Steel Company regimen married physical exertion with proper dieting, blubber evaporated and striations surfaced. Shoulders bulged like tight cannonballs. Chests swelled to majestic, romance novel proportions. Legs hulked beneath gym shorts. Abdominals appeared like angry cells. Confidence improved, too. Once-nervous nellies, now chalking their hands and throwing 150 pounds over their head, brimmed with élan.

But it wasn't all about the physical. Steel Company's biblical pedigree provided a greater sense of security and trust in the minds of Brad and Ellen.

Steel Company was heavily advertised in social magazines, including a full-page ad in the social slick *About Town*. Burning the orange-and-black logo, the shirtless hunks with chiseled frames, into the skulls of Magic City citizens. Luring them with the fleshy evidence of transformation. What Caine Hill saw in Steel Company as he scanned these advertisements was an opportunity to finally achieve some semblance of manhood. "I wanted to look like a man. Chiseled. Skinny," Hill said. "At our core as men, we constantly look to prove that we are worthy. Steel Company provides that opportunity for achievement. It allows you to say, 'Look at what I'm doing. I'm better than *you*.' I saw an ad for Steel Company, and all these guys were ripped, chiseled, and skinny, and I pictured myself with them. I wanted people to think, 'He's got it together.' It was all about validation. So I immersed myself in the culture and the people. I wanted to show people that I was doing a difficult thing and achieving. It brought about personal growth. Steel Company was responsible for that."

Over time, Steel Company began to take over Brad's identity. One of the prime indicators was how he dressed. Tight T-shirts advertising his visits to other boxes or competitions, mottoed compression socks, and minimal shoes became his common attire. Scuffed-up shins were displayed proudly. Brad liked Steel Company because it was hard. It was renegade. It was counterculture. It was addictive. It was unconventional. And if Steel Company had been a Jim Jones sect, Brad would have happily ingested the Kool-Aid.

Being a member carried certain exclusivity, and being "in" was better than being "out." Steel Company erected soft walls of exclusivity by placing a limit of 250 members per gym. So in Brad's view, it was the country club of workouts.

Yet the daily torment on Brad's body was worth it, because results were piling up and his body was developing into a strapping package. Mary Katherine Cabaniss, Brad and Ellen's next-door neighbor, said that Brad used to run shirtless down the street and bless the neighborhood with a peek at perfection in the flesh.

The problem was that Brad failed to understand the significance of boundaries and safety, or that Steel Company could be dangerous, even life threatening, if misused. Hill said that Brad's workout MO was to push himself "beyond what was healthy." "He would visibly get upset if he didn't beat me," Hill remembers. "I saw Brad as a rabbit to chase. As I got to know him, I realized he had a switch in his head, trying to be better. He looked at the world like, 'I can do this on my own.'"

Like everything else in his life, Brad threw caution to the wind. He could handle it. Results and achievement came before caution. Winning the day trumped technique, thereby whetting the blade on which he would eventually fall. A proper balance could have been achieved had he understood that Steel Company had a refining effect, helping Brad to surge out of the physiological, even psychological, doldrums, but not letting it consume him to the point that his life or identity was in peril. On its face, Steel Company was a salubrious exercise where health and physical fitness was possible. Unfortunately, Brad found out that obsession was possible, too, as he mindlessly climbed this Everest of mania. Instead of merely working out and going home, Brad wanted to build the persona and identity of a Steel Companyer. Strong. Athletic. Driven. Ambitious. He fell in love with the image of being a member of the elite.

The world peddled physical achievement as commodity of manhood, and Brad's concentration on physical strength bled over into family life. At home, Brad intimated to Ellen that he wanted to be the "family work-horse." He wanted to be the one the family counted on to haul heavy loads when no one else could, whom the extended family relied on for physical strength when a hefty crate or some other bulky object needed to be moved. Perhaps Brad believed that this new bravado would transfer over into other areas of life, making boardrooms or dinner meetings with a potential client seem less tense, or that it might steady the previously shaky podium moments when a speech had to be given. A warrior in all areas now, Brad thought that if he could survive and excel at Steel Company, he had the world licked.

More factored in. First, Brad was a little guy, and he was doing the things the big guys were doing. This lightweight, quasi-Napoleonic fireplug, who had always played bigger than he was, was being fueled by other guys at the gym. It wasn't infrequent to hear, "Holy crap, dude. You're killing it!"

This all may seem innocuous on its face. Pushing yourself to the limit. Reveling in the approbation of your peers. Enjoying the fruits of physical improvement. But there was one problem. Brad was desperate to become something else. Over the years, the voice of his inner critic had grown loud and overpowering. While he studied himself at the mirror on the morning of August 27, he did not see an internally strong man. If he were truthful with himself, he would have seen an ugly, gargoyle-like figure as he took inventory of his life. Consciously or subconsciously, Brad began to construct an avatar. Because Brad had been left at the maternal altar, so to speak, he felt he had to create a new identity that was the sole property of performance and physical attributes. Although he felt like a man when he stood in the mirror and bounced his pectorals up and down, indeed, he was focused more on looking like a man than he was on actually becoming one. Steel Company, he believed, was the mechanism to build Brad 2.0.

Indeed, the muscle came quickly. Brad applied fifteen pounds of beef to his thin frame over the course of ten months. Consistently, he scored in the top three in the gym. He felt that Steel Company, in terms of intense physical exertion, was the closest thing to track that he'd experienced in years, as he would often collapse at the end of a workout and lie on the gritty floor, his shirt soaked with sweat. Though others might be able to lift more weight, Brad, using rose-colored mathematics, felt if the athletes could be measured per square inch, he was perhaps the strongest member of the gym. He prided himself in his heart and determination and thought that his nickname needed to be "The Motor" because of his propensity to outwork the competition.

Steel Company didn't short its members on opportunities to compete. Indeed, competition was the rock that Steel Company was built upon, the agent that fed Brad's furor. Inter-gym competitions pitted teams of four against one another. At all events, Brad was nervous and even asked a few friends to stop by and support him. They did. But while others happily showed up to cheer Brad on from the stands, Brad was also losing a fan. His growing mania with Steel Company was beginning to get under Ellen's skin. "I was getting very annoyed with Brad's obsession," Ellen said. "The kids were one and three. We were trying to stay afloat with two kids. I wasn't sleeping. And there was a lot of stress. I didn't have a problem with him doing Steel Company; it was just his obsession that was the problem. I actually enjoyed it, but I didn't get into it like Brad did."

As the fetish grew, conversations between Brad and Ellen began to narrow on Steel Company. They were of the shallow variety, barely scratching beyond the epidermis of depth. Brad would rush home, eager to tell Ellen, "Hey, I cleaned this weight!" or "Hey, I deadlifted this weight!" as Ellen half listened while preparing dinner or taking care of the kids. Ellen admits that she talked about it only because she knew Brad loved it, because it was his hobby and passion, and because she wanted to be a good wife. She didn't want to be a meddler or discourager to Brad's fascinations, so she chose to be conciliatory and supportive, even though his Steel Company obsession was about to drive her insane.

Brad was trying to solve an internal problem with external means. But the truth was he was rotting from within. The fetid smells rising up from his boyhood. The decomposing walls of trust. The cracking foundation. While his insides were decaying, Brad thought that applying a little paint and sweat equity to the outside of the structure might do the trick. Every day, he worked on that exterior. A good performance on cleans might fix the broken shutter. A first-place finish might repair the door. A more ripped appearance would provide some spackle. Daily, he refurbished his home with the clanking of bars and plates. The purr of energy throughout the gym. The celebratory grunt after an important lift.

Brad's obsession, correlatively, occurred while he was living in the basement of his in-laws. Basement living created certain problems that would have been difficult for any young married couple, certainly one living in Mountain Brook with the kind of potential for success that the Hawleys had. Frustration from being exiled from your own home for months was toilsome enough, but compounding that was a distracted spouse.

So the marriage downshifted into survival mode, puttering along from day to day, unraveling proportionally to Brad's Steel Company fanaticism. Brad's mind-set on the marriage was that it was too much of a job. Factory-like. It was much harder work than he had anticipated. It was easy to love when you feel like it, much more difficult to love when you do not.

The Fall of Brad Hawley

Like the failing sun's head sinking into the distant horizon, the romance had waned. There was no excitement. No thrill. No sense of intrigue or spontaneity. No whizzing off for a day trip, just because. Married life had become drudgery. The newness had worn off, and the disappearance of that gush of euphoria he once felt in DC gave him cause for concern. His happiness began to win the war over his commitment, and there were times when Brad considered divorce.

Perhaps Brad believed that Ellen and the kids could not keep up with his pace. Everything was always push, push, push. Brad was pushing at the gym, pushing at work, pushing socially, but also pushing Ellen to reaffirm her commitment and loyalty to him. Brad had always found success in pushing, and found no value in reducing. In humbling. He feared that in reducing he would lose strength, lose manhood, so he forged wide-eyed ahead. As a result, he wasn't able to enjoy the simple pleasures of matrimony as he had in the beginning. Perhaps those old sentimentalities could have been revived by retreats into quietness or abstinence from materialism, but there was so much cacophony and distraction in his life that he could not focus on his family or reinvigorate that old romantic spirit again. His threshold had been pushed so far that he couldn't step back to the handholding, the kissing, the flowers, the chivalrous gestures, and the kind little words of encouragement. He hadn't thought of returning to romance, personified in small acts that spoke fluently in Ellen's love language. Gentlemanly acts, all of which could have provided spice, were viewed as "cheesy." Where had the days of Pinehurst, North Carolina, gone? Where was the elation of "See you on Tuesday"? Where were the happy days? The laughter? Theirs had become a stale marriage, falling flat and uninspired.

The upper-tier athlete is always searching for ways to achieve another level of performance, but interestingly enough, Brad did not apply those same benchmarks to his marriage. The litmus test of marriage was simply the way he *felt*. At the time, Brad never thought, "What can I do to get this marriage to another level?"

When Brad and Ellen were dating, Brad was very deliberate in dating her. Similar to a consistent workout routine, Brad worked daily at loving Ellen. After five years, he was no longer on the hunt for her. He wasn't pursuing her. Ironically, as the muscles continued to swell, Brad became more Paleolithic as a spouse, the *Homo erectus* hubs, Ellen tucked away safely in the cave. *Caveman Brad go hunt something else.* Back into the wild to feed his hunter/gatherer nature, his primal urges. Once he had captured her and the idyllic mountainside ceremony was over, once DC was behind them, once Webb and Marlen came into the picture, his grand adventure, his tour of pleasantries, was over. The suntanned, swashbuckling District of Columbia stud, sipping mint juleps at the Gold Cup, had turned into what many overstimulated college/young professional men fear: TDM—the domesticated male.

So many guys get into a rut. In their early thirties. Three, four, five years into their marriage. Many of them are coming out of their peak. Their prime. They go from funneling beers around hot chicks to this homey lifestyle. But Steel Company helped to pull me out of the rut. I remember having this vision. I remember thinking Ellen and the kids were in the rut, and I was walking on the ledge looking down on them. I never envisioned myself in the rut with them.

The spiced, comely atmosphere that represented those initial years had been traded for the storms of discomfort and frustration. Like many of their generation, they were two people drifting apart. Brad's attention had been diverted from his family to a workout, the distraction of Steel Company like a blinking, telltale eye to which his stare was affixed. Obsession became the enemy of marriage. As a consequence, he was no longer looking Ellen in the eyes. Surely they ached for him. He did not crave her touch. Surely her arms longed to hold him.

I became distracted from thinking about the depth of our marriage. I stopped wooing her. I didn't have to prove myself with her anymore. I was not pursuing her. When we were dating, I still had something to prove. After we got married and that three-to-five-year itch set in, I began to believe falsely that my physical being was sufficient for her. That my physical presence—my fitness, the aesthetic of my body, that I could labor and fix stuff, the physical stuff about me, that I was a fit, strong, sexual being—was enough. I thought that Ellen was fortunate that I didn't come home, crack a beer, sit on the couch, and eat chips. That I wasn't a fat slob. I thought, "I'm doing this all for you." I was consumed with the way I looked and what others thought. But Ellen didn't care about all that. What she cared about was my depth.

While the Hawleys were in turmoil, Steel Company offered stability. Steel Company offered family. Steel Company offered strength. So he ran to it.

The effects of Steel Company's rise to idolatry in the mind of Brad had far-reaching effects beyond disrupting his family life. During this bleak, unsmiling era, Brad's spiritual life was dormant. Life afforded only one slot for devotion, and Steel Company filled it, boxing everything else out in his life. He had no spiritual discipline. He had little left to invest in anything truly meaningful, because all of his discretionary time was spent working out or thinking about working out. Steel Company became an energy vampire, and because Brad had convinced himself that his identity and worth were found in what he could prove outside of his home, he began to slowly pull away from his family, like a ship detached from its moorings, grunting out into a dense, lightless sea. Brad's personal growth had little, if anything, to do with growing into more of a gentleman, loving his wife and children, or pursuing greater depths of the Christian life. Brad was rabidly concerned with building a new self, accomplished through physical extremism.

Thus home became a cold place, chilled by the unsaid. Brad sensed the unraveling of his family, but he refused to talk to Ellen about their problems. Steel Company was an outlet where he could dump his anxiety, but that only went so far. It was a Band-Aid that could not heal the dark, bleeding interior. He had friends, sure. But he felt that there was no one in his life he trusted enough to spill his guts to, no one to whom he could be fully vulnerable. He needed to find a wartime consigliore, a brother or mentor who could walk with him through the refuse of his past. Perhaps he was too afraid to show his true self to the ones who cared for him because he didn't want to be perceived as feeble and dramatic. That wouldn't have been projecting strength, as the world requires of men. Brad had a group to share in a workout, but he had no one with which to share his internal difficulties. Succumbing to the thought that he might need help was not a consideration. Showing emotion was weak. Outing the darkness, exposing it to light, was not even a consideration. Thus, avoidance was his defense mechanism. Running.

So Brad continued to feel increasingly alone, a man on an island to himself. "Brad found strength in self-sufficiency," Ellen remembered. "I think he wanted to continue the independence that he had had in DC. He didn't want to sacrifice that. I think he thought that changing for us would show a weakness in him. Brad seemed to have some trust issues. He kept saying, 'I need to know that you're on my team. That you're on my side.' Over and over."

Ellen quietly hoped things would turn around, and she thought by supporting him and his curiosities, the family might be salvaged. As he chased the world's definition of manhood and identity, he started to forget how much he truly loved Ellen and the covenant he pledged to her in the mountains of Pinehurst, North Carolina. His children, desperately needing a father, were left in the wake of his mania.

Like so many others of their generation, Brad and Ellen were growing apart. But *why* were they growing apart? What had changed in five years?

Brad had.

Forging deeply into Brad's psyche, one would find Steel Company was not the true object of his obsession. Steel Company was merely the mask. Brad's true obsession was himself. As he slowly succumbed to his "new self," a charlatan, unauthentic persona, the real Brad Hawley was being lost. What he thought was a Pilgrim's Progress up the mountain of manhood was instead a descent into the valley of mistaken identity.

The Fall of Brad Hawley

As he continued to sever himself from the family, Brad became increasingly icy toward them, unaware of the destruction of his actions. When Brad's mom bolted for Michigan, she had checked out geographically but not emotionally. She always loved her son. But although Brad was still living under the same roof as Ellen and the kids, even though the geography hadn't changed, Brad had checked out emotionally.

Brad seemed to trust the people at Steel Company more than he did his own family. Perhaps they couldn't wound him as badly. Since Sharon left, Brad had learned to push hurt away instead of leaning into the people who cared about him most when things got testy. If he got the sense that he might get hurt, he'd simply tomahawk the other person with a cutting word, grinding the person down into mush before he or she had an opportunity to volley. As this became increasingly more habitual, he failed to welcome intimacy in any form. Grace and mercy were concepts alien to him.

It gradually became clear that Brad wasn't going to reduce on his own. He had to be reduced by something far greater than his own will. And on August 27, 2012, Brad Hawley's metric was taken to zero.

FINALLY THE HOUSE WAS READY IN AUGUST, and it was a stunner. So drastic were the changes that if before-and-after pictures of the house were placed side-by-side, one would not think it were the same house. The contractor had taken a bland, uninspiring, broken house and made it picturesque. An elated Brad, Ellen, and the babies welcomed shutting doors and running water and toilets that flushed and unsullied walls. They walked barefoot across a brand-new deck and ran their eyes across the pristine landscaping and redesigning. The fresh brick retaining walls. The hardwood floors. Their own beds! Quite an improvement from the basement of the Magnuses, galaxies from where Brad had grown up in Cullman.

As the Hawleys settled in, the mountains of moving boxes slowly evaporated, pictures were tacked on the wall, and the furniture was arranged to suit their feng shui. Webb and Marlen had their own rooms upstairs. Things were back in Brad's grip, or so it seemed. Perhaps the marriage could be saved. Perhaps this was exactly the boost—the shot in the arm—that the family needed to set things straight and get back on the right path. At least the house was in order. Now they would find out if the home could be restored too.

Two weeks later, Brad fell.

Some might have said his determination to keep pushing was a hallmark of courage. But maybe someone was trying to tell him to stop pushing. Because sometimes, it's better for us to wreck than to keep going down the wrong path. Sometimes, we have to be taken to the brink of death to get our attention.

But it was more than that. Brad had built an altar.

"When Moses approached the camp and saw the calf and the dancing, his anger burned and he threw the tablets out of his hands, breaking them to pieces at the foot of the mountain. And he took the calf the people had made and burned it in the fire; then he ground it into powder, scattered it on the water and made the Israelites drink it." (Exodus 32:19-20 NIV)

When idols are built, atonement is coming.

Part II

*Fear not, for I am with you; be not dismayed, for I
am your God; I will strengthen you, I will help you,
I will uphold you with my righteous right hand.*

—ISAIAH 41:10

God is our refuge and strength, a very present help in trouble.

—PSALM 46:1

TRINITY

B ut only part of Brad died.

1:15 p.m.

Back in Hickory, North Carolina, a small manufacturing town an hour north of Charlotte, Ellen was trying to piece together what had happened to her husband. Like putting together a digital jigsaw puzzle, she began a rapid succession of phone calls, text messages, and e-mails that would blast out over the next several hours.

Save for her coworkers, Ellen was alone, completely blindfolded by geography. Mary Katherine Cabaniss, the Hawleys' next-door neighbor and unlikely herald who, in a text, asked, "Should I pick up the kids?" had no idea when she fired out the message that Ellen was unaware of the chilling events surrounding Brad. Minutes ticked by, and Ellen could not stop thinking about what Mary Katherine had said. *Why would she need to pick up the kids?* Ellen managed to keep a straight face in the meeting, but behind that veneer concern was escalating.

Ellen traditionally thought it rude and unprofessional to be fixated on a phone during an important business meeting. Today she wanted to seem impressive to her fellow sales associates and the president of the company, and she would have stepped away from the meeting only if she sensed urgency. Reading through the cryptic lines of the text, Ellen asked to be excused from the training room to step outside and make a call. In the vestibule, the news dropped down on her like a thousand-pound weight.

As Brad was being shipped to Trinity Medical Center, Jimmy Brady collected Brad's keys and cell phone and commandeered his Jeep. He tried to call Ellen from Brad's phone, but was frustrated when he discovered a four-digit code required to unlock the device. Of course, Jimmy didn't know it, so missives would have to be sent out to get word to Ellen.

Trinity, two miles away, was the closest hospital to Steel Company, but several capable options existed in the Birmingham metro area. St. Vincent's, UAB Medical Center, Princeton, Brookwood. Others. As the paramedics were loading Brad into the ambulance, Jimmy instructed them to "take him to the nearest hospital!" Whether or not the ambulance chose to take Brad to Trinity on the basis of that directive, one may never know, but Jimmy was right about one thing. Time was of the essence.

From Steel Company Fitness, there are essentially two routes to Trinity Medical Center. The first is to take Dexter Avenue to Church Street, turn right, make a left at the end of Church Street, and after an eighth of a mile, bear right on Montclair Road. The second is to turn *right* at the end of Church Street and follow Euclid Avenue before turning left onto Hagood Street, which snakes its way to Montclair Road. From previous experience, Jimmy deduced that a left at Church Street was the quickest route, so he sped in that direction. But the ambulance chauffeuring Brad was already ahead of him and had made a right. As it turned out, Jimmy's route was the fastest, the ambulance getting jammed up on Euclid by some annoying road construction—repairing gas lines—and having to take a labyrinthine detour through the cozy Mountain Brook suburbs. Jimmy, perhaps the more experienced Mountain Brook navigator, beat the ambulance to the hospital. The roadblock only added more minutes to Brad's quandary, increasing the desperation as the situation unscrolled, so that when the ambulance finally cleared the road construction, it wheeled into Trinity with the most critical of cargo. The paramedics loaded Brad hurriedly into the emergency room and began the steps toward emergency surgery.

The Fall of Brad Hawley

In a matter of minutes, Jimmy, harried but strong, had shifted from fellow gym member to acting family representative. He finally procured Ellen's number and phoned her, but there was no answer. Finally, after several thick, unnerving minutes, Ellen called back. Jimmy was still under the impression that Brad had a concussion, and if he seemed vague or optimistic to Ellen, it was because he didn't understand the severity of the injury. Besides, Jimmy didn't want to alarm Ellen if this was only a mere concussion. From that he could and would recover. There was little sense of panic in his voice as he retrieved Brad's pedigree information and tendered it to the workers, clad in bubble gum pink uniforms, at the desk.

But Ellen needed a fuller investigation, and it wasn't going to stop with Jimmy. Building her case file and feeling perhaps there might be another perspective, she phoned Coach Mark for more direct eyewitness evidence.

According to her, the first thing Mark said was "Brad got two twenty-five on his clean," followed by, "and he was doing toes to bar and he fell…he seemed like he was fine…he was talking to us, but then he started vomiting and kept repeating himself…he was not making sense…we called nine one one."

This is Ellen's best recollection of the conversation. She recalls Mark's tone being particularly stiff and matter-of-fact. Perhaps Mark thought that a discussion of Brad's performance would somehow assuage her emotions, but Ellen didn't care about how Brad had performed in the workout, much less how much weight he had lifted on cleans. Perhaps Mark, for Ellen's sake, didn't want to seem too distraught or apologetic if Brad was going to leave the hospital with a mere bump on his head.

As Mark spoke, the truth was beginning to unravel. "Stopped making sense" were words Ellen flagged. Could this be more than a concussion?

Detecting danger, Ellen hung up with Mark and immediately called her father, Milton, who was working at his office in Leeds. Ellen described the injury as a concussion, but Milton thought it best to take precaution and observe the situation himself.

"I'm on my way," Milton said firmly.

"As I was on the phone with my dad in the small vestibule leading to the exterior of the building, there was a short break in the conference," Ellen said. "I gave a brief update to my boss, Matt, but said that Brad likely had had a concussion, and he was probably OK. I stepped back into the conference with the group but sat in the back of the room, no longer focused on the furniture company. I couldn't sit still, so I quickly stepped outside the building to get some fresh air and to wait on the call."

1:46 p.m.
MEDICAL REPORT:
PHYSICAL EXAMINATION: DV3 08/27/2012 13:46
Computerized Technology Scan: Brain—Acute subarachnoid hemorrhage. Acute epidural intracerebral hemorrhage.

ED COURSE AND TREATMENT: DV3 08/27/12 13:47
Procedures: Intubation: Size 8.0 endotracheal tube place. Tube secured at 24 cm. Successfully intubated with a total number of attempts = 1.

Brad didn't have a concussion. Brad had a severe traumatic brain injury. The blunt force of the fall had shattered his skull, like a stone to a windshield. Brad wasn't knocked out. He was bleeding on his brain. In medical terms, Brad Hawley was hemorrhaging in the sub-arachnoid area of the brain, between two membranes known as the pia mater and the arachnoid membrane. It's safe to say that it was a much direr situation than what the Steel Companyers had initially believed. Brad was edging dangerously close to death, as, minute by minute, blood continued to pool dramatically in the interior of his head. Brad's injury scored a three on the Glasgow Coma Scale. For reference, this is the score you *don't* want, as this is the worst possible score, medical data suggesting that this score typically correlates to disability or death.

While Brad was being triaged, Jimmy wove through the halls to find his friend, the antiseptic feel of the hospital and its unexciting artwork echoing his mood. Finally, Jimmy happened upon Brad as he was lying on the gurney in a hallway. It was a startling scene, but one that did not put Jimmy in a substantial panic.

"He looked bad, but I didn't think 'Oh my God, he's gonna die,'" Jimmy recalled. Jimmy looked down at Brad and placed his hand on his shoulder. This was the real danger of extreme fitness, something no one wanted to see, but silently feared.

2:14 P.M. Ellen's phone rang. It was Milton.

"Ellen, I'm here with the doctor," Milton said. "I'm going to put it on speakerphone so he can talk to you."

Milton stuffed the phone into a doctor's hand. What followed was the type of nightmare phone call that, when you crawl in bed and say your prayers at night, you pray never happens to you.

"Hello? *Mrs. Hawley?*" the doctor said with an Asian-American accent.

"This is she."

"Hi. This is Dr. Nguyen. I'm a neurosurgeon at Trinity hospital."

The word "neurosurgeon" was an ominous clue, and Ellen's pulse began to race.

"Hello, Doctor."

"Mrs. Hawley, your husband is very sick. He has a subdural hematoma, which means he is bleeding in his brain. We are going to have to drill a hole in his head and evacuate the blood and stop the bleeding."

"Oh my God," Ellen uttered.

"I'm very sorry, but, Mrs. Hawley, I need your permission to perform this surgery."

For a moment, Ellen stepped out of her body. This couldn't be happening. This was a joke.

But it wasn't. Accepting the truth, Ellen gathered herself and tried to process the words.

Drill a hole in his head.
Drill a hole.
In his head.
In his. Head.

Imagine that. This was not a lazy Saturday when Brad might be building a deck with a cordless DeWalt drill he bought at Home Depot. This was an atrocious drilling. Past flesh and into a human skull. Her husband's skull.

Those words ricocheted across the canyons of Ellen's mind. She played them over and over in her head. She felt her body fall. Her heart hastened from the lethality. A montage of memories with Brad floated across her mind. See you on Tuesday. The gazebo in Central Park. The basement. The new house. She pictured his face. She wondered if she would remember it if he died. His eyes. The slope of his nose. How his mouth curved when he laughed. How he had once looked at her, full of love. The dark specter of injury was fully revealed now.

"My boss, Matt, had stepped outside to check on me, expressing his concern and support," Ellen said. "He was standing in front of me when I took the call from my dad. I watched Matt watching my face as Dr. Nguyen told me what was happening to Brad. Matt knew by my expression that something was really bad. He had a tormented look on his face that must have mirrored my tormented expression."

The color had bled out of Ellen's face. She was white with fear. She paused and thought about what to do. She began to converse with God. Her habitual, natural response. Because Milton was present with Brad, Ellen felt a degree of comfort that would not have otherwise existed. Her father had never let her down. He wouldn't this time. She knew he wouldn't.

"Do what you need to do," Ellen instructed the doctor. "Any decision that has to be made, I give my dad permission to make it."

As Ellen was hanging up with the doctor, her father grabbed the phone before Dr. Nguyen could hang up. Milton wanted to make sure that he expressed his love before the line was severed.

"Sweetheart, I'm here. Call me if you need anything," Milton said lovingly.

"I will. Bye, Dad."

Ellen hung up with her father and fell into Matt's arms. Weeping. Between intense sobs she explained to him what had happened to Brad. Matt's previous expertise in comfort had to do with how a sofa felt when a client sat in it, and rarely had he had the occasion to excel in the type of comfort Ellen needed. A rookie in these situations, Matt did his best to console her, and God used him as a soft place for Ellen to land in that harrowing moment.

As Ellen pulled away from Matt's embrace, she thought, *I might never see my husband alive again. I may not have the opportunity to tell him good-bye. There might've been things left unsaid. Our marriage was not in the best shape, and now there may be no chance to repair it. How am I going to live life if Brad dies? What are the kids going to do without a father?*

This wasn't supposed to happen.

This was a routine sales conference.

This was just another day.

This was an unwelcome aberration.

Ellen and Brad had been in a rut for almost a year. Ellen thought, hoped—*believed*—that the new house was just the refreshing the family needed, cause for a new start. But now this. Was it possible to have a long interval of peace in their lives, or were they going to have to navigate through perpetual strife and danger?

But there wasn't much time to think. Ellen zoned in on Birmingham, shifting into a higher gear to get back to her home city. To Brad.

The horrific news spread throughout the conference, and several coworkers rallied to assist her. Matt found a 6:00 p.m. direct flight from Charlotte to Birmingham and booked it. Ellen would need a car to take her back to the Charlotte airport. Joan handled that. Even in the midst of tragedy, love showed its feathers.

As Ellen readied herself for her unplanned return home, her thoughts began to center on the doctor. *Who is this Nguyen? What are his credentials? Is he any good?*

"A slew of thoughts entered my head," Ellen recalls. "How many people enter brain surgery without thorough research and history into the doctor? Testimonials, Google searches. They travel to the best in the world. I knew nothing about this man who held the key to my husband's survival."

Medical Report:
CLINICAL IMPRESSION: DV3 08/27/12 14:19

1. **Fall**
2. **Acute Fracture Skull**
3. **Subarachnoid Hemorrhage**
4. **Epidural Hematoma**

Condition: Critical
Certified Med Emerg: Patient's condition represents a certified medical emergency. Discussed care with patient and family. Explained findings, diagnosis, and need for follow-up care.

Respiratory failure.

PLAN: Will take the patient emergently to have a right suboccipital craniotomy for evacuation of subdural hematoma. Will place a ventriculostomy due to his severe traumatic brain injury. Risks and benefits of performing this surgery was explained to the patient's wife and his father-in-law. They wished to proceed with this procedure.

The Fall of Brad Hawley

Matt waited with Ellen for the taxi back to Charlotte as a tyrannical dread reigned over her. It seemed like an eternity waiting on that car. Nothing was breakneck, waiting on tragedy.

The car finally arrived, a late-model Mercedes sedan. Matt loaded Ellen's bags into the trunk and offered prayer. He wished her well as she ducked into the backseat, looking up at him with eyes inundated with terror.

As the driver sped away, Ellen sat nervously. She shot out a hard breath. Her hands quaked. She didn't want to be alone. There were people to call. She thumbed a number. Her first call was to Brad's best friend, Rich Campbell, who was totally oblivious to the events that had befallen the Hawleys. The toughest part for Ellen was admitting it out loud.

"Helen!" Rich answered cheerily as he received the call. "Helen" was a nickname given to Ellen by Brad's friends, always proffered as light-hearted razzing.

Not wanting to disregard Rich's benign attempt at humor, Ellen let out a conciliatory chuckle. After all, she needed a laugh.

"Have you heard anything about Brad?" Ellen asked.

"I have not," Rich said. "What's up?"

"Brad fell at Steel Company."

"Oh, Jesus."

Rich had heard this before. Doubtless he thought this was simply another "Brad moment" and that he'd be fine and up again in no time.

"Rich," Ellen said with a more macabre tone, "you're not going to believe this. He hit his head, and they are about to do emergency surgery. I'm headed home right now."

"Wait...for real?"

"Yes."

"Where are you?"

"I've been at a sales conference in North Carolina. I just got here today, but I'm in a cab headed back to Charlotte. I have a flight booked for Birmingham, tonight."

"You've got to be kidding me. Oh no! Oh my God, Ellen! Is he going to be OK?"

"I don't know, Rich. I don't know. At first, they thought it was a concussion, but I just spoke with the doctor, and they are about to take him back into surgery. They said he was bleeding on his brain. I'm so worried about him. This is awful."

"Where is he?"

"Trinity."

"What do I need to do? Can I do anything?"

"Rich, I'm worried. I think we need to call in a priest, just to make sure. Will you get Father Bazzel?"

"Goodness. OK. OK. Yes, absolutely, I'll take care of it."

As soon as Rich hung up the phone, he placed a call to Father Kevin Bazzel of Saint Paul's Cathedral in downtown Birmingham. Bazzel was a young erudite priest who would later be called to administer last rites, including an anointing with oil known by Catholics as "Extreme Unction."

Brad, unwittingly, was about to engage in one of the seven sacraments.

"Ellen called me and was absolutely in tears," Rich recalls. "She got me at the office. I think she actually said, 'Will you get Father Bazzel?' So I called the church office. The diocese. I got a secretary. I said, 'Here's what's going on. You have gotta get Father Bazzel.' I basically told her two things: either tell him to call me back ASAP or get him to Trinity Medical Center, because it is incredibly important. Father Bazzel got me when I was on the road. Called me on my cell. I told him, 'I need you there quickly.'"

Rich arrived at the hospital and found several concerned Steel Companyers perched in the ICU waiting area. Father Bazzel arrived minutes later, and Rich led him hastily to the triage room, where he found Milton standing over the scene. Behind him, nurses were cutting off Brad's shirt, and machines were being hooked to him like tentacles.

Then the room stopped.

"When Father Bazzel and I walked in, everything stopped," Rich said. "Everybody stepped back away from the table. People had respect for the process that was about to happen. Everyone joined in prayer. They formed a circle. They had total respect for faith. Not many things in this world would have stopped that room, but the room stopped, and there was total silence. It was amazing."

The room fell reverent as Father Bazzel readied for prayers and ministrations. After he blessed the oil, he began,

> *O Holy Hosts above, I call upon thee as a servant of Jesus Christ, to sanctify our actions this day in preparation for the fulfillment of the will of God.*

> *I call upon the great archangel Raphael, master of air, to open the way for this to be done. Let the fire of the Holy Spirit now descend, that this being might be awakened to the world beyond and the life of earth and infused with the power of the Holy Spirit.*

> *O Lord Jesus Christ, most merciful Lord of Earth, we ask that you receive this child into your arms. That he might pass in safety from this crisis.*

> *By this sign thou art anointed with the grace of the atonement of Jesus Christ, and thou art absolved of all past error and freed to take your place in the world he has prepared for us.*

Father Bazzel swabbed the oil and with his thumb painted a cross on Brad's forehead. As prescribed by Catholic liturgy, he then delivered a prayer of universal thanksgiving. The solemnity of the moment concluded with nurses wheeling Brad, cross forward, into surgery. There was nothing more to do.

He was in the hands of Providence.

2:45 p.m. "When I was in the car, I sat down and took a deep breath and pulled out my iPad," Ellen said. "I sent out an e-mail to about twenty of our closest friends with the subject line PRAYERS. Rich was my first call because I knew I needed to get a priest to the hospital. After that, I called Brad's mom, but couldn't get her. So I called her sister Sandy but didn't tell her what was happening right away. After several unsuccessful tries to get in touch with Sharon, I called Sandy back and asked for help. She was amazing and assured me that she would find Sharon and get her to Birmingham."

The next phone call was to Brad's dad, Bob Hawley. Starkly contrasting Sharon's emotive outbursts, Bob was not one to be consumed by hysteria, distress, or rage. The numbness was evident when Ellen phoned on August 27.

"OK, well, I'll get by tomorrow to see him," Ellen remembered as Bob's response.

Tomorrow? Ellen thought. *Tomorrow?*

More calls were placed from the back of the Mercedes. Ellen was reaching out to anyone who would talk. Silence, she felt, was brutal. "The whole time, I was in shock," Ellen remembers. "I knew it was bad. I knew it was bad, but I didn't want to think about it. I was crying while phoning my closest friends for the entire one-hour drive back to Charlotte for that six o'clock flight to Birmingham. Each of them tried to calm me and assure me that it was going to be OK, but none of them knew if it would be. I was scared, because I didn't know what was going to happen to my husband. Brad had had lots of injuries, but he always seemed to pull through."

When the car arrived at the airport, the driver had been listening to Ellen's mortifying predicament for almost an hour. One had to be heartless and unfeeling not to feel sympathy for her, and the driver's reaction as he unloaded her bags assured that the once-professional drive had now turned personal and emotional. "When I got to the airport, the driver pulled my bags out of the trunk and gave me a hug with tears in his eyes," Ellen said. "He hadn't turned around once during the one-hour drive, but he heard my strife, and I knew he could feel my pain."

Ellen checked her bags at the airport and went through security. She clutched her cell phone and revisited it every few seconds for new texts and calls. *Where is God in the midst of all of this?* Ellen wondered. Right here. Her faith had assured her that He was walking with her every step of the way, and in the terminal she soon received a reminder. In the Charlotte airport, the incredible would happen, something Ellen would later perceive as a "Godwink," something truly astounding and incomprehensible that would let her know that she wasn't trudging through this valley of the shadow of death alone, that the promises in Psalm 23 applied even to Charlotte.

"Ellen?" said a voice from the masses.

Ellen turned around. She was startled to hear her name, so far away from home.

In the terminal, Ellen was very aware that she was crying, but she was trying to walk discreetly. To not to draw attention. Then a woman approached her. Ellen was startled, until she saw that it was her elementary school music teacher! "She recognized me," Ellen said. "And it was definitely nice to have someone to talk to. Later on, my friend Cobbie told me she'd been praying that I'd find someone at the airport. Someone to talk to. Someone who could help me."

God was affixing a ribbon of comfort at every post. Her coworkers. Matt. The cab driver. Her music teacher.

After this encounter, Ellen boarded the plane and sat uncomfortably in her seat. When she began to ponder what might be found at the end of this flight, she caught herself, not allowing her thoughts to go to that mental destination. Forming a gate in her mind, she checked her thoughts there, allowing only the positive and lovely to access the interior places that were aglow with the peace and satisfaction of God. "People shouldn't be alone in times of crisis," Ellen said. "I boarded the plane not knowing if Brad would live or die. But throughout the whole process, I tried to stay ignorant to what could happen. I didn't allow myself to think about what might happen or what could be."

Ellen was not a writer, but on the one-hour flight home, she penned a letter to her husband, his life in flux, a detainee in the omnipotent hold of the Almighty. Ellen felt the urge to write, for writing has a special attachment with the great and serious moments of our lives. It is an old form of expression—letter writing, that is—an archaic, seemingly dead method of correspondence, and even though it was unclear whether Brad would ever read what she had written, Ellen needed this for her own sanity. She thought for a moment about composing an e-mail, but there was something more personal, she felt, about a handwritten letter. For Ellen, writing was catharsis, peace, love, faith, fear, disbelief, joy, grief, sadness, and mercy rolled up into one. She had to make some sense of this mess, to untangle the tangled, to out the inner thoughts and waking imaginings that were dancing their dance of despair. Writing would allow bright transcendent hope to rule her mind, instead of the unnerving alternative.

She began.

Brad,

I am flying home from Charlotte now wishing I were with you. I have so many thoughts going on in my head right now. Knowing how determined you were to crush your score. Knowing how you always strive to be the best. Knowing how you always push to prove yourself. This was a freak accident. It could have happened to anyone. But it happened to you.

What is God telling you? He is enough. He loves you. I love you more than you can know. Right now, I don't know if you're going to be okay. All I keep thinking about is how much I need you. How you always encourage me to be my best self. You know that I sometimes get upset by your methods, but there is love behind it and perhaps a lot of frustration. I need you to be a leader to Webb & Marlen. And a leader to me. You are the head of our home. You are the provider. We would be lost without you. We also need you to be the spiritual head of our family. God has sent us too many signs, too many chances, where we did not react to. He needs to be put first in our marriage & our family.

If by God's grace & love you pull through this unharmed, what are you/we going to do with this life? I am prepared to care for you in sickness & in health. I will stick by you if you have permanent damage or walk away unharmed. I want you to continue to live life to the fullest. To enjoy every second of every day, but live knowing that you have a wife that respects you, loves you, and wants to honor you (hence my 40-day challenge to get organized).

Let's use this trauma to be better. Better Catholics, better spouses, and better people. Let's live with renewed purpose to serve God first. Let's live a life that's fun and full of adventure. There will be more accidents, more injuries, and more illnesses. I don't feel that I am always as compassionate as you need me to be. I am often overwhelmed by my responsibilities as a wife, mother, & sales rep. I feel that I don't focus on your needs & am not as sympathetic as I should be. Our communication has room to improve. I feel that I have been difficult to live with this past year. I am sorry. I want to be better for you & for the kids. No matter what happens. How severe the damage. I am here. I will nurture you through this,…until death do us part…in 60 years.

I love you.

The Rest of Monday

E llen gazed out the plane's window as the sun strafed the oak-and-pine-draped hills of Appalachia. The pristine sunlight washing the South was a stark contrast to Ellen's morose face. Tucked inside the pill-shaped cabin, hundreds of strangers would never know what forged the passing tears of the woman sitting in an aisle seat who was not supposed to be there in the first place.

After she penned her letter, Ellen stuffed it in her purse and bounced a disquieted knee in the seat. Her hands trembled with anxiety. She felt the beginnings of a sweat. She filed through magazines sticking their necks out of the backs of seats. She sipped on ginger ale. She hurled several prayers to the heavens.

"God, if it's in Your will, please don't let Brad die."

While Ellen was hovering above the clouds, Brad had been anesthetized and was on the operating slab, where Dr. Nguyen went to work. Nguyen removed part of his skull, the "bone flap," in order to access and treat the cranial hemorrhage. That was accomplished with a drill, which burrowed into the bone like a miniature jackhammer. The doctor then separated the pliable membrane covering the brain called the dura mater and witnessed the brain itself. Using a drain, he evacuated the fugitive blood on Brad's brain. It would not have been a moment for the weak stomached, the nervous Nellie, or the blood-averse pansy. Nor would it have been a good opportunity for a social media post or selfie.

Brad was lying on a table, in a hospital gown, with his brain exposed.

The Fall of Brad Hawley

During this primal event, the worried trio of Milton, Jimmy, and Rich, waited nervously outside. Their presence marked with overarching concern. It was all so surreal. Father Bazzel had also remained to offer prayer and comfort. It is worth noting that none of these men—Milton, Jimmy, Rich, Father Bazzel—were related to Brad by blood. These were men who, at different times and through different people and events, had come into Brad's life. For Milton, it was a son-in-law-type affection. For Rich and Jimmy, it was a *philos* affection. For Father Bazzel, priest-parishioner. Yet they all could relate to one another in their mutual affection for Brad. And as much as these men wanted to believe that Brad was going to make it, the high likelihood of life without him oscillated in their minds.

When the plane hit the Birmingham tarmac, Ellen powered on her phone and frantically waited for the series of voicemails and text messages that would appear like buoys. She grabbed her belongings from the overhead compartment and unloaded the plane. Oblivious to the stores chocked with magazine racks and T-shirts with "BIRMINGHAM" stitched across the chest, the bars dotted with lonely travelers slow-sipping whiskey, Ellen raced through the airport corridor. She processed through baggage claim, and with bouncing bags hurried out to short-term parking to find her brother, Mack, waiting on her with the car. He had the door swung open conveniently to shave a few seconds off the trip.

Assuming Brad survived the three-hour surgery, there was a high possibility that he might never be the same again. Ellen began to prepare herself for the worst possible scenario if he did make it through surgery: that Brad would be alive but in a vegetated state. No matter the outcome, Ellen was prepared to accept it, and she silently renewed her commitment to him.

The vehicle Mack was driving coursed Interstate 20, hopped onto Oporto-Madrid Boulevard, and negotiated the maddening series of Irondale stoplights before arriving at Trinity, where Milton was waiting for them at a side entrance. As Ellen walked swiftly toward the hospital, she saw her father standing in the doorway. His face strong but beleaguered. She could always count on her father in times of distress, and she would lean on him heavily this night.

Milton greeted her with an impassioned hug and led her through the halls and up the elevator to the Neuro ICU waiting room, where Ellen's mom, Gail, ran to her and embraced her. Because Ellen didn't want to face the growing crowd, she was quickly escorted back to the ICU, where Brad had just returned from surgery.

Ellen learned that Brad had survived and Dr. Nguyen had saved his life.

It was just beyond twelve hours since Brad had dropped her off, and the last image Ellen had of her husband was an intact, standing-up-straight Brad kissing her good-bye at the airport. Now she stood at the doorway of the ICU room, looking down on her husband, who had survived brain surgery. Brad's head was wrapped in a turban-like dressing, but it was nothing similar to the bandanas or headbands that might have been displayed at Steel Company. "When I walked in for the first time, Brad was intubated, hooked to machines, head wrapped in a bandage," Ellen said. "Nothing was moving. He could slightly move his head. His eyes looked at me. I could see in his eyes that he was behind there somewhere. He looked really confused. I feel like, at that point, I wasn't thinking about the future or potential outcome. I was thinking he's alive and he's here."

Ellen felt a potent similarity to Brad's previous medical visits, but this trip was unique. *This is Brad. So many surgeries. So many ER visits. Here we go again. He'll get through this, and we'll be OK. Or will he?*

Though she had mixed emotions, she felt an underlying doom. Yes, Brad was alive and looking at her, which was quite a relief, but something told her that there was to be a long journey ahead. Maybe Brad's long string of luck had finally run out.

As he lay in the hospital bed, Brad woke up groggily and received the first two-second glimpse of his new life. Ellen reached out her hand and grabbed his as Brad's eyes blinked open for the first time.

"Hey, sweetheart," Ellen said softly.

Brad's eyes began to fill with water. He heard her. He didn't fully comprehend why he was lying there. Perhaps it was the fog of a dream. Perhaps it was a cruel memory from his subconscious, playing a trick on him. But as he became aware of the position of his body, his extremities, his vital functions, as he felt the itch of the tube in his throat, he realized that this was no dream.

As Ellen clutched his hand, Brad brushed his eyes across the room to gain inventory of his surroundings. The back wall, where a TV was affixed. The window. The ceiling. Charts and beeping things. The people behind Ellen who had gathered.

Where am I? Why are these people here? Brad thought.

The sun began to set on this strange and challenging day. As Monday waned, the full tide of emotion, the realization of what had happened— that this was not some suffocating dream—began to surface. Ellen knew that August 27, 2012, would be stamped in her mind forever. Although Brad had survived, at the very least he had secured a long-term ticket to the ICU. He was not leaving the hospital anytime soon.

Ellen looked at the road to recovery and saw it running out of sight. There might be no end to this trauma. For the foreseeable future, this was their life.

Sure, the family had been threatened before, but nothing like this. Emotional cracks had been discovered in the dike of marriage, all of which Ellen—and to some degree, Brad—had worked to patch. But now, a physical injury was threatening them.

Why was God touching their lives with this injury? What was He trying to tell them? Ellen would continue to ponder these thoughts.

Brad was lucky he wasn't dead. Doctors and nurses would claim that it was a miracle he was even alive. A nurse who was present for the gruesome matinee would later admit, "When he went into surgery, I didn't think he would get up off that table."

Dr. Nguyen, the hero of the hour who had just Lazarused Brad from the dead, appeared in the Neuro ICU waiting area, where a choir of supporters had collected. It was perhaps the most physically ripped convention of individuals in the history of Trinity Medical Center. Jimmy Brady remembers the scene:

"The surgeon came out and said that everything had gone well. There were probably twenty to twenty-five people in the waiting room, and I remember that the surgeon came in and went to the center of the room. He even joked, saying, 'It looks like he needs to find another hobby.'"

Everyone chuckled. Knowing Brad, they understood that he wasn't a neophyte to this sort of thing. Brad being Brad. The levity loosened the air, but only momentarily. A few dozen yards away was a very sick patient.

For much of the night, Ellen remained bedside with Brad—semiconscious, a throat tube installed—holding his hand for comfort. Although she didn't want to leave him, she felt she had to make an appearance in the waiting area. Wanting to show her appreciation, she would occasionally walk down to the Neuro ICU waiting area to address the torrent of friends and family clustering in support and mountain-moving prayer.

Around ten o'clock, Ellen was informed that the ICU was closed, and she was encouraged to go back to the waiting room. Ellen said that the demeanor of the nurses—an intense, hawklike concern—gave her little comfort.

The waiting room was an austerely decorated brown-scale room with a long window on the south side overlooking a more austerely decorated patio painted a yellow-flesh color. Smoke, produced by twitching visitors from a supposed "nonsmoking" patio, would eke into the waiting room when the turnstile-like door was opened and closed. Rows of hooked-to-gether chairs ran over a leaf-themed carpet, and JCPenneyish artwork was fastened to walls. Shutters winked up and down, depending on the time of day, and there was a tall breakfast table and several end tables displaying King James Bibles, *Readers Digests*, a work by C. S. Lewis, and advertisements for a Power Chair with a registration box and attached pen and string.

Visiting hours were posted on a wall placard:

MICU Visiting Hours
8:00 a.m.   5:00 p.m.
12:00 p.m. 8:00 p.m.

Visiting times are for 1 Hour
Two Immediate Family Members (May Rotate)
Children Under 12 Are Not Permitted

In truth, these visiting hours at Trinity were soft. Rules would be broken for the Hawleys. Not that the folks at hospital showed favoritism, but perhaps they did not want to seem insensitive either. The atmosphere in the ICU waiting area was leaden enough. No need to make things worse by acting like the hospital SS.

In preparation for a long and troubled night, Ellen's family brought blankets, pillows, and sleeping bags to the ICU waiting area. Standards would have to be loosened in terms of billeting. Milton, sentry-like, spent the night sitting upright in a chair, reading an iPad with one eye while keeping the other peeled on the entrance to the room. Just in case a nurse or doctor appeared. Friends Rich and Hank were there, lending their love, their heartfelt encouragement and succor, doing what they could, offering to get something or to make a call. Whatever was needed. Anything. Many others did the same.

Brad continued to sleep through the night with the hose that was breathing him life. When she wasn't tending to Brad, Ellen bivouacked in the waiting area, attempting to sleep but finding only fitful tossings.

Eyes gravitated to Ellen as if she was the default home of stares. She tried to remain stoic, her internal torment masked by her public face. She had to broadcast herself as strong, with it, together. Unbreakable.

"Those first few hours in the hospital, I just felt numb," Ellen remembered.

Laura Carlson, Ellen's cousin who was also present that night in the ICU waiting area, agreed that the mood was "somber." Although Brad had successfully made it through surgery, things were still classified as "touch and go."

"When I got there, I kept asking the doctors what to expect," Ellen says. "The first night was a big night, and all we could do was just wait and see. That night was scary—seeing how he would respond to surgery. I think, medically speaking, that first night is always the telltale."

Ellen wondered how she would see him on Tuesday. Never in her most unimaginable dreams could she have envisioned that any of this would happen when she leaned in his ear on the DC street. There was no portent of things to come. No guarantee of ease when she signed up for life with him. No promise of an unbroken continuum of bliss. And if she could have returned to that moment when she whispered in his ear and write a revisionist history of her life without Brad in it, she would still choose to marry him anyway, no matter the outcome.

For Ellen, covenantal marriage held no contingencies. She made a vow. She made a promise.

And Trinity was watching.

TUESDAY

God moves when we are immovable. An old Sunday school teacher once shared his take on the Twenty-Third Psalm: "Scripture says, 'He maketh me lie down in green pastures.' And why does He make us? He makes us because there are times we don't want to."

When Brad woke up on Tuesday, the scene didn't look much like green pastures. It looked like a muted, sterile hospital room. It looked like unpleasantness beset by a daylong curriculum of immobility. Regardless of whether Brad would regain his physical strength, would walk again, something inside him began to die that Monday. Brad would not change overnight, but the fall began the process of dying.

No, the killing of Brad Hawley was not literal death. It was the death of pride. The death of self-reliance. The death of ego. The death of the man he had been constructing the majority of his life. The death of the man he had been assembling as a reaction to family tribulations, toughening through minor injuries, armoring through the brainwashing of the world. The death of his ability to fix everything. The death of his perception of true strength.

Author Pat Conroy once wrote, "American men are allotted just as many tears as American women. But because we are forbidden to shed them, we die long before women do, with our hearts exploding or our blood pressure rising or our livers eaten away by alcohol because that lake of grief inside us has no outlet. We, men, die because our faces were not watered enough." Though tears would eventually fall, Brad would have to traverse a lake of bitterness before he would realize he needed to let go. Through this bone-chilling event, he would discover the necessity of tears. He would realize, to pull out of this mess, he would have to rely on forces much greater than he. That he couldn't just muster up enough strength or through sheer willpower work his way out of circumstance as he had done for the last thirty-four years. He couldn't simply grunt and strain his way out of the quagmire. Due to the gravity of the situation, he was forced to rely on supernatural strength. In the past, the ceiling of life was relegated to things earthbound. To human grit. Now he was going to have to rely on God, because it wasn't his call whether he lived or died. The fall exposed how weak Brad really was.

Ellen had already been in the habit of posturing herself in that manner. She had a deep faith and her heart was inclined to Christ. If there was trouble, she gave the situation over instead of trying to manage or manipulate by her own accord. God was central to her life, not just an obligatory box to check. Her Christian walk wasn't simply confined to the hour-long Mass on Sunday morning. A weekly duty to collect eternal brownie points so she might earn heaven. Every day, she put on the raiment of Christ, and as she bonded herself with Almighty God, obedience flowed.

But Brad's faith journey was different. Brad had to learn to fall before he walked.

To die before he lived.

"On the flight home, I prayed that God would take control of the situation," Ellen said. "In the past, when I would give situations to God, I would always have peace about it. Through the process, even though I was upset about what had happened to Brad, I had peace that it was going to work out. That everything was going to be OK. Faith and reliance on Him had gotten me through several things with Brad in the past and life in general. We didn't have a peaceful home. Brad would yell and snap often. But my faith kept me calm and at peace through the chaos of life."

The Fall of Brad Hawley

Brad slept most of the day on Tuesday as family and friends continued to populate the ICU waiting room. Love was manifest, tears were shed, and large doses of prayers and hugs were dispensed.

"The waiting room was full of people, and it was a lot of waiting," said Ellen. "That first day was really quiet."

Most of the speaking was done from the ICU room as Brad clung to life. Ellen's day consisted of marches back and forth between Brad's room and the ICU waiting area, the space like a parade ground, her life confined to that sorrowful radius. The flow of affection was contingent on which space she occupied. In Brad's room, Ellen was the one giving affection. In the waiting area, she was the one receiving it.

Sleep came in fits and starts. While awake, Brad's eyes vacillated from grey and empty to brimming and alive. This was his only method of communication. He couldn't speak.

"When he would awaken, I could look at his eyes and tell he was there," Ellen said. "He would talk back and forth with his eyes."

The surgeon, a squat Asian-American man who spoke fluent English, gave the family encouraging updates as Brad remained intubated throughout the morning. "Dr. Nguyen, for better or for worse, stayed positive," Ellen recalled. "He never once made me think it wasn't going to be OK. He was positive and said Brad was going to pull through it. That he'd be fine. So I wouldn't let myself think that it wasn't going to be OK. I wouldn't let myself think that he would be a vegetable or that he would be disabled or wouldn't survive. Dr. Nguyen encouraged me, and I fed off that. Brad was on life support, but I tried to not think of it in those terms. I kept myself naive intentionally. I chose to listen to the doctor who literally said he would be home in three weeks. I'm not an idiot, but I just chose to think that. Just take this one day at a time. I didn't think ahead. I was living in the now, just being there, doing what I could do. There was literally no thought to the future. At that point, I chose not to talk to anyone else who had experience with brain injuries because I knew enough to know that every situation is different, and I didn't want false hope or to be falsely discouraged."

Sharon caught the first available flight to Alabama and arrived from Michigan at 9:30 a.m. on Tuesday. A slow process of forgiveness had been taking place since Sharon's exodus from the Cullman house, but recently, her relationship with Brad had been tenuous at best. Brad had bristled when he perceived Sharon attempting to play the victim card, utilizing a babe-in-the-woods narrative to her advantage.

Brad's relationship with his mother was yet another halfhearted effort, something he felt he had to do out of obligation. Anything that had wounded him, he approached with kid gloves. Sharon. The church. Friends. And by elevating himself over the perpetrator, Brad could exercise a level of control. Besides, he felt that simply letting her back into his life was forgiveness enough, that he was being "kind" in doing so. Doing her a favor. He felt he needed to continue to punish her for the transgression of leaving him, and his attempts at reconciliation did not extend to full forgiveness. Because he lugged the unhappy freight of bitterness across the years and kept a record of wrongs, every argument was like knifing at the original wound. Sharon could never seem to get a clean slate. She tried unsuccessfully to draw near, but because Brad had erected a barrier to his heart, their relationship remained superficial and robotic. Transactional. He subconsciously didn't want to get hurt again. For Sharon, his breastplate was thickest. It protected his deepest wound.

When Sharon arrived in Birmingham, there would be no verbal brawls, no histrionics or high drama between her and her only son. Brad was asleep mostly and during his short waking minutes could produce no more than a gesture with his panicked, grief-heavy eyes. "When Rich brought me to the hospital, I could not see Brad," Sharon remembered. "I was told that Brad was not going to survive. I was absolutely petrified. I went right to the hospital. I didn't think anyone thought he was going to live. I kept praying, 'Lord, just let him survive.' I was constantly thinking about Ellen and the kids—what they would do without him. I wondered,

'Will I get to talk to him?' but my main concern was Ellen and the kids. I thought about just how much I loved him and how sorry I was for things that had occurred. The feelings he had toward me. I was sorry maybe that I hadn't told him about his life. Who his dad was. That I had kept things from him. I wondered if I had waited too late. The whole thing—I just—as I think now and think about these circumstances, the bottom line is that I was operating like 'he's here.'"

Indeed, Brad *was* there, but only a notch above death. If he could somehow clear this thicket, Sharon saw this as an opportunity to fully repair her relationship with her son. She hoped by offering herself in service that grace could wash away the black particles of bitterness from his heart and they could begin anew. Yes, that was her hope. And while other family members were filing into their respective positions, it was decided at the hospital that Sharon was to take care of the house and kids. She accepted proudly. Sharon was content with any help she could give. She would have done anything for her son, completed any reparation or penance.

Treatment, at times, came in the form of trial and error. Brad had been using a breathing tube for the last twenty hours. Tuesday afternoon, the doctor attempted to extubate the breathing tube, but Brad threw up savagely, vomit seeping into his lungs. The tube was immediately shoved back down his throat.

Many of those who stayed closest to the situation were not afforded the luxuries of proper hygiene. Ellen hadn't showered since Monday morning, nor had she seen her children. Ellen's sister Claire brought some face wash and a change of clothes, and Ellen had a few private moments to wash away the grime that she had accumulated. The tumult could not be washed.

By afternoon, Ellen felt the first signs of fatigue. She had been running on adrenaline for a full day. As the shock began to wane, the weariness eventually ran her down. Late in the afternoon, she found a window of time to slip out and return home for the first time since she had boarded the plane to Charlotte.

Ellen walked into her house and up the interior stairwell leading from the garage. She greeted Marlen and Webb, now safely under the care of their nanna, Sharon, who had alerted them of their father's condition in language that was understandable to infants. "When I got home, Webb started asking about Brad," Ellen said. "He asked, 'Does daddy have a big boo-boo?' I told him yes. Then he asked, 'On his head?' Again, I responded yes. Then he so sweetly asked, 'Was he jumping on the bed?' My mom had recently given him the book *Five Little Monkeys.* We had been preaching not to jump on the bed. It was so sweet. I wish I had it recorded."

After a quick shower and a short visit with the kids, Ellen returned to the hospital, where she was encouraged by Brad's progress. "Brad was starting to get stronger and more aware of his surroundings," she said. "Tuesday morning, he could barely squeeze my hand. By Tuesday evening, he was starting to lift his arms."

As the day went on, Brad was able to lift his hands higher. Each time, he would get closer and closer to grabbing the throat tube, and Ellen would kindly reach for his hand and pull it back. No, Brad, no. By nightfall, the nursing staff grew concerned that Brad would yank out the tube. So they restrained his arms with straps that were affixed to the bed. "This was very upsetting to me," Ellen remembered. "Watching my husband be tied to a bed was the first glimpse into what could be."

Tremors of Brad's injury and subsequent hospitalization were felt outside of Trinity, and a growing audience needed to be apprised of Brad's condition, his loved ones concluded. When the curtain of evening fell on Tuesday, Rich Campbell created a Brad Hawley–dedicated page on CaringBridge (www.caringbridge.org), a website that provides a message board for family and friends to receive updates when a loved one is ill. CaringBridge is useful in that written updates on the patient's condition could be made to a corporate body, instead of relying on the often-laborious word of mouth. Doubtless many close to the situation wanted to see how Ellen and the kids were faring in the midst of this grievous ordeal and CaringBridge would prove to be an invaluable communication tool for the Hawleys. Since Ellen already had enough to worry about, Rich volunteered to be the first courier of intelligence. His first post, a primer entitled "Let's start from the beginning," was the first public glimpse into Brad's injury and demonstrated a point-in-time snapshot of what the family understood about the grim event. They would find out later that some of the information they had relied upon for the message was not entirely true.

Yesterday, August 27, around 12:30 p.m., Brad was working out at Steel Company Fitness (a CrossFit gym.) He was finishing up a challenge with a "toes-to-bar" exercise and was just shy of his goal when his hands gave out. Brad fell from the bar, and his head was the first thing to make contact with the ground. He suffered a skull fracture on the lower back side of his head, and the fracture severed a vein. Thankfully, his friends at Steel Company knew that something was wrong and knew what to do. Because of the quick response of his friends and a great EMS and ER team, he was in surgery within two hours. By 1:30 p.m., Brad was in the ER and getting prepped for emergency surgery to drain the blood and fluid from his brain and to repair the vein causing the massive internal bleeding. The surgeon was able to drain all the blood, find the vein, and stop the bleeding. He remained intubated postop and all through today. This afternoon, the doctors extubated him (removed the breathing tube), and since lunch, Ellen has been able to stay in the room with him as long as she wants. The surgeon spoke to us this morning and felt good about the procedure and was encouraged that blood and fluids had not gathered at the base of the skull. He told us that Brad will be in the hospital for at least two weeks, and as he begins to breathe on his own and "wake up," they will begin cognitive assessments and try to establish a better prognosis.

We are just shy of the 8:30 visiting hour and have a waiting room full of visitors. There has been a constant flow of friends and family, all showing their love and support, and the Hawleys will be forever grateful for that. Brad was just reintubated as a precaution so he is getting some help breathing again.

Rich also encouraged friends to bring meals to the hospital, upload pictures of Brad, or sign Brad's guest book on the site. Any small gesture would be appreciated, Rich assured. An image of Brad and Ellen standing on the runway of *Top Gun* in San Diego, with sleek gray majestic jets in the background, was posted on the site as their profile picture.

Later that night, Rich made another post, entitled "This is just a cut-and-dry explanation of the medical side." Cregan Laborde, a family friend who had recently completed his gastroenterology fellowship, had been called upon by Ellen to explain the intricacies of Brad's injury and condition to the interested masses. Dr. Laborde was one of many friends who would step up and shine through the dark cave of tragedy.

Rich copied and pasted Laborde's medical dialect and personal reflections, with a notation at the very end that brought a ray of hope: "He is already responding to commands, which is a good sign."

As the day unwound, friends and family were already taking their stations. Like pieces of a chessboard, the king could barely move, and the queen had the most versatility and power.

WEDNESDAY

The eyes revealed much. On Monday, Brad's eyes were wide and filled with tragedy. Ellen could see behind the dark-brown discs, the fear-smothered irises, and although there was not ample lucidity, she knew that her husband—could *feel* that her husband—was with her. By Wednesday, when Ellen gazed into those same familiar eyes, she felt that he had begun to drift into a despondent abyss. "That Wednesday and Thursday, I could tell he wasn't in there anymore," Ellen recalls. "His feet and arms began to pronate. I couldn't see him in his eyes anymore. I had him, and then I lost him. That was the first time I really started to get scared, that I thought maybe he wasn't going to be OK."

Brad's lungs were also of paramount concern, though he was sleeping peacefully, heavily sedated, his breathing performed by the ventilator. Wednesday morning the doctors performed a bronchoscopy to scope the small pockets of fluid in the lungs. They eyed suspiciously an emergent blood clot on his brain.

Ellen no longer wanted to remain naïve. Ignorance wasn't bliss, and she began to collect as much information as she could, utilizing family connections in the medical community, which, at first, seemed invaluable. Advice arrived on two fronts. The medical and the logistical. *What is Brad's prognosis? Is Trinity the best option for treatment?* These were the two most pressing questions. Ellen even went to the trouble of sending scans to a neurosurgeon in Michigan who was a close friend of the family. From Ellen's point of view, Trinity Medical Center did not have the best reputation in Birmingham (not a bad one, just not the best), especially for neurological care, although the doctors and staff at Trinity probably would have argued differently. As Ellen consulted a variety of friends, many of whom felt their voices and opinions were tantamount to chief, she began to feel overwhelming pressure to transfer Brad to UAB Medical Center, believed by many to be the best hospital in the Birmingham metro area. "There was a lot of pressure to move to UAB, because Brad started having issues postsurgery," Ellen said. "That was the most stressful of our hospital time, and it is when I started to second-guess myself. I had a lot of pressure from Brad's friends to move him. But the doctor told me that if I moved him, he could possibly not make it. He was so unstable that they couldn't even move him on Tuesday to get a CT scan."

Second, third, and fourth opinions from family friends were offered, and as Ellen began to feel discussions turning adversarial, she called in the big guns. "It got so contentious that at one point my dad got so upset with the way my friends were pressuring me that he blocked them out for me. Cregan became the filter, and he would disseminate information and give it to me as fact, not as emotional persuasion."

Ellen liked Dr. Nguyen and did not believe Trinity had done anything wrong. Initially, she thought that by putting a swarm of heads together she was exercising logic, but as time went on, she began to feel more burden than benefit. A tangled web. "At first, I wanted these opinions but not when they became commands instead of sound advice," Ellen said. "Because of the strong opposition, I began to question my decisions. I felt by leaving Brad at Trinity, essentially I was giving him a death sentence. But I had to rely on my own feelings in the matter, even though I received some long, strong-worded e-mails."

Rich was Brad's best friend and had, in the past, been a voice of reason, a wise influence when life called for discernment. Folks knew that Rich had Rasputin-like influence with the Hawleys' Royal Court, and used that relationship as a point of entry for their strong sentiments. "Some of the doctor friends who essentially were taking the reins were filling Rich's head with a bunch of information," Ellen said. "Everyone had the best intentions in mind, but I was being bullied to move him. People weren't giving me their opinions; they were *telling* me what to do. I wasn't asking for that. I was asking for advice."

Late into the night on Tuesday, Dr. Nguyen, Ellen, and Ellen's mom had a lengthy conversation about options. They sat cross-legged on the floor of the ICU waiting room for the better part of an hour. If, in the back of her mind, Ellen wasn't pleased with the overall medical treatment at Trinity, she was at least pleased with the caliber of care offered by Nguyen. She described Nguyen as having a great bedside manner. A compassion, she felt, neurosurgeons often lacked. "I approached Dr. Nguyen about moving Brad to UAB," Ellen said. "Brad was not stable, and we talked about the pros and cons of moving him or keeping him. Dr. Nguyen tried to instill our confidence in him, and the conversation was back and forth. Dr. Nguyen was very personable. I was still debating at this time whether or not to move Brad, but Dr. Nguyen made me feel confident in him. He talked about his background at a level-one trauma center in Jackson, Mississippi. He told me he was prepared and left me with no doubts about the quality or level of care at Trinity."

In the midst of undulating emotion and chaos, Ellen longed for some semblance of peace. That night, Nguyen provided it. "I went to sleep that night with peace," Ellen remembered. "We were OK where we were."

But Wednesday, Ellen felt more pockets of pressure, mostly from Brad's friends, who thought they knew, better than Ellen, what was best for Brad. Thinking back, Ellen does not take these uncomfortable moments from expert voices as anything but serious concern for a friend. Certainly there was no malefic intent for glory, nor was it an attempt to wrestle control away from the ultimate decision maker. But that did not make the situation any less difficult when it was actually happening. For Ellen, all signs were pointing to remaining at Trinity. As the current ran against her, Ellen kept her eyes fixed on the cross.

Bolstering her decision to stay was the assent by other doctors to the capabilities of Trinity. Ellen spoke to both the chief of neurosurgery at

UAB and the CEO of UAB hospital while considering her options. "The CEO said, 'I don't know if we have a bed for Brad,'" Ellen said. "And he essentially said if the doctors at Trinity thought they couldn't handle Brad, they would have transferred him. That no doctor wants a bad result under his or her watch."

Yet the pressure seemed unrelenting, as some of Brad's friends now adopted a bull-by-the-horns approach. "They started to go around me, and they eventually got him accepted at UAB through another department," Ellen said. "His friends were telling me that Trinity was holding him captive. But Dr. Nguyen insisted that he was not transferring Brad out of his care to someone who was not a neurosurgeon."

Notwithstanding opinions or demands, the buck stopped with Ellen. No one else had the authority to make decisions on Brad's behalf, and as much as others desired her to yield to their demands, Ellen was equally unyielding. "I felt comfortable with the doctor at Trinity and trusted him that he couldn't move. So I was comfortable leaving him there. And the nurses were amazing," Ellen said.

Those living in the suburbs of the ordeal would not be privy to information regarding Brad's potential transfer. It wasn't merely that the nucleus of care simply needed to present a strong front to their audience. There were layers of intimacy that needn't be crossed. Concerned parties could download the CaringBridge app, where Ellen and others kept them updated, but a committee closer to the situation continued to vie for Ellen's ear.

Ellen felt on Wednesday that friends of the family needed to hear from her, and she was comfortable stepping away from her bedside duties to pen a few verses. That Wednesday post, rich in emotion, allowed access to her state of mind:

Friends,

Brad had a pretty good night last night. As you read, we had to reintubate him yesterday. He just wasn't quite ready to breathe on his own. He was having trouble clearing the fluid in his lungs.

The Fall of Brad Hawley

They are a little concerned about a small pocket of fluid in his lungs, so the pulmonologist is doing a bronchoscopy right now to clean out his lungs. This is about a fifteen-minute procedure. He is sedated now, which makes me happy. It has been so hard watching him struggle with the breathing tube. Though many people tell me he will not remember this, to me, he really looks to be suffering. Because he is getting stronger, last night he kept trying to reach for the breathing tube. I tried to gently hold his hand back, but then he would start to reach with the other hand. I finally had to take the nurses advice and let them restrain his arms.

We have been so blessed to have friends here around the clock. They don't seem to encourage overnight guests in the ICU waiting room as evidenced by the hard floor. At least it is carpeted. Rich, my dad, and I spent the night on the floor here on Monday night. Hank and Rich split the night last night, while my mom and I slept on the floor. Though they do allow me to stay in the room with Brad as much as I want; sleeping is not really an option in the ICU.

We have been very impressed with the doctor who saved Brad's life. He comes from a level-one trauma center in Mississippi. God was obviously in control of the timing, having him here when Brad arrived on Monday.

Please continue to pray for his recovering and the wisdom of the doctors and nurses. We have loved our nurses Cameron and Jeremy. They are taking great care of Brad.

Thank you again for all of your love and support.

Ellen, Brad, Webb and Marlen

It was the closest the Hawley tribe had been in a year.

THURSDAY

The blood was back. Just when Ellen thought they might be out of the woods, things turned staggeringly for the worst. Thursday, an early-morning CT scan revealed a 1.8–2.2 mm pocket of blood on Brad's brain. This was shattering news.

"It was devastating, because we hoped he was on the mend," Ellen said.

By Wednesday, Ellen had secured a hotel room located within the hospital, in the building adjacent the ICU, third floor. Wednesday night, she went to bed at 10:30 and got up around 5:30 Thursday morning. By the time she arrived in Brad's room, the staff had already taken him for a morning CT scan, and he was back in his room, sleeping soundly.

Ellen had settled into her chair—one she described as "semicomfortable"—when Dr. Nguyen walked in with a clipboard full of results. By this time, Ellen and the good doctor had developed a rapport. "I remember he would sit in the ICU with the nurses and put his feet on the table. We developed a friendship," Ellen said.

Dr. Nguyen, wearing his trademark blue scrubs, held the results of the morning CT scan in his hands. As he stood there, licking his thumb and probing the pages that hissed at every turn, an ominous and explicit fog began to descend upon the room. Nguyen looked up from the results and tendered the news to Ellen in his ever-optimistic fashion, saying something like, "Ellen, we need to go in and repair this blood clot...the bleeding hasn't stopped...we need to go back in." The dark vapor of the words lingered behind his front of sanguinity. Nguyen was certain, matter of fact, nonnegotiable. He ordered emergency surgery as surely and unilaterally as if he were ordering his own lunch. A second—this time larger—craniotomy to drain the blood was his morning mandate.

"When we got the CT scan results back, they called for another emergency brain surgery," Ellen said. "I didn't want them to cut his head open again."

But cut they did. Brad was whisked away immediately, so swiftly that Ellen had no time for consultation with friends and family. This time, she would not beg for second opinions. And although Nguyen had essentially commanded the procedure, Ellen felt that the decision fell broadly on her shoulders.

"I was really upset," Ellen remembered. "I was physically very upset and at that point needed to be by myself."

While Brad was being prepped for surgery, Ellen went into the surgery waiting area, her rapturous love for Brad undying through each station of the turmoil. "I remember there was a big TV screen in the surgery waiting room that told you where the patients were in the process," Ellen said. "I talked to some other people, who were following their loved ones. Beside the name, it kept saying 'Waiting for surgery.' That morning, they bumped several people who had brain surgeries because of the emergency nature of Brad's situation."

Soon, Ellen would disappear. While waiting on surgery, she made a quick post on the CaringBridge site from her phone before retiring to a stairwell to text her mom. For three days, Ellen had been canopied by love and grace, a refuge supported by the pillars of wonderful friends. She had listened to their comforting words and allowed them to saturate her. She had prayed her prayers. She had trusted Him. But she had yet to be silent.

She told her mother that she wanted to vanish for a while. She didn't want to see or talk to anybody. "I wanted to be by myself where I didn't think anyone would find me," she remembered. "I just wanted to be alone. I wanted peace."

Ellen then remembered there was a chapel nearby. The chapel, carved into a hospital nook, was an oddly shaped, round room with 1970s yellow brick walls. There were chairs fashioned into rows, and an altar. The carpet was wine colored and worn. Literature was dotted about, and resting on the altar was a cross. The privacy of the stairwell had served as a nice respite, but it lacked a naturally sacrosanct ambiance. It was in the chapel, this sacred place, that, for the first time in many days, she became still.

As Ellen knelt alone and began to pray in the quiet of the morning, the light was pouring in through the defined colors of the stained glass. Reds. Greens. Blues. Ellen found peace in solemnity. Felt a washing. From her position of bent knees and cupped hands, in the silence and reverence, her mind was able to clear, as if all the discussions and all the opinions were somehow canceled out in favor of one divine voice. The only voice, in the end, that mattered.

She knelt for quite a while, praying to her God. Exquisite tears began to fall from her eyes, the silence and prayer ringing them out like a dishrag. She asked the Lord to uncap His heavenly mysteries, His omniscience, and allow her to think clearly through this situation. This unlikely sojourn with her partner in life. She now cried for comfort and discernment because she had begun to second-guess her decision to keep him at Trinity. "I felt it was fine for Brad to recover there, but I wasn't prepared for a second surgery," she said. "I also didn't want to face all the 'bullies' who had tried to persuade me to move Brad."

Ellen was wrapping up her prayer time, and as she began to rise from the altar, she heard footsteps across the floor. She turned around and it was Monica, Webb's teacher's daughter. Ellen had not met Monica before the hospital, but Monica had been popping in each day to check on the family.

"How are you?" Monica inquired, offering her best smile.

"Hey, Monica!" Ellen said, brushing her face. "It's good to see you again!"

"Good to see you!"

"You've been so sweet to come by."

"Well, thank you. Can I do anything for you? Have you eaten?"

"Actually, I haven't eaten. I got up early, and I've been in the chapel. I've been in here for a few minutes. You know Brad had a second surgery this morning."

"I didn't. I'm very sorry," Monica said compassionately. "Can I get you anything? Anything to eat? Breakfast?"

"Aw, Monica. You don't have to do that."

"No, no. I want to. It's no problem."

"That's so nice of you."

"What would you like? They've got biscuits down in the cafeteria. How 'bout I get you one?"

"That sounds pretty good, actually," Ellen said. "I'm starving."

Ellen and Monica laughed. For Ellen, it wasn't that what Monica had said was necessarily that funny, but laughter had become a necessity for her sanity. The last time she remembered laughing was the conciliatory chuckle after Rich called her "Helen." After three joyless days, it felt good to laugh.

"I bet," Monica said. "I'll run down to the cafeteria and get you a biscuit."

Small things done with great love. Those were the things Ellen cherished the most. "Monica didn't even have to pop in that first day and let me know she was there," Ellen said. "I had a lot of respect for Mrs. Marzella, her mother, who was Webb's favorite teacher. She was someone I really respected and admired. It meant a lot to me that her daughter came to check on us."

After Monica returned, Ellen ate quietly in the chapel and stayed for a little while longer. Being in the presence of the Lord seemed to be the safest place she could be. Though her life was raining turmoil, the chapel provided an adequate coat of solace that helped her to weather the storm. "At that point, I was completely distraught and upset," Ellen said. "I didn't know what was going to happen. I just had to trust and have faith."

Having to recapitulate the surgery was perhaps more excruciating than having to endure the first procedure, because the oasis of survival, dangled in front of her for two days, was now jerked back. She had him, now she might lose him.

If Brad died, Ellen felt she would always have to answer for her decision to keep him at Trinity.

Brad was in surgery for two hours. Ellen learned that, for the second procedure, Dr. Hrynkiw had replaced Nguyen, who had been the attending surgeon the entire time. A year later, Dr. Hrynkiw made the news when he walked through six miles of snow to perform brain surgery on a patient. Hrynkiw performed the craniotomy with Nguyen's assistance.

Ellen was back in the waiting room when Dr. Nguyen appeared around nine o'clock and relayed that the surgery had gone well. Sharon and Bob were listening too. Ellen's mood had been zigzagging all week. Once again it changed dramatically, from gloom and uncertainty to sheer happiness and elation from answered prayers.

Ellen didn't know what to expect from day to day, and routine was lost to uncertainty. Her days were beginning very early, while nights lingered late. On the day of the second craniotomy it wasn't yet ten o'clock in the morning and Ellen had already experienced enough drama for a lifetime. Each day seemed to run together with the next, and she often wasn't sure what day it was, as if the days were threaded together with no real beginning and no real end. Time drew out methodically, yet it seemed that each day had no life of its own. Some days had elicited unimpeachable joy, while others were funereal. Some days had been filled with high drama, followed by boredom and nothing. These were the effects of the great pause of their lives. It was just one long moment of trying to survive.

The Fall of Brad Hawley

"For the rest of the day, I was just peacefully waiting," Ellen said. "It was like a waiting game. I spent a lot of the day in peace and quiet, not wanting to talk to anybody. I just sat in his room. The nice thing about it was that I was isolated from visitors."

Ellen was the gatekeeper to the ICU, as nobody could visit unless Ellen approved. "The nurses gave me a lot of power. Technically, it was supposed to be family only, but they allowed me to have some other people," she said.

It was appropriate that Ellen shielded Brad from all discomfort.

"Brad, do you want to watch the football game?" a nurse asked, leaning over to her distressed patient. Around seven o'clock, Brad awoke with successful surgery number two tallied on his ledger. Another showpiece to add to his increasingly thick medical résumé. The dreaded throat tube had been reinserted, and nurses had cocooned his head again with that terrible-looking bandage.

Thursday was the opening day of college football season, and two SEC schools, South Carolina and Vanderbilt, were pitted in a contest on ESPN. It wasn't his Auburn Tigers, but given these morbid circumstances, it would more than do. Ellen and staff would rely on small bonuses such as these to lift Brad's spirits.

When the nurse asked him if he wanted to watch the game, Brad blinked twice to indicate assent. Brad found that tasks such as speaking, swallowing, and walking were now impossible. Functions he had taken for granted in the past. He would have to discover other ways to communicate. Food would have to be routed to his stomach. Bathroom breaks were nonexistent because his digestive system was no longer receiving signals from his brain. "Number one" was accomplished with a catheter, and "number two"—well, number two was not an issue since he was unable to eat. All bathroom duties occurred within the square feet of his hospital bed. Showers were out of the question. And working out? Forget about it. Kettlebell swings? Not even a worldly consideration. Cleans? Andromeda.

Ellen posted that night on CaringBridge:

Brad is slowly starting to wake up. He has been opening his eyes, and as he looks around, I can tell that he is aware of his surroundings. Every time he opens his eyes, I remind him of what happened. He looks back at me with a confused, blank stare. He has been moving his feet around and just squeezed my hand on demand. It has been a long slow day, but Brad did have major brain surgery this morning.

Brad had not spoken a word in four days. He hadn't had a solid meal. A tube was down his throat. He'd had not one but *two* brain surgeries. He was totally immobile, save for short and tedious movements of his arms and the wiggling of his feet. The hot friction of his body against the hospital bed. He stank. He ached. He had little comprehension of his surroundings. He floated in and out of sleep. Through all these trials, he realized something. His dreams were better than the nightmare of awakening.

The Weekend

The waiting game continued. For most of the day on Friday, Ellen remained in a chair beside Brad's bed, looking down on his supine melancholy. Nurses, touring the halls, would scoot in and out at random times with a test here, some medicine there, fetching things, checking vital signs, and offering encouragement. The nurses worked twelve-hour shifts and came to know the Hawleys intimately. Ellen believes that Trinity encouraged such a structure— "They do that on purpose so you can get to know the patients."

"Cameron was awesome," Ellen said. "She was one of my favorites. She was young, late twenties, and had brown hair. She got engaged while Brad was in ICU. I remember she was very comforting to me while I had pressure to move Brad. She assured me they could handle it. She was very sweet, and I knew she had a strong faith. Courtney was another one. She was sort of cut and dried. Young, blond, and twenty-something. Matter of fact. But I was completely comfortable with her in the room. Brooke, when she came, she moved all of her stuff to Brad's door, parked herself next to his room. She was very diligent and on top of things all night long."

Though Ellen had high praise for those three in particular, not all of the nurses made her feel warm and fuzzy. "Some of the night nurses made me nervous," she said. "They would be at the nurses' station, cutting up and getting on YouTube. They were not very serious."

As each nurse rotated off her shift, Ellen said good-bye, adding, "Hopefully we *won't* see you next week!" Nothing against the staff. Nice place and all. But Ellen was ready to go home.

Uneventful in terms of Brad's physical progress, Friday was a day when the family received the greatest emotional boost of the week. It was another "small things done with great love" moment that demonstrated that protectionism could be used for good. As superiorly cloistered as it may seem, Mountain Brook folks take care of their own, and as word spread throughout the community, neighbors took action. When Milton drove Ellen home on Friday to put Webb and Marlen to bed, they were surprised to find a gallery of green bows affixed to mailboxes on Ellen's street. The bows were in Brad's honor.

The neighborhood had rallied, and as Milton drove slowly past each house, every house, left and right side of the road, he and Ellen were awestruck by the symbolic unity of neighborly affection. An unknown someone, someone with great alacrity and love, had taken the time to organize this effort. They had gone to a local five-and-dime and purchased the bows and taken the time to stop by every house to ask permission for a green bow to be attached to the mailbox. "I cried as we slowly drove past each mailbox, every mailbox," Ellen said. "Having all this support and knowing so many people were praying for us, willing and waiting to help us, and ready to have us home gave me strength to make it through another day and night by Brad's side."

This was a small, simple gesture that made a profound impact on Ellen and emboldened her immensely.

SATURDAY WAS THE OPENING WEEKEND of college football season, and Ellen hoped that watching the Auburn game in the hospital room might help to assuage the slow, torturous intervals of the hospital stay. Before the game, Ellen went for a long walk and spent time praying in the chapel. Later, she had a "serious talk with Brad, showing him pictures of Webb and Marlen, reminding him of his family and how much we love him and need him."

That afternoon, a PICC line was installed. The PICC line was necessary because Brad needed nutrients to survive, and the only way was through intravenous means. Physically, there were no major changes in

Brad's condition that Saturday, and the ventilator remained. Physical therapists had been visiting from time to time, but since hospital therapists did not work over the weekend, Ellen begged for help in one of her CaringBridge posts. Ellen the Caretaker was busy filling in the gaps left by medical staff. Ellen the Griever was busy trying to remain positive amid the calamity.

Around four o'clock in the afternoon, friend Jon Delk, a physical therapist, arrived in response to Ellen's post. "He showed us some very basic movements, but it seemed to really light a fire in Brad. He left, and Brad's determination started. He worked to move his arms for the next two hours. He had a little more difficulty with his feet," Ellen said. These exercises weren't the kind of pregame festivities that Ellen had imagined leading up to the kickoff of a college football season.

Around seven o'clock in the evening, Ellen thumbed the remote control to ESPN and hit the mute button. Brad couldn't handle the sound of the TV. That year, Auburn was ranked number twenty-five in the coaches' preseason poll, and the team was opening with fourteenth-ranked Clemson at the Georgia Dome in Atlanta. Ellen and Brad were big fans, Auburn football adorers, and the biggest event every fall was always the Auburn football season. By the end of the night, things would already be looking grim for Brad's alma mater.

There were no tickets to sell. Brad and Ellen hadn't planned on going to Atlanta, even though it was a big game and a mere two and a half hours from Birmingham. They had carved out space in their weekend schedule for the game, of course, and were planning on watching it at the house and grilling out. But that was before the Fall. And since Brad was stock still, the best Ellen could do was to fit an orange-and-blue shaker into his limp hand and hope that his spirits might be energized. Just before kickoff, however, "Brad slowly lifted his arm straight up into the air," Ellen remembers, as if to give his own muted acknowledgment, rallying cry, and assent to the Auburn family. When Auburn did well, Ellen cheered, hoping even a first down might rouse some internal euphoria within Brad that would spread like wildfire to other parts of the body. A "football is the best medicine" mentality. Yet as the TV in the ICU room teemed with pigskin, Ellen quietly wondered if they would ever go to a game again. She had fleeting thoughts of handicap passes and pushing her husband into the stadium on his wheelchair, but she quickly dismissed those pendulum swings toward the terrible in favor of the hopeful, eventual pyramiding toward normalcy.

Auburn lost 26–19 that Saturday. Luckily Brad didn't witness the final outcome. Before the game was over, he had fallen asleep with the Auburn shaker in his hand.

Ellen:

Most of the day was slow, with no change for Brad. He still seemed miserable, uncomfortable, and empty inside. Brad's nurse for the day, Diane, was here when he arrived on Monday. She told my mother-in-law that they really didn't think he was going to survive when they brought him in.

Sunday's plan was to tackle the breathing-tube issue. The first attempt at extubating Brad had not yielded the results for which they had hoped. For the last few days, Brad was being weaned off the ventilator, as directed by his pulmonologist. The lung doc surmised that Brad was ready to come off the ventilator by Sunday, and he was successfully extubated around one o'clock in the afternoon with no fluid leaking into his lungs.

It was the end of a long week in the hospital. While Brad bounced in and out of consciousness, Ellen was fully awake and lucid throughout the entire ordeal. In just one week, the family dynamic had flipped. Brad was still the man of the house, but was incapacitated. Ellen was now the decision maker and leader. She rose valiantly to the challenge. The whole terrific mess had staggered her but not permanently. Through crisis, life revealed the best of her. Through darkness, she reinforced her commitments to God and to her family. Strengthened them, even. Through darkness, her faith was increased. Through darkness, the light of God was shining.

The Fall of Brad Hawley

And in terms of marital resiliency, this unpleasant shaking made it abundantly clear that Ellen would be by Brad's side, no matter what. When Ellen took her vows to love Brad Hawley in sickness and in health, she meant it.

Brad had once said that he needed to know that Ellen was "on his team." The Fall would erase all doubt. When Brad Hawley needed a partner, God sent Ellen. Her daily walk with the Lord wasn't just preparing her for the good times, the highlands that lay ahead. Ellen's walk with the Lord was preparing her for times like these, the valleys of life, the ordeals and savage torments that would inevitably occur along the way. And in the midst of this walk of faith, God was not just promising that He would never leave or forsake her, even in the blackest moments of these distresses. God had been preparing Ellen for something.

Her finest hour.

Week Two

There was an oak tree outside the window of ICU room number three at Trinity Medical Center in Birmingham. Soaring up through the bricked patio and rising eye level with patients who called that room a temporary home, the tree's beauty was respite for those who would one day be released and for those who do not have an iota of hope. This was Brad Hawley's view as he clung to life.

In just one week, Brad's perspective had dramatically shifted from what he couldn't do to what he could do, from one of the top Steel Company athletes in all of Birmingham to simple movements seeming ambitious. He couldn't walk. Couldn't talk. Couldn't breathe. Couldn't move his legs. His bathroom was a catheter. He could barely move his arms and wiggle his toes.

Systems had to be created to function. Brad and Ellen worked against the language barrier by developing their own nonverbal vernacular. Their friend, Kapi, put together a board to convey thoughts. They used eye signals for assent and pointed at icons. There was a picture of a toilet.

Medically, Brad faced a litany of complications. The primary concern remained the lungs, as stingy secretions blocked airways. The pulmonologist performed a procedure to clean out these routes, and a BiPAP mask was affixed to his face to increase oxygen levels. The BiPAP, a loud and cumbersome device, would aggressively force air into Brad's lungs, and every two hours, a pulmonology aide would perform breathing treatments using vapor medicine. The aide held a mask to Brad's face for three to four minutes at a time and instructed him to breathe deeply. Another breathing procedure involved the use of a mallet with a padded top, similar to the Whac-a-Mole game at Chuck E. Cheese's. The therapist would hold Brad upright and bang on his chest to loosen the secretions. Two minutes in the back, two minutes in the front. Even the slightest pounding was uncomfortable and annoying, and the family, quietly wishing the procedure could be skipped, wondered why such rudimentary devices had to be used. After all, this was 2012, not 1950. Surely inventors could have developed a more technologically efficient device other than a mallet, they concluded. Further, a ventricular drain had been fitted to relieve cranial pressure. With all the obstacles in the way, it seemed that Brad might never be normal again.

When recovery did occur, it was snaillike. Day by day, there was an uptick in movement, but often Brad's internal fight to get better impeded his progress. The stronger and more flexible he became, the more he warred with the machines. His agitation with the BiPAP mask and breathing treatments did nothing but increase discomfort while slowing recovery. By the end of Monday, Brad was able to clap his hands together for the first time. As he slowly came to, rockets of anger that had been rumbling inside him were unleashed, and everyone—nurses, Sharon, Ellen—was suddenly at his beck-and-call.

More issues persisted. Legs had to be constantly massaged. Ellen spent a considerable amount of time performing leg calisthenics. Pushing, pulling, bending, rubbing, raising, and lowering. Up in a frog position, stretched out the length of the bed. Back and forth. To prevent drop foot, Brad wore compression socks and boots. The footwear had to be removed before the therapy began. For Ellen, the job was exhausting, and others had to sub in to help. Even Brad's friend Andrew became a champion leg rubber.

"Brad was a very high-maintenance patient, even when he was very sick," Ellen said. "His legs were in so much pain. He was used to working out every day. He would insist that I—or his mom—constantly massage his legs to ease the pain. There was no rest when we were in the room with Brad. He always had us up doing something for him, and it was exhausting. He would clap to get our attention."

Pain medication had to be taken religiously. Brad received his Dilaudid every four hours, alerting the nurses at least ten minutes before the medicine was due. "He would watch the clock for his pain meds and send us out in the hall before it was time, to make sure the nurse was ready," Ellen remembered. "He barely let Sharon and me sit and take a breath, unless he was sleeping. We had about one hour of peace after each dose of Dilaudid."

On Tuesday, September 4, eight days in, Ellen received good news. The ventricular drain and the BiPAP could be removed. Brad graduated to a regular oxygen mask, but the lungs still had to be closely monitored. He was still "teetering dangerously close" to going back on the dreaded BiPAP machine.

By the end of Tuesday, the nursing staff advised Ellen, now totally exhausted, that it would be best if Brad was left alone for a while. Ellen sneaked in a short excursion to see Webb and Marlen, who were oblivious to their father's condition. She relished the ability to slip away and see the kids, if only for a brief while.

Sharon had been maintaining the house and taking care of the kids since her arrival on Tuesday morning. During the day, Webb and Marlen were sent to preschool at South Highland Presbyterian Church, a large Romanesque edifice tucked into a corner lot in downtown Birmingham, beside a row of bars and former bars with windows pasted with "FOR LEASE" signs. When possible, Ellen was present in the car line to pick the kids up and take them home. She had developed a close relationship with many of the parents and teachers at South Highland, and she tried to project a sense of strength as bouncing, backpacked children retired to cars at the end of a long school day. Although Ellen didn't want the extra attention, many of the parents had been following her CaringBridge updates and were anxious to get a personal update as well. Even the least bit of normal life seemed to help Ellen during this bleak era, and seeing Webb run into her arms with a huge smile on his face was the highlight of her day.

Nights, Sharon cooked dinner and split duties with Mary Katherine, the next-door neighbor, who tidied the house and made sure everything remained in order. One would have thought with Ellen gone for such long stretches of time that Webb and Marlen would have pined for her, but Sharon was doing such an admirable job in relief that Webb was enjoying every minute of it. Kids were constantly coming over to play. A close family friend, Mrs. Stetler, sent Webb a care package filled with gifts. It seemed that Webb got a new gift every other day.

"It was like a big party," Ellen said.

Marlen, a one year old at the time, was simply too young to understand what was going on. It was respite to Ellen for Sharon and Mary Katherine to have control of the house and the kids. She didn't have to feel guilty about attending to Brad.

Yet, a feeling of doom followed her everywhere she went. Ellen had expressed concern on CaringBridge that Brad's stomach was "quiet," and relayed that the doctors were giving him medicine to "wake it up." This was code for "Brad's digestive system isn't working properly."

Brad couldn't swallow because his epiglottis was paralyzed, and any particle that entered Brad's mouth went straight into his lungs. From time to time, a nurse would stop by and offer Brad a small suction straw to suck out the saliva. When the nurse was absent, Ellen would administer it to him personally. Initially, the straw was attached to the wall, but once Brad's arms gained more strength, he was able to rest it in his hand loosely. The straw was yet another annoying contraption. As Brad clumsily tried to operate the device, the straw would frequently fall under the covers, whereupon he would mouth, "Where's my straw?"

Brad was eventually able to muster a measly cough, but since mucus couldn't trespass into the lungs, it, too, had to be suctioned out. Brad's tongue had become white and flaky due to lack of moisture. His saliva thick. "We would peel big flakes of dried white skin off his tongue," Ellen recalled. "Brad's mouth was extremely dry. His tongue had turned into a white crust, and it would flake off in large pieces. And it hurt." It pained Ellen to witness this parched terrain, and she begged nurses to give Brad something to alleviate the discomfort. They eventually provided a small sponge and some cream. It offered little relief.

Since Brad had been rendered mute, Ellen became his interpreter when the nurses had difficulty understanding his commands and groans. Not only was Ellen taking care of his physical needs but she had also become his voice. Perhaps for the first time in a long while, Brad realized that Ellen's voice mattered.

Ellen also confessed to a little tomfoolery in the ICU. One particular night, the hospital staff scolded her when she clandestinely snapped a few pictures of Brad on her iPhone. Although pictures were expressly forbidden, Ellen knew that those images would remind the family of the affliction that was so powerfully affecting their lives. "I explained to the nurse that I don't plan to show them to anyone except Brad," Ellen said. "I am holding them for next year, when he tries to go base jumping or skydiving. Hopefully he can find another way to satisfy his sense of adventure."

By Wednesday, the teetering tilted in the wrong direction. Brad was back on the BiPAP machine, finally succumbing to its present necessity in his life.

That afternoon, he wrote his first words. A big step forward. Since the TV was on constantly, Brad was fed a steady diet of pizza and Coca-Cola advertisements. He heard soft drinks fizzing over cubes of ice, and pictured himself having one out of a curvaceous glass. He motioned Ellen over and instructed her to hand him a piece of paper so he could scrawl something down. Holding the pen awkwardly, he bore down on each letter. The first attempt was no more than chicken scratch or a crude cuneiform. This was the first time anyone noticed that his motor skills were largely absent. The final draft read "Coca-Cola" in broken penmanship, similar to a three-year-old's. Perhaps no better than Webb's.

Ellen produced a Coke and fed it to him on a tiny sponge. He choked on it.

The small amount of liquid that went down tasted like salt. Brad had lost his sense of taste. This spoke to the powerful nature of the human brain. Holding full autonomy over Brad's taste buds, the parietal lobe that controls human taste had been affected by the Fall, such that the sensors telling Brad a Coke tasted good were now down like windswept power lines, signals failing to transmit from lobe to tongue.

Wednesday night after the preschool-like writing exercise, Ellen went home. Her children needed her, and she sensed that they were having a hard time coping with the nightly estrangement. Ellen was having a hard time coping too. She missed her children intensely.

The next day, the condition of Brad's lungs had regressed, and he was now alternating between the BiPAP and a regular oxygen mask. Physical therapy—including the awful mallet—was the order of the day. Midday, Ellen posted on CaringBridge.

> I asked him if he knew why he was here today, and he said no. I was pretty discouraged by his response. I tell him daily about his accident. On a brighter note, his spirits do seem up today. I spent the morning trying to encourage and build him up. I told him I would take him anywhere he wanted to go once we get out of here. He motioned for a piece of paper and wrote "Vegas."

Vegas. A far cry from his current treachery. An almost unattainable goal that would require traversing actual as well as bodily geography. Yet for all of Brad's demerits, there was a fighting spirit within him. A heart as big as a tractor. With God's help, he was capable of pulling this heavy load. Brad was at the epicenter of suffering, but still pumped adrenaline for a cross-country trip. This wasn't just lip service. He desperately wanted to get there.

For Ellen, the battle for survival occurred on two fronts: the physical and the metaphysical. As she saw Brad's slow upticks and disjointed milestones, she attributed much of the progress to the availability of medicine, to technology, and to the acumen of hospital staff. But she also believed her prayers were being answered. Ellen would do all she could to help Brad physically, but she believed that the coupling of prayer to her physical assistance gave Brad his best shot. Drawing Almighty power, Ellen continued to batter the heavens with her pleas.

Alas, there were back-steps. Ellen was able to pick up the kids from school on Thursday and spend a couple of hours with them before returning to the hospital that night. When she arrived at 7:45 p.m., an odd scene startled her. When she turned the corner into his room, Brad was lying half in, half out of his bed. He was almost in the floor, attempting to yell for help, and his oxygen mask was off. Ellen frantically called for nursing staff. Later, she expressed her concern:

> How did he get like that? How long had he been there? Perhaps he tried to move and just got stuck, and there was no one here to help him. Not being able to talk has to be terrifying. It makes me not want to leave him alone again, but I can't spend the night in his ICU room. I will make sure he has the nurse call button in hand before I leave.

Ellen stayed at the hospital that evening to ensure no further roguery occurred, watching with the gallantry of a mother protecting her young, nest-weary eaglet. The adrenaline rush of shock carried her for the next few hours. Now ripe with energy, she worked to reposition his legs and pillows until three o'clock in the morning. She found it no coincidence that she had been praying earlier that day for a renewed vigor.

Although there were setbacks, his lungs were clearing and his stomach was waking. Good signs. On Friday, doctors performed another bronchoscopy, a procedure that helped Brad's lung function. The procedure had gone so well and Ellen was so encouraged that she began preparing for the next step in a long recovery process. If all went as planned, Brad would graduate to Lakeshore Rehabilitation Hospital, a leading-edge inpatient rehabilitation hospital just a few miles away.

Minute as the steps were, they were steps regardless, and though it seemed that Brad wasn't ready to phase out of Trinity, Ellen knew he couldn't stay there forever if indeed the end of this was his survival and not his death. Eventually, Brad would have to transition out of the hospital, and Ellen started to reconnoiter the environment at Lakeshore, scheduling a tour of the facilities. When she got there, she wasn't impressed, a sense of gloom falling on all sides of her. In her opinion, Lakeshore was a depressing and austere environment. As she toured the halls, she found the environment to be drab and uninviting. Not to mention the median age of the patients was around seventy. "I felt like I was in a nursing home," Ellen said. "But from everything that I had heard, this was the best place for traumatic brain injury patients."

There was, however, a stark contrast between appearance and reality, and as she met with staff—several therapists and a clinical director—her spirits were lifted. Ellen hoped for some younger, spryer patients who could "challenge and encourage" Brad. She hoped for like-aged, like-minded individuals who, together with Brad, could stir a bit of synergy. A Steel Company–like sociology, minus the obsession. Still, a muddled path ran from ICU to Lakeshore, a crucible to pass through before Brad could enter Lakeshore.

Saturday, Ellen was further encouraged by Brad's improvement. Now Brad was off the oxygen mask and using a nasal cannula, a lighter and less intrusive device. Lucid thoughts and intelligible words were beginning to form more steadily, even though medication often made him loopy. Dr. Nguyen even suggested that Brad might be moved to a regular room.

Great energy was required to keep the dyad marching through the wilderness, and on Sunday, one of the members of the brigade suffered a setback. Ellen's body was weary, her immune system vulnerable from the lack of sleep and overall stress of caring for Brad for two-plus weeks in the hospital. Her once-sturdy body was physically and emotionally torn down from the never-ending duties in the ICU, from taking care of kids, asking for prayer, sleeping in strange beds, posting online updates, managing sitters, battling fitful sleeping patterns, calling friends and family, and being without her loved ones for large chunks of time. "I wouldn't stop," Ellen said. But her body was telling her indeed it was time to, as a sore throat, fever, and headache curtsied menacingly to her on Sunday.

Ellen's survivalist nature had gotten her through the fourteen-day peril, but now she needed rest. As she convalesced in her home, a group of family friends arrived at the house unexpectedly. The yard had been neglected and needed serious tending. So the pop-up landscaping company of Lindsey, Brian, Shaun, Ben, and Patrick put on their work clothes and cut the Hawley's yard. The makeshift crew spent hours trimming hedges, mowing the grass, weed eating. Mauling and slicing the yard into perfection. Ellen was deeply humbled by the gesture.

Ellen was able to make a feeble post on CaringBridge that Sunday night, describing Brad's status as a "step back." She had learned in her bedridden miasma that he was back on the BiPAP machine. Although it was not the news she wanted, she knew that the peg of Brad's overall health continued to move in a positive direction, and "the good days outnumbered the bad."

The regular room would have to wait for now. The Hawleys would have to be patient and believe, for this was all in God's timing. Patience was something to which they had grown accustomed. And the lessons. They came slowly and powerfully, crystallizing in their mind as they passed before them, one by one. Had God waved a wand and fixed Brad, perhaps they would have missed the importance of what He was trying to say. Thus they learned about grace. The green bows, the yard work. Yes, even the biscuit. Through the wait, they felt the stirring poeticism of small things done with great love. The foot rubbing, the gifts for Webb, the umpteen volunteers who donated their time to this recovery effort. The wait, Ellen believed, was the Lord's way of revealing Himself.

The Fall of Brad Hawley

"I want to inspire people to fight," Brad Hawley once said. Brad had come a long way in two weeks, though to a casual observer, the progress would appear indiscernible. He was still in the ICU. He was still, in large part, immobile. The bed continued to exhibit mastery over him. True, making it this far was a miracle, but from a motor standpoint, he had yet to exhibit overt, skyrocketing change.

And now, staring into the approaching otherworldliness of a regular room, the worst part seemingly over, Brad would realize the real fighting had not yet begun.

Rebirth

Out of the pitiless hinterland of despair, the revenant began to emerge. Brad would write again. From one simple phrase, "Coca-Cola," to "the cold steel that held my life in its knurling," describing the bar he fell from, the descriptions and themes of Brad Hawley's recovery would include maddening, overlong, extensive, harrowing, excruciating, frustrating, and transformative. From a knee-high march through the swamp, he would shout hallelujahs and praise, and out of the muck, a finer specimen of a man would emerge. The dross of his life would be swept way, the unfruitful branches pruned, the metal refined.

The months from late September 2012 to May 2013 would be even more arduous than the weeks in ICU. Again Brad was battling himself, only this time progress would not be measured in how much he could build himself up but, rather, in how much he could empty himself out. Brad would learn that growth in the Christian life meant constant dying to self, that his old ways—living for self, feeding the flesh—were crucified. Christ in, Brad out. This concept of displacement had not previously been a consideration, but through the fall Brad would learn the surpassing greatness of knowing Christ as Lord. Before he could do that, he would have to walk through an emotional and physical hell.

On Monday of the third week, Brad, with the liberal assistance of physical therapists, stood for the first time since the accident. The goal was to get him up and get him into a wheelchair so he could take a short tour of the ICU. Outside of a quick trip to get a CT scan, he hadn't seen around the corner of his doorway. He hadn't seen the hall. He hadn't seen the other patients.

It was an unbeautiful effort. The nurses wrapped a gait belt around his torso to assist with standing. Brad felt as if he were on a human leash. Then they set him down in a wheelchair. His oxygen tank riding shotgun. The thirty-foot ride was choppy.

Ten feet, stop.

Ten feet, stop.

Ten feet, stop.

Through the Neuro ICU to the Cardio ICU, Brad waving to a panel of observers as if he were in Victory Lane.

But the pain was unbearable. "Take me back!" Brad thundered in his loudest whisper. "I gotta go back to my room. I can't stand it. Take me back!"

Why is it so hard to sit in a chair? he thought. *It doesn't make sense.*

Ellen grimaced at the whole exercise, but she was smiling on the inside. Seeing her husband having to be aided by a team of nurses and watching him sit laboriously was indeed difficult, but it was pure joy to see even the smallest progress. "He got all the way to the Cardio ICU, thirty feet away, and hit a wall," Ellen said. "He immediately asked to be wheeled back to his bed. We turned around and got back to the room as quickly as we could. Even though we didn't make it very far, getting out of his room was a big step. The thirty-foot ride was too long for him to bear."

Brad was now off the BiPAP machine, and vital signs were looking promising. Writing was more legible. Regarding his steps to recovery, he was able to communicate more effectively with the doctor. Dr. Nguyen even attempted to feed him a bite of chocolate pudding. As the doctor held the spoon to his mouth, Brad thought, *Are you serious?*

Nguyen offered, "Your epiglottis is not paralyzed."

Well, it is! Brad thought.

Emotionally, Brad remained testy. He hissed at Ellen that morning for the venial sin of drinking coffee and bottled water in front of him.

Simple, everyday activities had to be handled with caution, for it was torturous for Brad to witness the ease with which others operated. Ellen would, in the future, tread lightly while drinking in front of him. These were the first signs of the kind of hell Brad was capable of administering.

Brad still hadn't seen his kids in over two weeks. He missed them dearly and wondered when he might be "normal" enough for the kids to get a look at him. The closest Marlen had been to seeing her father was a picture that hung on the wall of her classroom at South Highland. From time to time, Marlen would walk by and kiss the photo.

"She obviously missed her dad, and Webb did too," Ellen said.

Tuesday was September 11. Ellen described the day as "steady." No shocking milestones or setbacks. She spoke with Dr. Nguyen, who said that he needed to see several consistent breathing days to parole him to a regular room. Brad was slowly gaining a greater understanding of what had happened to him. He claimed that it all seemed like a "bad dream." An acute, surreal terror invading their lives.

Brad's weight had dropped significantly since he entered the ICU because he had not eaten solid food in over two weeks. He was narrowing into a gaunt shell. Before the Fall, he was used to five meals a day and several intermittent snacks. Protein bars and the like. He was precise in his caloric intake. Now, he didn't have a choice whether or not the food pumped into his body was Paleo, amino acid shakes, protein-enriched chow, or other "clean" food. Those days were over.

Devices such as the feeding tube, while life-saving and providing daily fuel, could be particularly irritating. However, on Wednesday, the feeding tube was removed. A PEG tube procedure in the gastroenterology lab fitted Brad with another—praise God—less invasive feeding machine. The PEG ran through his belly at an insertion point into his small intestine. Ellen relayed that the procedure went "perfectly."

"The doctor sat me down to explain the procedure and noted that this tube would be good for about a year. This was another dose of reality to my ever-positive, Brad-is-gonna-be-OK attitude. The reality of having to feed Brad through a tube for a few weeks, a year, or perhaps a lifetime was another realization of our new reality," Ellen said.

Milton and Gail, present for the procedure, provided crucial support and encouragement, their presence demonstrating that Brad and Ellen were not on an island unto themselves. Bob, who had doused his passive attitude like a finished cigarette, was also there to lend support for his son. Perhaps this was an opportunity to build the family Brad had always coveted. It took tragedy for Brad's dysfunctional family to come together.

Once the PEG tube was installed, either Ellen or the nurse would take all of Brad's medicine and place it in a mortar, creating a proverbial salad of pills. Then they would chop up the concoction, grind it into a powder with a pestle, hold up the tube, pour the mixture in, and chase it with water. The tube would often clog—another nuisance—and Ellen would come to the rescue.

On Wednesday, the family decided to allow Webb to see his father for the first time since the accident. That afternoon, Ellen prepped Webb by telling him that his father had a "sore throat"—which was, in fact, the case—and couldn't talk. She also lured him with the promise of ice cream.

So Ellen carried Webb, clutching a Barney doll that had arrived as a gift from Aunt Sandy, into the room. Webb was very quiet as he viewed his father from his three-year-old eyes. Brad was trying heartily to remain alert and appear as normal and dad-like as possible, given the inherent difficulty in that endeavor based on his bony appearance and that Trinity was all hospitaly and such. Brad had prepared for the moment he would greet his son by being propped up in the Cadillac chair. A big leather chair with a high back. But Webb wasn't convinced. As he looked down upon Brad from his mother's arms, his eyes grew big as coins as he gazed confusedly, suspiciously at his father.

Because he couldn't stand letting his son see him in that condition, Brad blazed on the inside. "Get him outta here!" he wailed from the disguise of a whisper.

As Ellen took their child away, a slew of thoughts began to cement in Brad's mind. He felt that he was no longer a strong and protective father. Powerful. A man Webb could look up to for physical strength. As much as Brad wanted to be strong for Webb, he felt feeble and pathetic. He felt Webb had seen him as some sort of monster, mirroring the way Brad truly viewed himself on the inside. Since he had been masquerading as Mr. Tough Guy, as Motor, he failed to see the value in himself outside of his physical characteristics. That there was a very bright, capable, and valuable person within. In Brad's mind, he wasn't a father unless he looked like a father, his mind still wrapped around the cosmetics of manhood.

Making matters worse, when Brad's mind pulled back in focus, he was reminded how uncomfortable it was to sit in a chair. "Get me back in bed," Brad commanded. "I can't stand this chair."

And although it was only a three-minute meeting, something clicked inside Brad. A small visit from a child—*his* child—was like flipping a breaker switch. That short exchange provided all the motivation he needed to get the engine running again. Seeing Webb gave him the will to keep fighting.

As the nurses helped Brad back into his bed, he thought about fatherhood. He thought about the kind of father he had been to his son and the kind of father he now wanted to be. At this moment, all the deficiencies of his past came crashing down on him, and he purposed at that moment to be the kind of man whom Webb could look up to. Seeing Webb had warmed his heart, yes. But more than that, Brad understood how much his son—that wonderful little boy—needed him.

THE HAWLEYS HAD MORE UNEXPECTED PROBLEMS with which to contend. Wednesday night when Ellen took Webb and Marlen home, a dark house greeted them. The power had been disconnected due to nonpayment. Ellen was trying to keep up with all the bills, but the stacks, piling high, seemed to keep growing and somehow the light bill had gotten lost in the shuffle. Ellen immediately called the power company and paid the bill. Thankfully, the lights flickered back on within a couple of hours. Ellen was learning to rely more on eternal light than on Alabama Power.

But Ellen was tired. Managing the chaos had become overwhelming. Simply too great a load to bear. Still, she continued to find little encouragements along the way. Scattered throughout the same heap of bills were uplifting letters, verses, and prayers. Someone had even sent a packet of bath salts and some banana bread.

Ellen shared the following verse on CaringBridge that night:

Have I not commanded you? Be strong and courageous. Do not be afraid. Do not be discouraged, for the Lord your God will be with you wherever you go.

Jobs were also on hold. Both Brad's and Ellen's companies extended courtesies, granting an unspecified grace period to take care of the cumulative details of recovery. While at the hospital, Ellen caught up on a few work duties, another rubber ball in the air for her constant P. T. Barnum–like juggling act.

By Thursday, medical staff intimated that Brad might be moved out of ICU, chief among the reasons being that his lung condition had improved. Breathing and speech were better, and the awful Cadillac chair was now much more agreeable. The pace of Brad's recovery encouraged Ellen. It was more marathonish, no stopping and starting, backing up, or threatening to drop out of the race altogether.

It was around this time that Brad thought, *I can get better.* God was opening a door, he felt, and it was up to Brad to walk through it. Before, it wasn't his call. Around week three there was a growing sense that he could get better, but he was going to have to fight. Certainly, Ellen and the kids were motivation enough, but Brad also wanted to do it for himself. Because Brad had had a previous sense of invincibility, he had a hard time grasping the true severity of his injury. He wasn't just going to walk out of there and return to normal, pre-accident Brad. Realizing the extent of the injury was an important moment for him, but he also understood that he could get better and that he had to do so for his family.

Two important milestones occurred on Thursday. First, Brad was taken completely off the oxygen for a period of time, and second, he stood up and ambled thirty feet across the floor with the help of staff and a few sporadic breaks. Brad's inpatient therapist had attempted to get him to stand up on many occasions, but this time was different. Using a gait belt and leash, the therapist lifted the wobbling patient to his feet. This action, in itself, was enough to stoke a fire within Brad. This was the moment when Brad's mental attitude shifted from "it's not your call" to thinking "God has brought me this far. Now it's my turn." For the first time in a long while, Brad felt God was speaking to him: "If you want your life back, you've gotta fight."

The best headline of *The Hawley Times* blared on Friday:

DOCTORS APPROVE BRAD FOR ICU RELEASE

Bye-bye, ICU.

At eleven o'clock in the morning, Brad was taken to room 816, a virtual Shangri-La compared to the Spartan accommodations in intensive care. Ellen asked friends to kindly allow Brad to rest over the weekend, but that didn't stop the intrepid duo of Rich Campbell and Hank Powers from volunteer work late Friday night. Friday was Ellen's mom's birthday, and Rich and Hank relieved Ellen so she could celebrate with her mother. Around eleven o'clock, Hank brought coffee into Brad's room. It was going to be a long night for Rich, who had given up time with his wife and kids to stay with Brad at the hospital.

Hank shoved a warm cup into Rich's mitt and sat down. The two men chatted quietly with the TV volume at a low level. Then, something astonishing happened. As the men were talking, Brad opened his eyes and looked up at his two friends through the glow of the TV screen.

"What are y'all doing?" Brad asked.

The Fall of Brad Hawley

Hank and Rich spun around in total shock. They had had no idea Brad had been paying attention, much less that he would—or could—insert himself into the conversation. This was one of the first occasions when Brad had spoken loud enough to hear. Most of his speech had been relegated to no more than low-decibel whispering or, at the most, furious muttering when be barked at his nurse to get him out of the Cadillac chair.

A MAJOR PLAYER IN THE SAGA left on Friday, one whose absence would create a tremendous void in her wake. Sharon had agreed to stay throughout the entire stint in ICU, and now she felt Brad had reached such a plateau that it was safe for her to return home. Sharon didn't want to leave but knew that she couldn't stay forever. Her impact had been immeasurable, her presence a godsend.

The day on Saturday was relatively uneventful, but the night was filled with restlessness. Ellen had shipped the kids to the family's lake house at Lake Martin with Milton and Gail, and she devoted her evening to caring for Brad. That is, waiting on his beck and call. Brad was more "with it" now and employed a take-charge, demanding attitude. If he needed something, he resumed his clapping motif.

Pain in his legs? Clap.

Pain in the hips? Clap clap.

Pillows needed readjusting? Clap clap clap.

Ellen had no experience as a masseuse, but she did her level best to rub out the shooting pain in his legs and feet. He was still using a catheter and a "poop pad." Changing out the pad required considerable work. Brad would roll over and grab the bed bar and pull himself up so they could change out the pad. It was painful, and often he would demand that the nurses get off their haunches and pull it out from under him quickly: "Hurry, hurry, hurry!"

Instead of a daily hot shower, Brad submitted to sponge baths to prevent bedsores. He longed for the warming cascade of a shower. To stand on his own and feel the water rushing over him as he soaped himself. To let the soft pellets connect with face and body. To be cleansed by the warm flow of water across his skin. Showering was yet another activity he had taken for granted in his past life, and the sponge baths would assure that if he made it out of here, he would more greatly appreciate the little intricacies of his day.

Now a week later, Ellen was still trying to shake her cold, and a sleepless night on Saturday didn't help matters. Ellen needed another break, so she hired a sitter and a massage therapist to fill in for her on Sunday. Brad wasn't happy. Sitters and other caretakers were not adequate substitutes for Ellen's presence. Brad wanted, demanded his wife by his side.

Brad also gave an interesting revelation on Sunday. He mouthed to Dr. Nguyen that he had been "seeing double" for the last two or three days, and later told Ellen "I see two of you." Later on, he whispered to his friend Kapi that he had been seeing double the entire stint in the hospital. Brad was soon diagnosed with double vision, a condition known as diplopia.

An MRI was scheduled for Monday. When the results came back, his brain appeared to be normal, but fluid had built up in his sinus cavities. A visit from an ENT doctor provided essentially no prognosis, but Ellen read from his face that this was quite a sad situation.

It seemed as though little could be done for some conditions that were plaguing Brad. Little except wait. Brad would get better in the natural course of things, but how long it would take, no one really knew. Dr. Nguyen was encouraging. He left little doubt in Ellen's mind that Brad was going to be all right. But perhaps Nguyen was too encouraging. Relying on Dr. Nguyen's positivity, Ellen braced for a quick recovery, believing Brad would be back to normal within a couple of weeks.

Myriad issues remained. For now, double vision took top billing, but looming in the background were the dreadful supporting cast of the lungs, legs, feet, and epiglottis.

But had anyone considered Brad's emotional and mental well being as frustration continued to mount? Had anyone been consulted about the behavioral effects of traumatic brain injury?

The Fall of Brad Hawley

Brad had a long way to go and was as ready for the next step. He had come a long way over three weeks. Growth, measured now in terms of medical milestones, had nothing to do with Brad's material successes or number of reps. Injury had sucked the value out of his toys. Those things were unusable in the hospital.

Simply making it through surgery, through ICU, and out of the hospital was a miracle in itself. Anyone close to the situation believes it was by the hand of God that Brad had made it this far. Yet the road ahead was paved with cautious optimism. Brad was coming out of the first stage of his own personal hell. But as her husband was pardoned to Lakeshore Rehabilitation Hospital, Ellen would soon discover they were far from heaven.

PURGATORY

Brad found purgatory. On Wednesday, September 19, he was transferred to Lakeshore Rehabilitation Hospital in Homewood. In Ellen's mind, Lakeshore did not live up to the bill, at least as flaunted in the picturesque literature presented to her and which, in all likelihood, gave her a ray of hope for the next step of Brad's Pilgrim's Progress back to normalcy. Lakeshore, remembered by her as a drab, austere place, very depressing and gloomy, looking like the worst nursing home you have ever been in, mauve themed with early-1990s carpet, ill lit with low ceilings and seventies VCT tile stretched throughout, was complemented on the outside by an old gray/brownstone edifice no gaudier than a paper grocery bag, emitting a rather draconian vibe, psych-wardish and severe, and, had Igor or the Hunchback of Notre Dame lived there, no one would have been surprised. Of course, much of this description is hyperbole, but serves as a window into Ellen's memory and is created largely from her reflection on that time in their lives. A time clouded eternally by the grim nature of their visit. In sum, she does not reflect on it fondly.

The most disconcerting aspect for the Hawleys, aside from all the aesthetic drawbacks of the hospital itself, was that Brad had garnered the coveted prize of youngest patient. And that by a long shot. Lakeshore was home to several septuagenarians and octogenarians receiving therapy for hip fractures, joint replacements, strokes, diabetes, arthritis, and Parkinson's disease. Brad was the atypical patient. For instance, when

The Fall of Brad Hawley

Ellen was greeted by the Lakeshore welcoming committee, the kind woman at the front asked, "Are you the daughter?"

Ellen nor anyone else involved in the Brad Hawley saga was afforded the luxury of choosing the fellow clientele, nor should they have expected the center to house a caucus of young athletes. Like it or not, the passage home went through Lakeshore. That Lakeshore lacked like-minded and like-aged individuals was something they'd have to live with. Injury carried with it a new sociology.

Transport to Lakeshore proved to be a difficult errand. As a precaution, Brad had to be shipped by ambulance. To get him there, he was loaded up on a gurney, hauled into the back of the ambulance, and taken to Lakeshore by paramedic escort. Ellen followed in her car with Brad's belongings and effects. Toiletries, paper work, a few CrossFit T-shirts, some gym shorts, and undergarments.

Brad was learning about new numbers. New metrics. Not PRs on toes to bar or overhead squats, mind you, but rather the various room numbers at the ascending stages of recovery. His new room number at purgatory, the "middle place" between Trinity and the comforts of home, was 226. Like that intermediate world where sin-sick souls are suspended and purified, where prayers for the dead matter, Brad was undergoing his own form of purification. The process at the hospital and at Lakeshore worked primarily through physical and verbal incapacitation. He literally couldn't move, and by having to hold still through alone time, through solitude, Brad's near-dead spiritual life would eventually kick-start into motion.

Ellen's expectation was spot on: she anticipated a three-week stay at Lakeshore and that was exactly what she got. Unfortunately for Brad, it was no longer possible for Ellen to stay with him throughout the day because she needed to get back to her job. The courtesy of reprieve from work, she felt, had extinguished. Coupled with that, Sharon was gone, and Brad would have to spend nights at Lakeshore alone. Ellen needed to be home with the kids. Thus, aloneness became Brad's new normal. Ellen shared her concern on CaringBridge:

> Brad is getting settled into his new home at Lakeshore. I stayed with him the first three nights in his new home, but last night I stayed home with the kids. They have been passed around for the past month and have not done well with the constant change of scenery and people. They don't sleep well and seem very confused. It is very hard to balance the kids and Brad. Brad is the first one to say that the kids come first, but I also know that he gets very bored, has trouble communicating, and still needs a lot of help. I hate leaving him, but then I hate not being home with the kids. I am honestly really struggling how to balance my time.

Ellen encouraged friends and family to pop in during the visiting hours of 4:00 p.m. to 8:00 p.m., to keep Brad company and prevent him from descending into depression. His mind was one of the few things still completely intact, and the family couldn't afford to lose it now.

Once Brad was finally settled in to his new home, Ellen began to realize the immense gulf of recovery Brad would have to cross. To recap, Brad was gaunt and emaciated from losing thirty pounds. He couldn't walk, could barely talk, could not stand up on his own accord, and couldn't swallow. He had to use the bathroom on a pad and had a catheter in his penis. He was suffering from double vision, had lost his motor skills, and was ingesting a cornucopia of medication each day. In addition, he couldn't shower, couldn't bathe, couldn't shave, couldn't drive, and couldn't wipe his own behind. Even his wheelchair had to have a special headrest installed because his neck was too weak to hold his head upright.

Within the first few days of his stay, a mystery person left a helpful book for Ellen. The book was entitled, *Living with Brain Injury: A Guide for Families*. Out of all the works Ellen could have expected to read in her lifetime, this would not have been on her list. Richard Charles Senelick,

MD, speaker and author of several works, penned this valuable guide for TBI survivors, advertised as a book on "how to cope with the physical, cognitive, and behavioral changes that take place after a brain injury occurs." The book proved to be a great tool to help Ellen understand the monster they were up against.

As if there was any doubt, this was holistic recovery. It wasn't as if Brad had, say, a broken arm—a largely physical injury. Brad's physical manifestations were obvious, legion, and many of the physical ailments had a neurological root. Brad's injury would require therapy that arrived in many forms. Occupational, physical, music, and speech. And his recovery on a triumvirate of fronts: physical, cognitive, and behavioral. A witness mark to his condition at this point in the recovery was that he had crumbled to the point of having to toss a ball to a physical therapist to improve his hand/eye coordination. He was rail thin. His weight was nose-diving with each day he remained on the PEG tube. His epiglottis was still paralyzed, and there was no telling if or when it might reactivate.

Brad's emotional health had to be constantly massaged. Particularly troubling for him was the solemnity, the tedium of Lakeshore. During the day, there was absolutely nothing he could do. He literally was on an island to himself.

Maybe I'll read a book?
Oops, I have double vision.
Well then, I think I'll work a crossword or Sudoku puzzle (someone actually bought him one).
Oops, I can't write.
Maybe I'll call someone.
Oops, I can't speak.
Get out and get some exercise?
Oops, I can't walk.
Oh, I know. I'll sit up in a chair.
Oops, I forgot. Sitting up is excruciating.

This was the point when Brad hit severe depression.

"It was the darkest period of my life," he concludes. "I was so lonely."

His days were chopped up into halves. Therapy was conducted in the morning. Occupational therapy included learning how to shower and dress. Physical therapy included learning how to walk again with the aid of a gait belt. Music therapy included using a xylophone to recognize notes and the strumming of a guitar helped rebuild motor function. And speech therapy included learning how to talk and swallow. Since therapy did not take a massive enough chunk out of the day, concluding around noon, Brad began to dread the day's second half, a time often imbued with monotony. For the rest of the afternoon, he just sat there and listened to the TV. He listened because he could not watch it, an infirm condition caused by double vision. If misery loves company, Brad's best friend for the good part of a month was a small flat-screen television that wasn't even his own.

The afternoon silence forced Brad to think. Angered at his condition, Brad scanned the fields of his faith, once verdant but now a drying-up wasteland. Intermittently, he would pray. Pray for continued recovery. Pray for the ability to be a dad and husband again. To see again. To eat again. To be the workhorse again. He still clung tightly to the thought that one day he might lift weights again. That he might walk again. And, by the grace of God, he might run again. Brad wondered if these mustard-seed conversations were being heard, or if they mattered at all.

He missed Ellen. She would stop by and visit during her lunch break, but could no longer afford to leave the kids by themselves at nighttime. Friends and family continued to visit sporadically, but the turnstile was slowing. Even when people did show up, Brad wasn't so sure he wanted them there. "There were only three or four people he was comfortable with keeping him company," Ellen remembered. "Others, he just wasn't comfortable with them staying for long periods of time. I think it was his pride. He didn't like people seeing him that way. I was not at Lakeshore that much, so I was worried that Brad was getting depressed and lonely because he couldn't do anything. We added Zoloft to his medication. At that point, it was just another pill."

The Fall of Brad Hawley

The ambiance didn't evoke euphoria. Brad's room, plain as a Mennonite's dress, was colorless save for a few medical notes clipped above his bed in sheets of blue, yellow, purple, and red. The blinds remained closed, primarily because his view to the outside was not some splendid vista as he enjoyed at Trinity. Rather, it was the alluring view of a trash Dumpster. Ellen and other friends brightened up the room by leaving little notes on his door, and visitors were welcome to sign a guest book to note their arrival.

Yet friends and family lent their assistance in the most basic of human tasks. Either nursing staff or Ellen, who wheeled him into a shower stall and used a handheld showerhead and a bar of soap, accomplished bathing and showering. Bob, Ellen, or the nurses performed shaving. On at least one occasion, family friend and local stylist, Brooke, took time out of her day to drive to Lakeshore to give him a trim.

Bathroom duties were particularly problematic. He couldn't go on his own, so the nurse had to cath him. "He was dependent on the nurse to relieve his bladder," Ellen said. "And he would blow up the bed, and the nurses would have to clean his poop. When he couldn't go to the bathroom, we'd have to give him copious amounts of Milk of Magnesia and laxative. Then poop would explode everywhere. I was changing Marlen's diaper at home and Brad's at Lakeshore. It was like I had two babies in diapers. There was a point that I thought I would have to insert the cath in Brad, but I didn't want to do it. That scared me."

Doctors prescribed an eye patch to assist with Brad's double vision, and his uncustomary appearance created a divergent reaction from the two kids. Webb loved it and even procured his own eye patch, which, if not being worn, remained on Brad's bedside table. It was cool having a buccaneer as a father. Marzella Huffman, Webb's 3-K teacher at South Highland Presbyterian Preschool and mother of Monica the Biscuit-Bringer said that Webb often wore his eye patch to school. "I think this helped Webb to have a connection with his father," Marzella said. The blue latex gloves that engulfed his little hands as he wrestled them on awkwardly also enthralled Webb. He still talks about them, to this day. Marlen, on the other hand, was frightened by Brad's odd visage, refusing to crawl into bed with him, spending most of her time at Lakeshore curled up in the bosom of her mother. Leery of the scary man with the eye patch who stared back at her. Brad did once muster a smile from her, however. On another occasion, a high five.

Most days, the kids were there to visit no longer than five minutes at a time. Brad tired quickly trying to keep up appearances. But the kids were coming around more, hallelujah, and they were able to see their father in a better state than the shell that smiled back at them at ICU.

The whole family was affected by Brad's collapse. Even Rocky, the four-year-old German Shepherd, seemed lost and listless without him. Brad had trained Rocky since he was six weeks old, and ol' Rock was out of sorts without his master. Brad missed Rocky too. The pair of pals had a special attachment, and Brad was eager to get back home to see his buddy.

Six days after arriving at Lakeshore, Brad was taken by ambulance to visit an ENT doctor. The doctor examined his vocal cords and determined that his right vocal cord was completely paralyzed. There was "weak movement" in his left, and the palette, tongue, and cough were also feeble. Since these issues were neurological, the ENT could offer little help.

Later that day, Brad walked the longest distance he had walked in a month. With the assistance of a walker and a watchful physical therapist holding the gait belt, Brad hobbled a distance of 150 feet.

As the days went by, Brad's left vocal cord was improving. That crucial membrane for speaking, singing, and laughing was poised for a renaissance, and this small victory garnered praise from Ellen on CaringBridge:

I am very thankful to God for hearing our prayers about Brad's vocal cord. It is a small victory, but perhaps a wink from God reminding us that He is in control and He will take care of us.

The Fall of Brad Hawley

Ellen trusted that God welcomed all prayers, general and specific, large and small, even those offered for improved vocal cords. Instead of subscribing to the concept that God, the distant, silent overseer, created the world and ignored it to its own devices and ruin, Ellen believed that God was concerned with the most intimate details of their lives. The minutiae, she believed, was a concern for Him, even the very hairs on her head were accounted for, and no matter presented was too trite or insignificant.

Back at home, Webb, the tiny pirate, was becoming more nocturnal. Ellen grew distressed because she could not get him bedded down before ten o'clock. The Francis Drake–like, swashbuckling tyke was developing a habit of getting up around three thirty in the morning, rattling around the house, rattling toys, appearing in a daddy-less bedroom, climbing in bed, frustrating Ellen.

I have a new respect for my single-mom friends, Ellen thought.

Brad was the disciplinarian of the family, and the effect of his absence had trickled down, even to sleeping patterns. Normally, Brad would have just said, "Go to bed!" and that would have been the end of it. But Ellen was the sweeter and more grace giving of the pair. When her son wanted to crawl in bed with her, it was heartsease. She couldn't bear to say no.

By Saturday, September 30, Brad was turning a corner. He had more *umph*. More zip. He was walking farther. His dizziness had improved. He looked stronger. Not only did Marlen sit on the bed with Brad but something extraordinary also happened. That afternoon, father, son, and daughter took a ride on the wheelchair, looping the second floor at Lakeshore three times like *Ben-Hur* charioteers. Brad had chucked the eye patch and was now wearing special goggles that gave a nod to the old Ektelon racquetball specs, masking tape affixed to one of the lenses.

THE HAWLEYS GREETED OCTOBER, not with typical autumnal pleasantries and the anticipation of tumbling leaves and colder weather, but with the glitz of a barium-swallow test. Brad failed it. He could eat ice chips, but because he could not swallow, those pizza and Coke commercials on TV remained torturous. Brad wondered if he would ever eat a solid meal again. In fact, his mouth watered for a fat slice of what he considered the best pizza in town, De Vinci's. This was a pie that could not be shoe-horned into the classification of Paleo, but at this point, who cared?

Wednesday, Ellen walked into Brad's room and was surprised to see her husband wearing an Independence Day T-shirt. Unfortunately, this was not the Fourth of July or a memento of the movie starring Bill Pullman and Will Smith. Brad donned the shirt because Wednesday was Brad's "Independence Day." His supposed last day of therapy. Unbeknownst to Ellen, the administration had concluded that Brad's time was up at Lakeshore. Flabbergasted, Ellen thought he had at least another week in therapy. Now they were about to kick him out? Why were they releasing him? Ellen laughed at a note that was left in his room, outlining all the requirements to graduate from ICU: dressing himself, walking to the restroom, feeding himself, shaving. A hefty inventory. Had Brad been released under those pretenses, he would basically been gifted release, similar to an F-student walking across the auditorium stage to receive a diploma. Ellen panicked.

She says she phoned a case manager four times before she finally got an answer. Once they connected, the case manager assured Ellen that there would be at least two days of clemency and that he would leave on Friday at the soonest. But that didn't completely comfort Ellen. Later that night, she approached the attending physician, who extended the grace period through the beginning of the following week. The doctor described Brad as a "dream patient," one who does everything until he gets it right and follows instructions religiously. This taxonomy was a di-rect contrast to Trinity. Brad, the incorrigible patient at the hospital, was now—wait for it—a *dream* patient?

The mere threat of release helped Ellen to understand how unready they were for his arrival at home. The house would have to be in or-der. New accoutrements would have to be installed, including grab bars and ramps. A wheelchair, a walker, and an adjustable bed were needed.

The Fall of Brad Hawley

Brad's head would have to be positioned at a thirty-degree angle to prevent vertigo and to facilitate feeding through the feeding tube. A catalog of accommodations.

With the influx of friends stopping by to visit, Brad received varied reactions. Some were able to keep their composure. Some bore tears at the sight of their withered friend. Ellen remembers a visit by family friend Jason Hutto: "Jason came to Lakeshore one Saturday to watch the Auburn game with Brad. At one point, Jason suggested they go for a walk and wheeled him out. Jason was a happy-go-lucky guy, and I remember him sitting outside balling but trying to pretend he wasn't crying. I guess he just couldn't stand to see Brad in that condition."

A visit by Bryan Thompson produced another impressive display of waterworks. Thompson, one of Brad's closest confidantes hailing from Jasper, Alabama, was one of the guys at Auburn who always invited a little lighthearted needling. But on this day, as Thompson witnessed the malaise of his friend, there was no stopgap for tears. Thompson broke down in front of his friend.

"Thompson, you gotta stop, man. Come on, dude," Brad said.

Regardless of their propensity for tears, Brad began to appreciate those vital visits, a welcome reprieve from the leaden atmosphere of a hospital room. Ellen did reserve a few nights to spend with her husband, and even though she had to sleep in a chair, Brad preferred this type of sleeping arrangement. He looked forward to the nights Ellen could stay over. It was almost like a date. For instance, Brad circled October 4 on his calendar and made it abundantly clear that he wanted her to spend the night. The night was significant because it was Ellen's birthday.

"I had a quick dinner and spent the night in a chair at Lakeshore. Gosh, Brad was in such a bad place in his life," Ellen said.

Since insurance allowed the Hawleys to extend their stay, Brad was able to spend another week at Lakeshore. This time was not without incident. On Thursday, October 6, Brad buzzed the nurses because he felt the urge to go to the bathroom. They were "unresponsive," as he recalls, and his stubbornness quickly took over.

Fine. Screw them, Brad thought. *I'll do this myself.*

Brad clutched the side railing and pulled himself up, making it to the side of the bed unassisted. He pressed down on his knees and paused. His breathing laborious. Beginning again, he somehow managed to stand with the walker. He dragged himself just a few feet forward, to the toilet. Oddly, he felt a sensation to pee, even though he hadn't peed on his own in six weeks. He eventually made it to the seat, where he sat "flaccidly" for fifteen uneasy minutes. He was unable to produce even a trickle.

"Nurse!…*Nurse!*" Brad called, giving up on the bathroom and hoping someone might hear him and help him back to the bed. But there was no answer.

Screw them, he thought again.

Upon standing, or attempting to stand, not a second or two had passed before he fell. He slammed face-first onto the floor. When nurses finally discovered him, his front tooth was gone, and blood was pouring out of his chin. Luckily, he had fallen forward, not backward. Ellen was livid when she heard about the spill, and decided to spend another night in the chair.

But every day, he was walking farther and doing more than he ever had since the Fall. He made a crude attempt at playing a Coldplay song on his guitar as part of music therapy. In anticipation of the ride home, he had to practice getting in and out of the car.

As dangerous and stupid as the bathroom effort was, it demonstrated Brad's progress and determination to recover. Yet this type of recovery would require baby steps, not broad jumps. Every day, Brad would have to face a bar that kept going up. He had been humbled such that the most basic of human tasks were his bar.

TUESDAY WAS INDEPENDENCE DAY (number two) when Brad was paroled from purgatory: *We're home!*

After two lovely ambulance rides—one from Steel Company to the hospital and the other from the hospital to Lakeshore—Brad was finally able to travel in a car. In fact, the last time he had been in a car, Wiz

The Fall of Brad Hawley

Khalifa was thumping the Jeep as he made that foreboding drive to Steel Company Fitness on August 27.

The practice getting into the car paid off. After Ellen supervised him into the passenger seat, she cranked up the vehicle and putt-putted out of the parking lot and onto Lakeshore Drive. Brad took a deep breath and smelled the sweet perfume of freedom. He noticed the sights and sounds of Birmingham with freshness and newfound novelty, as if he were a first-time visitor to the area. The places he had once whizzed by mindlessly he now noticed. He smiled and closed his eyes as everything sank in like a silvery dream.

As they got closer to the house, Brad's heart began to pound unceasingly through his chest. There was great excitement within him to put an end to this long six-week journey away from his home. As Ellen made a right off Cross Hill Road onto their street, Brad saw the green bows fastened to every mailbox on both sides.

"What happened?" Brad inquired. "Who are these ribbons for?"

Ellen, keeping her eyes on the road as she broke a grin, said, "They are for you."

Brad was overtaken with disbelief. He didn't say anything, but began to cry when he realized that neighbors would be so good-hearted as to honor him during this time of trial. Making a greater emotional impact was that he did not know the names of many of them.

Ellen would recollect that special moment on CaringBridge:

It was pretty emotional driving him down our street, as he looked at all the green bows. He was very touched by this. Thank you for your thoughts and prayers. They have truly helped to sustain us through the last month and a half. The first phase of this bad dream is ending. Though we have a long road ahead, this is a major milestone in our road to recovery.

Brushing the tears away, Brad steadied himself as the car scuttled into the driveway. He glassed his eyes across the front of his stunning home. The cream color. The front patio. The windows and doors. It meant more to him now than when he'd first laid eyes on it after the renovation.

Ellen did not pull the car all the way down to the garage, as she normally would have. The stairwell leading upstairs would have been too difficult to climb. Instead, she parked the car in front of the house and walked around to open Brad's door for him.

Brad creaked out. He straggled to the door as Ellen opened it for him. He looked inside. He discovered that the house was essentially the same way he'd left it. There was little fanfare, save for the reaction of his kids and his wife. It didn't make the local newspaper. No members of Steel Company greeted him at the door. Just his family. And that was enough.

When Brad walked into his home, he was anxious to see Rocky.

"Rocky?" Brad whispered anticipatorily.

There was a moment of silence before Brad heard Rocky's feet pattering against the floor. The jingle of his collar. But as Rocky rounded a corner and closed the month-and-a-half gap between them, he sniffed at Brad as if he were a stranger. Clearly, seeing Brad should have sparked a memory in him, but this was not the same Brad. This was a skeletal facsimile.

"Hey Rocky!" Brad mouthed hopefully.

Rocky continued to sniff skeptically, his hesitation making Brad immeasurably sad. He had become a stranger in his own house. He realized it was time to reintroduce himself to his family, even to those who he thought knew him best. He knew it was time to pay more attention to them.

IN CATHOLIC BELIEF, the soul expiates its sins in the realm of purgatory. As believers pray and the fires of cleansing snuff out the filth, the soul moves closer to heaven. Once a requisite level holiness is reached, the soul may enter through the beatific gates to greet the Lord.

Brad Hawley had paid for his mistakes. He had spent four weeks in hell and three weeks in purgatory, and believers prayed him out. He would learn that often, the greatest refining occurs when we cannot move.

Part III

REDEMPTION

*Though you have made me see troubles, many and
bitter, you will restore my life again; from the depths
of the earth you will again bring me up.*

—PSALM 70:21

*But when, through the open door of the cross and the name and
power of Jesus Christ, I commend myself to the father's heart,
then God cancels all my past, accepts all my present, swears
His holy name for my future and the love of God take me over.
Then fear goes out of my heart, because love has come in.*

—A. W. TOZER

No Light

H e had been home for only an hour. Things were back to semi-normal at the Hawley household. Brad had been released from purgatory and was now lying on his own sofa, watching TV. Beside him was his once-estranged son. His wife and once-estranged daughter were in the front yard. His once-estranged dog out back on the deck. The doors of the house were swung wide open, and a buoyant breeze sailed in the scents of autumn. If this wasn't post-TBI bliss, nothing was.

Historically, Rocky the German Shepherd would often surprise houseguests who froze in their tracks at the ears-erect, stealthy beast. Although his menacing appearance often belied his happy demeanor (guests, upon discovering that Rocky was amiable and not lethal, let out a deep sigh of relief), Rocky was the guardian of the house, no less, and on this October day, something aroused his suspicion.

As the 131-pound father lay on the sofa and held clumsily his son, Rocky started barking uncontrollably. At the time, Brad was rotating between a walker and a wheelchair, and as soon as Rocky started to bark, Brad jolted up, grabbed his walker, and hobbled over to the french doors leading to the deck.

"Rocky, be quiet!" Brad said, attempting to roar. The decibels producing no match for the extent of his fury. Thrusting his body forward to increase force in his voice, Brad had momentarily forgotten that he was a TBI survivor. He began to fall and, before he knew it, was tangled up in his walker on the floor. When he looked up, Webb and Rocky were standing over him, their pitiful father.

"Ellen!" Brad screamed from his interior, producing little more than a whisper.

Ellen, hearing the thump, rushed into the house with Marlen still in her arms. Finding her husband upside-down like a tide-washed starfish on the living room floor, she sat Marlen on the couch, ran over to Brad, reached down and hooked her arms in his armpits. She then boosted him up, forklifting him to a standing position. As she engineered him back on the couch, Brad shot a spray of expletives.

It was like this for a while. Brad wanted to be a dad again. He wanted to be normal again. He was sick of his body not being able to do what he commanded it to do. His happiness had been cruelly bled out in a nearly two-month-long process. Cells of frustration and wrath now racing through his bloodstream.

Relinquishing control of his body proved to be difficult, but now Brad realized that he must relinquish control of duties within his own home. He would have to defer to Ellen for discipline. For all matters of the house. As a result, he was considerably short and snappy with Ellen. Hisses were common. He resented her for being able to take care of the house and kids. While living in an architecturally beautiful house, Brad resided in the slums of emotion on the inside.

"It was terrible. We were terrible," Ellen said. "He was very angry, difficult to talk to. Mean. He was a controller."

Ellen suggested that they see a counselor, but Brad huffed it off as an unlikely option.

The frustration was particularly palpable every morning when Ellen left for work. Around seven forty-five, Ellen and the kids loaded out for the day, trading places with Brad's new in-home nurse, LaShon. Ellen was still trying to balance the kids, Brad, and her job. So for her, LaShon provided a much-needed breather. Nursing-wise, LaShon was there to crush up the roiled patient's pills, help him shower and bathe, and be there to lend a hand if Brad fell. Though LaShon was merely doing her job, Brad often viewed her as an unwelcome, nagging crutch. Brad believed LaShon's mere presence underscored that he was in a pitiful and helpless state, and he grew to resent her.

Ellen was back at work, but what should have been a welcoming milestone was met by acrimony. Seeing his wife seize daily the title of breadwinner was painful and humbling to Brad. Ellen had encroached on his turf as the leader and head of the household. Brad had been ousted as the family czar, not by unkind overthrow but by his own demise. So he watched her, morning after morning, dress their children and head out the door while the incapable Mr. Mom convalesced. Every day from that vantage point, he could see them down the hall from his station in the marital bed. A noxious, sobering view. A sense of dread would set in as he heard Ellen's heels clicking on the hardwood floor, knowing that she was ready for work and that soon he would be left alone with wayward thoughts of silence. With LaShon. Ellen would tell the kids, "Let's go!" and, like that, they were gone.

Perhaps it was the silence he feared most. Silence cut into him like a dull blade and forced him to think critically about life. Silence forced Brad to face himself. To face God. In the past, his life had been filled with the luxury of white noise, noise that he could hide behind. He had been surrounded by the constant flow of family, friends, and numerous stimuli. Being quiet and still was anathema to Brad. His life had become too loud. But once he was immobilized, noises of the quiet house began to haunt him.

The lengthy halt of his functions made Brad realize how the family could operate without him, and frustration continued to escalate as he longed to recover his place in the household. Brad wanted to be the provider, but his idea of the full nature of providing was fundamentally skewed. His mind was still focused on the physical and disciplinary attributes of his contribution, while emotional and spiritual leadership took hind teat.

Physically, Brad wanted to battle back. He measured growth by his ability to physically move, and since any movement throughout the house was thorny and delicate his growth seemed stagnated. Brad could get up and amble around, but only with the help of LaShon and that old trusty apparatus, the gait belt.

From a motor-skills standpoint, the direst issue was that Brad could not sit up all the way. This meant that he was unable sit on a couch, because he couldn't hold up his head. His only option was sitting in a wheelchair with a built-in headrest. Coupled with the double vision, he was unable to read, watch TV, or write. He literally sat idle all day, long enough for the anger to turn nuclear as he waited on Ellen and the kids to return home.

In addition to Brad's own feeble attempts to move, physical and occupational therapy bolstered his daily routine. Friends lent their services. Jon Delk frequently dropped by and performed physical therapy. Kapi assisted with occupational therapy to try to fire up the hands. Brad also performed exercises in a wheelchair with small weights to rebuild musculature in the limbs. "WODs" included moving from the bed to the couch and back. No stopwatch was used.

Through extensive physical therapy, Brad eventually graduated from the wheelchair to a full-time walker, and though these milestones were encouraging, the physical improvements did little to pull him out of his emotional quandary. His vision would eventually improve, allowing him to surf the Internet for hours at a time, but that temporary salve could not fulfill his need to be a valuable contributor to his family and to society at large.

It was a humorless time. The injury was like adding poison to the residue of Brad's childhood, and the combination was toxic. While Brad insists that his frustration stemmed from his overwhelming desire to contribute, Ellen suggests that Brad had entered his "angry stage" trying to "control" (manipulate?) more than contribute. Ellen claimed that life with Brad during this time would aptly be described as a "living hell."

"If a toy was left on the floor, he'd get furious. It'd drive him crazy when something was out of place. He tried to control me and keep me from working. He'd go off on LaShon. He never did anything to make things easier on people," Ellen remembered.

To be fair, Brad wanted to be a father again. Understandably, he wanted to be the head of the household again. He wanted to discipline the dog. He had been a clean freak before the Fall, and he had lost his cleaning privileges. All these factors made Brad's emotions particularly combustible.

In all honesty, Brad didn't think he was trying to control Ellen. Control anyone, for that matter. The verbal zingers, he claimed, were his way of "channeling" control *through* Ellen—setting up a form of agency—all while he was learning to deal with this new paradigm: the real Brad 2.0.

The line of demarcation had been clearly drawn on August 27, and Brad was slowly becoming cognizant of this new life. The Brad who couldn't walk. The Brad who couldn't sit up on the couch. The Brad who had survived but was physically a shell of the man he had once been. The Brad who was developing anger issues.

In retrospect, Ellen believes the family was ill prepared for the severe emotional effects of TBI. She claimed that she hadn't been instructed that patients often exhibit mood swings, uncontrollable anger, and depression—depending on which portion of the brain has been affected. A simple Google search will show that patients who experience TBI are often prone to the following: verbal outbursts, physical outbursts, poor judgment and disinhibition, impulsive behavior, negativity, intolerance, apathy, egocentricity, risky behavior, lack of empathy, depression, or anxiety.

While Ellen and Brad didn't realize it at the time, the behavioral effects of TBI were taking a major toll on Brad. Brad had gotten a lot meaner. If he was hard before, he was unbearable now. Ellen knew something was wrong, but, having little time to process the situation, did not give TBI proper culpability.

Reflecting on the trying era, Ellen concludes there was a "misstep" in treatment. She claimed that there was a "gap" in the continuum of care, a blind spot amid the flow of doctors, therapists, and paper work. She pointed out that the first doctor, Dr. Nguyen, was a neuro-surgeon and that his job was to perform surgery, not to treat psycho-logical ramifications postop. Other doctors focused on treatment of myriad physical issues. Few, if any, Ellen believed, focused on behav-ior. Indeed, Brad's mental and emotional rehabilitation were as para-mount to his recovery, and to Ellen's knowledge, no post-home-arrival counseling services were offered. Unfortunately, the manifestations were dark.

When his voice returned in late October, the family was introduced to his full-throated fury. If there was a verbal filter before the injury, that filter was now removed. Damage had been done to the fontal lobe of the brain, and thus he had no impulse control. Whatever Brad thought was belted vociferously and pell-mell. No trooper regulated the delicate highway from brain to mouth. And, as Brad's vitriol and hair-trigger tem-per loomed daily, Ellen walked on eggshells.

One severe behavioral symptom was Brad's change in attitude to-ward the kids. Ellen says that Brad couldn't handle the kids' misbehav-ior. Ever on edge, Brad disciplined, not by firm scolding or tough love, but by yelling. The kids even noticed the new paternal change and were becoming exasperated with the shrill reprimands. "He did a lot of disci-plining during this time," Ellen said. "I remember he would whack Webb on the leg. He took discipline way too far. The kids would say 'Daddy, stop yelling!'"

Things reached a boiling point that Halloween. The neighborhood was festooned in orange and black decorations and other playthings for the children, including a big JumpyKidz inflatable in the Hawleys' yard. Earlier in the day, Ellen's mom had taken Brad to the doctor, while Ellen and the kids went trick-or-treating. Later that night, there was a party at the neighbors' house, the whole family attending. Marlen dressed as a ballerina and Webb as Spider-Man. There was a cookout and plenty of hopping, reckless, shaking, sugar-brimmed children.

The Fall of Brad Hawley

Midway through the party, Brad, clutching a walker, was helped home by a few neighborhood friends. Earlier that day at the doctor's office, the cantankerous pedestrian underwent a barium-swallow test. His epiglottis movement showed ever-so-slight improvement, and he was allowed to suck on pellet ice. A new luxury. After the party, Ellen and the kids went home. They were tired and needed something to eat. Ellen was trying to cook dinner, but Brad was fixated on his new amenity. He kept insisting on going to get ice.

"He kept saying, 'No, we have to get ice. I need my ice,'" Ellen said. "Brad was being totally ridiculous. Mom came over and sat me down in the back room. Since Brad wanted to go get ice, she had to cook the food. She was pretty upset about me not standing up to Brad."

So Ellen took him to get ice (did she have a choice?). Brad knew that Sonic fast-food restaurant, while not the most convenient in terms of proximity, used pellet ice to cool their sodas and Route 44 cherry limeades. "Take me to Sonic," Brad thundered, loading himself into the passenger seat before Ellen started the car.

Silence permeated the interior as they turned out of their driveway. Ellen made a left turn off their street and a right turn onto Old Leeds Road. She veiled her anger as she negotiated the roads, but then, breaking silence, said, "Brad, do you know how selfish you're being? The kids haven't had dinner. They're hungry, and we need to get them to bed!"

That ignited Brad. His eyes became glossed with rage. He leaned over from the passenger seat and began berating Ellen with a rapid succession of vitriol. Ellen, aghast at the behavior, knew then that they needed to seek out professional help.

He still got his ice.

Ellen made an appointment with a counselor, hoping that communication with a third party could somehow mitigate the feud. Brad, to be expected, was wishy-washy. At first he said he'd go, then backed out. While he could barely walk, he proved to be an expert at somersaulting around counseling.

It came down to the day of the appointment, and the pendulum had swung in a radical way. Brad had become unrelenting in his decision not to go. He didn't think the family "needed" counseling. "I remember going back to the bathroom, and I was bawling, crying," Ellen said. "I started to pray, 'God, help us. Help change Brad's heart.'"

Then something even more radical occurred. "After I calmed down, I got in the car, backed out, and started out the driveway," Ellen said. "Brad came out with this walker and got in front of the car. He said, 'You can't go by yourself. Fine, I'll go with you.' But once we got there, he was very quiet and didn't really talk about what was going on. Everything was surfacy, and he acted like everything was normal. And I didn't want to say anything that would ignite another firestorm at home. We ended up going to the counselor, but never really got below the surface."

There was nowhere for Ellen to turn. Even in those rough days before Brad was injured, Ellen always had hope. She never wavered on her commitment to her husband. She had put up with the egomania, the workout obsession, the injuries, the cars, the global thrill seeking. Now all of that business seemed rather meek. Now the light of their marriage was but a trembling flame. Ellen began to wonder if she could make it through this dark period, or if her days with Brad were limited.

The miserable month of October was the worst time in the history of the Hawleys' marriage. It was "the Dark Ages," a Medieval-like epoch. Ellen had signed up for "till death do us part" but was beginning to wonder if the definition of death could extend to the death of sanity.

INCORRIGIBLE

In the fall, when the trees overlooking Old Leeds Road unload their leaves, off in the distance you can see a cross. That cross is affixed to Trinity Medical Center, where, for three weeks, Brad Hawley lay in a hospital bed, clinging to life. As miraculous as it was for Brad to make it out of the hospital, out of Lakeshore Rehab and to his house, the Hawleys would need perhaps an even greater miracle to save them. Quite naturally, one would think that "home" signaled a huge sigh of relief for Brad and Ellen, that making it out of a six-week morass to the couch would spur a slow-but-sure incremental healing. Not so. Their situation had become even darker.

While Brad historically claimed that he felt as if he was on an island, Ellen was the one who was truly alone. In the nightmarish months of October and November, she was like a lost traveler in the moonless night of marriage. These were frontiers that she would have never considered when she penned her famous letter affirming her commitment to Brad on the airplane. Now she wondered if the darkness would consume her.

"There was only so much a person could take," Ellen said. "I had close friends with whom I shared things and to whom I could vent. I told them what was going on, but I didn't tell my family. I even talked to some of Brad's friends, but I guess they didn't feel close enough to talk to him."

So as Brad continued down the jagged path of recovery, Ellen staggered along beside him.

Anger and frustration were not the only manifestations of TBI. While Brad was in the hospital, Ellen sold his $40,000 Jeep. She did this for two main reasons. They needed the cash as a cushion for the next several months, and she feared that Brad would want to drive prematurely. Indeed, increased mobility encouraged Brad's desire for vehicular transportation, and in November, his fixations had shifted from pellet ice to a new truck.

While canvassing the Internet, Brad spotted a fully loaded, white Ford F-150 pickup truck at a car dealership in Trussville, Alabama, only thirty minutes away. Apparently, it was the "best deal" on a fully loaded truck, since, of course, car dealerships would never fudge nor engage in the slightest of puffery. It didn't take much for Brad to be convinced he needed it. The tan leather. The four doors. The four wheel drive. All the amenities.

By pure happenstance, the family scheduled lunch at Ellen's aunt's house at Lake Logan Martin. On the way, Brad suggested they "swing by the dealership"—which was sort of close—for a quick test-drive. When the Hawleys arrived at the car lot with kids in tow, a slick-talking salesman greeted them in the parking lot. It wouldn't have taken deft of salesmanship to convince Brad of the purchase. He was already salivating at the thought of a new ride. Sneakily, Brad withheld the material information that he was a TBI survivor, and, after letting the kids crawl around in the voluminous cab, loaded up in the driver's seat and whipped out of the parking lot. The salesman, riding shotgun, found himself in an on-and-off-the-shoulder affair that would have measured a peg above a child manipulating the vehicle. All over the road, wide eyed, still two months away from being cleared to drive, Brad felt the elation of a driver in his first race at Daytona.

Ellen wasn't laughing. "I was pissed," Ellen said. "We were on the way to eat at my aunt's house, and Brad said, 'Take me to buy this truck.' I said, 'Brad, you don't even have a job. You can't even drive.' That was when he became especially focused on the truck. He said, 'If you don't take me to get the truck, we are getting a divorce.' He threatened to divorce me several times. He was furious. Then he said, 'Call Rich. Rich will take me to get the truck.' After he test-drove the truck, that was when

The Fall of Brad Hawley

I started to sort of detach myself from him, because I thought he was going to kill himself."

This renewed sense of reckless abandon was debilitating Ellen. Being a thrill seeker in his previous life was something that Ellen liked, if not cherished, about Brad. Now that the circumstances had changed and one nick on the head could end him, Ellen wondered how much longer he was going to last. Brad simply couldn't have the same outlook or unmitigated daredevil mind-set anymore. He needed to be cautious, aware, restrained. New vocabulary to him. The joyride at the dealership was a kind of frightening theater into what Ellen feared most about Brad's new version of himself: that there was too much old Brad left.

Before the Fall, Brad had been the vice president of sales for a start-up intellectual property company. When their chief sales guy (Brad) went down, the company lost important revenue streams. Since the company could not hire Brad back at the same pay grade, they attempted to lure him back, he said, in a less lucrative capacity. "It felt like they offered me a charity case," Brad said regrettably. "You can come back but at a much lesser job." He respectfully declined and began to look elsewhere.

With Ellen pulling the heavy haul, Brad knew he would need to eventually find gainful employment to supplement the family income. He wasn't even close to ready to getting back to work but concluded that the search should begin immediately. If anything, he needed it for personal reasons. A man cannot feel like a man if he doesn't work at something.

Brad had so improved physically that he became a very accomplished Internet user. His aggressive surfing led to a Skype interview with an intellectual property company with a home base in Belgium. Due to an eight-hour time difference, the 2:00 p.m. interview in Belgium meant a 6:00 a.m. interview in Alabama. Brad barely had time to roll out of bed before he was in front of the computer screen.

For the proceedings, Brad got duded up in a jacket and tie. But that was only from the waist up. Beneath the threshold of the camera, he sported a pair of boxer shorts.

During the interview, Brad kept up appearances and tried to project a sense of normalcy. He had always been good at "turning it on" when the time called. Yet again, he did not disclose that he was a TBI survivor. A minor omission, he thought, if he could perform the duties of his job.

The interview was going well until Brad, who had virtually no authority over his bodily functions, sensed that nature was calling. Thankfully it was number one and not number two. He had a choice. He could (a) ask to be excused, get up, and expose his boxers as he hurried to the bathroom or (b) relieve himself in the chair. He chose to let 'er rip. The luke urine soaked his boxers, then filled the chair, and then ran down onto the floor. Brad's face remained still and stoic for the camera as the urine splattered against the hardwood. Lava of laughter building within, he feared he might erupt as his face turned ruddy. He somehow managed to hold it in, and as soon as the Skype call was over, he got up and laughed embarrassingly all the way to the shower.

En route, Brad ran into Ellen in the hallway. She had been listening.

"You sounded pretty good," Ellen said. Then she glanced downward and saw his soaked boxer shorts.

"Oh," Ellen sighed.

Completely unaware of Brad's injury and obviously impressed with his performance, the company in Belgium asked Brad to fly in for a second interview. There's something to brag about. "Peed in the floor. Made the cut." While trying to coordinate flights, Brad was requested to produce a writing sample, a short dossier to demonstrate his ability to communicate via the written word. Instead of penning an actual sample, Brad referred the company to the CaringBridge site. Now bloodhound-like to the subterfuge, the company eventually decided on a tasteful rebuff. "We're going in another direction."

Before the Europeans finally rejected him, Ellen saw that her husband's interest piqued at the thought of a new job, and she feared that Brad would actually consider a trans-Atlantic flight. The thought of Brad getting on a plane horrified her. "Thank God they said they wanted to go in another direction, because he would have gotten on that plane,"

Ellen said. "He could barely make it around the house and wouldn't listen to reason."

If Brad thought he was cute, Ellen still wasn't laughing. Her previous amusement at Brad's antics had turned into a glower. She knew that the road to normalcy would take time and that it needn't be rushed. "He was determined to be back to normal," Ellen said. "People were wondering why I wasn't posting updates on CaringBridge. I took Webb to get a checkup at the doctor, and the pediatrician said, 'You haven't posted in a while. I love positive stories!' I stopped posting during October and November because there was nothing positive to say. It was such a dark time."

Brad's vigorous Internet work also involved an exercise in hero creation. He longed for affirmation from his Facebook friends that he was a miracle, and he began to embrace the identity of hero/survivor in his online profile. He started CrossFitting again. That is, lifting five- and ten-pound dumbbells and posting his inchwormish progress on social media. Great reinforcement came from the Steel Company community. One individual even encouraged him to come back to the gym as soon as December, a decision that would have been recklessly premature. Brad wanted to believe that because so many people were following his recovery, he was posting to try to keep them "updated." But in reality, he was doing it for himself. He fueled off of the increased renown and felt he needed the affirmation to keep going. When people would say, "You're a miracle!" or "You're amazing!" Brad ate it up. He would make a post on social media, continue to refresh the screen, and watch the likes pile up. During the recovery, he always got a lot of likes, especially from Steel Companyers.

Whether or not Brad had good motives for his increased social media presence, he was right about one thing. He was a walking miracle.

Still, Brad reveled in the thought of walking into the gym with no assistance. Of tossing that dreaded walker to the side and walking unaided again. The thought of being ready for a workout turned over in his mind. He began to think that he could be a Steel Companyer again. But mostly, he wanted to prove people wrong. Even after a horrific injury, even as far as he'd come, he still felt the need to prove himself to the Steel Company community.

Perhaps there was a bit of embarrassment that accompanied the nasty fall.

Perhaps Brad felt he had humiliated himself, and he needed to prove he could come back and succeed again.

Brad thought *People don't know how good I am.*

So for Brad, Steel Company remained the litmus test for manhood. If he could just get back to Steel Company, he'd be all right. "I had begun to worship it," Brad said. "It almost became a vehicle. Some people kept hitting the lock button on the doors and would not let me out. The power of that community is amazing, and they don't even realize it. It's almost like the culture traps people in it. There was this pull that was trying to pull me back into it. It's like riding a vehicle at an off-road rally, and it's incredibly fun, and all you wanna do is get back in it. It's like you're going ninety miles an hour on a dark, rocky road, but a simple turn into a tree, and it'd kill you."

Brad's hermetic distance from Steel Company finally came to a close that fall. In November, the Brad Hawley Invitational was organized by Steel Company to raise money for Brad and his family. Ellen remembered the Steel Company headman called her to pitch the idea. She says he intimated an event featuring "elite athletes" in central Alabama had already been scheduled and wondered if it might be changed to benefit Brad. Ellen and Brad happily agreed.

To plan the event and program the WOD, a Steel Company coach soon arrived at the Hawleys' home. He brought coffee but unfortunately Brad couldn't drink it. Brad thought it was a nice gesture, though.

Brad and the coach sat on the living room couch, poring over the particulars of the workout. But this was no team effort. Basically, Brad retained carte blanche to do whatever he wanted to do. Doubtless anyone would have disagreed at this juncture. "It was me basically saying, 'Here's what I want to happen in the WODs,'" Brad said. "The coach was enthralled with the handstand walk. There were elite guys coming, and I wanted to make them do it. I didn't want them to think this was a simple event. I wanted to program something to convey that I wasn't soft. That I hadn't gone soft. I wanted to enforce that by saying that I wished I were well enough to compete. That I was in it to win it. Totally down with the Steel Company thing. It had nothing to do with me being angry at the sport, but I remember I wanted them to work really hard, if not punish them."

Similar to the themes with Sharon, Brad had been wounded and now, rightly or wrongly, wanted Steel Company to pay for that wound.

The WOD for the Brad Hawley Invitational
#1a for time: (12 min cutoff)
50 overhead squats, 135/95#
40 kb swings, 70/53#
30 ring dips
2 shuttle runs (~300m total)
rest 1 min
#1b In a 60 sec time frame
handstand walk for distance

Before the event, word of Brad's injury had spread throughout the Steel Company community and the Birmingham community at large. Brad had become known as "the guy who fell at Steel Company," as many in the Over the Mountain community had heard someone was seriously injured while exercising at Steel Company. The details and the man's name were a bit hazy.

At the event, it was good to run into old friends who expressed their encouragement with Brad's progress. Many hadn't seen him in a while and were both impressed and saddened by Brad's frail appearance as he hobbled around on a walker. They wanted to shake his hand and tell him they were pulling for him. Praying for him. Brad had become a celebrity within the Steel Company community and was even interviewed on their online television network.

The host began: "We have a very special guest, Brad Hawley himself, joining us. We're here, and behind us is the first-ever Brad Hawley

Invitational event. He was on hand today to watch, but he's going to be competing in it next time. We're very excited about that."

As the city of Birmingham stood in the background with an orange-and-black pull-up bar looming, Brad responded. "Well, it's been really humbling, and it's been amazing to see these athletes. Everybody's so good—all these guys and girls are up for it. It's just been really humbling to have all these people out and, I know, in support of me. I've been, you know, trying really hard to get back, and I really look forward to competing in it next year."

If this seems awfully presumptuous, that's because it was. Brad was thirty pounds lighter, had a PEG tube sticking out of his belly, couldn't drive, and couldn't walk on his own accord.

As Brad toured the event, he noticed that crash mats were installed under the pull-up bars.

For the first time, Brad viewed Steel Company through the lens of a voyeur. He was able to step out of the situation and witness the workout through new eyes. And for the first time, he thought it a bit silly. "I remember there was this guy who had a Mohawk," Brad said. "He had a bunch of tattoos and had his shirt off. He thought he was a warrior. But when he was doing pull-ups, he fell off the bar. There was great irony in that. I remember he fell on his side, and he sort of grumbled: 'argargar-rahhh!' He sounded like a Viking."

This moment was part of an important learning process for Brad. Part of the hard perspective shift. As he watched another man fall from the bar, he thought, "Dude, get a grip."

And he realized that was once him.

Was Brad worried about inspiring people through his recovery? Maybe, maybe not. Brad says that he "embraced" the idea of being an inspirer and used that to rebuild a sense of new self-worth. Being a hero carried a certain amount of responsibility that, truthfully, Brad wasn't sure he wanted or deserved. He didn't mind being enthroned as a hero. He simply didn't want to accept the inherent charge and duty that heroing entailed.

The Fall of Brad Hawley

At that point in his recovery, Brad hadn't crossed the mental bridge that God was the real hero in all of this, but instead he vied for that classification for himself. Brad wanted the credit. It was *Brad's* strength that had gotten him this far. Brad wanted to prove to everyone that he possessed the strength within to overcome the most difficult of circumstances. That he could rep out TBI, setting a new personal record. Others might be able to lift more weight, but could anyone recover from traumatic brain injury? Yes, if Brad could overcome this disruptive, sweeping event, he could be perceived as the strongest of them all.

But then there were little moments, something Brad said in the television interview, which cemented Brad Hawley as a voice for truth and inspiration. Where one could tell that inside of Brad a transformation had begun. Where God turned his mess into his message: "Well, I tell ya. The one thing I've gained from all of this is perspective, and you know, I was in the best shape of my life when I fell, and I really do attribute part of that to why I'm here today and why I'm sitting here talking to you. But the one thing I want everybody to have from this is—I want them to gain humility; I want 'em to be thankful. I mean, this Thanksgiving should be a time when you spend it with family and friends. You know, it's great to be in shape. It's great to be strong, but man—kids need a father; a wife needs a husband. You need to be there. And that's one thing I've gained from this: while it's all great and it does act like a drug for me, it's great to just be alive and be breathing."

The Mad Dr. Shaffer and the Excruciating Bliss of PEG Tube Removal

The epiglottis is an underappreciated organ of the human body. It is like the man who works at the water department and supervises the flow of water into your household: you might live without him, but you wouldn't want to. As well, the ability to swallow is often taken for granted, and Brad Hawley ultimately realized his epiglottis's value when it ceased to work, when the beautiful symphony of the human body was silenced. By November of 2012, he was at the apex of frustration. Yet, no matter how dire an outlook, Brad was still in the business of setting goals. This year, his goal was simple: he wanted to enjoy Thanksgiving dinner with his family.

The alternative and remedy for patients who have lost the ability to swallow is the installation of a device called a PEG tube. PEG stands for "percutaneous endoscopic gastrostomy," and the tube is inserted into the body through different access points. In Brad's case, the stomach. Nutrients are administered into the stomach via the tube, and the goal is to provide to the patient the requisite level of "food" in order to survive.

By November, Brad had already failed several swallow tests and was still not eating in the traditional sense. He hadn't had a solid meal in more than two months. Before, Brad would have simply bulked up, pushed harder, and strained to get where he needed to be. Now, there was nothing he could do to make his epiglottis start working again. No amount of training would be able to bring that essential life function back to normal. And, with another swallow test looming, Brad wondered if the epiglottis would recover, or if he'd be burdened with the PEG tube for the rest of his life. That, and a sub-130-pound frame.

The lifestyle he had developed—the diet regimen, the shakes, and the Paleo-driven program—no longer existed. Before the accident, he was ingesting six or seven small meals a day. The type of food he was putting into his body had become a vital part of his workout, and the phrase "you can't outwork a terrible diet" had been drilled into his head. Because of the influence of Steel Company, Brad viewed exercise as a holistic endeavor. He was 100 percent committed to eating healthy and even went to the extent of ordering his meals, shakes, and protein bars online. With this mind-set shift, his body began to transform. His desire for processed food was squelched, and an organic diet replaced the junk he'd consumed previously. The kind of stuff most Americans eat. While other flabby men sauntered through town wearing their Sansabelt pants and Van Heusen shirts, boasting their big, fat guts, Brad's face and body were chiseled down into a svelte, Adonis-like form. He looked healthy as a horse. He felt terrific.

Now with a paralyzed epiglottis, Brad could not control the foods going into his system. Paleo or not, the food that pumped through his PEG tube was life sustaining, and as alien and unconventional as it was, the device was keeping him alive.

Brad also continued to battle the problematic symptom of double vision. "To me, double vision was the worst symptom of my TBI," Brad said. The morning of the third swallow test, as Brad and Ellen were leaving the house, Brad glanced at a tree in the yard and noticed that, miraculously, his double vision was gone. Doing a double take, he noticed that the tree was still there in singular form. Wary of jumping to the conclusion that his vision was restored, Brad wondered if this was an outlying moment of visual clarity. He felt a tingle of excitement in his gut but quickly dismissed it.

But as Brad and Ellen climbed onto Highway 280, he realized this was no mirage. "We got onto Highway 280. Before, the lanes in the highway would overlap, and it looked like we were going to hit cars," Brad said. "But that morning of the swallow test, 280 was clear as day. I said to Ellen, 'Oh my gosh, my vision's back!' In an evening, overnight, my vision was back. I woke up to clear vision. It was an emotional moment."

The swallow test, his second outpatient test, was conducted at Lakeshore Rehab. A nurse and a speech therapist led the proceedings. As Brad describes it, they sat him in a chair, held his neck up, and positioned an x-ray from his upper chest to his lower chin. He was then fed a brownie.

"I remember being very, very nervous," Brad recalled. "I worried that I was going to choke. I couldn't breathe. So when they fed me the brownie, I was chewing very slowly. You know, it's funny now. It was a hospital brownie, and it felt like cardboard in my mouth. I remember thinking with all my might that I would do anything I could do to make my epiglottis work. I was chewing very deliberately. Slowly. I swallowed gently, and all of a sudden, I saw the speech therapist. She said, 'Ah! Look at that epiglottis move!' When she said that, I lost it. I broke down. I cried. I think about the magnitude of that moment. An hour prior to that, my vision was back. Then my swallowing was back. The emotion of the moment was too much to bear. The speech therapist and the nurse started crying. Ellen burst in, and she was crying. The nurse in the room was a nurse who had been with me when I arrived in trauma. She said that no one in the room thought I was coming off the table, and there she was, watching me pass the swallow test."

Brad's first order of business after the dramatic swallow test was to fetch the Birmingham-famous "Mona Lisa" from De Vinci's Pizza. The Mona Lisa was Brad's go-to on a "cheat day" when he broke off from the camp of healthy regimen. "I was craving a Mona Lisa pizza, in my opinion the best pizza in town," Brad recalled. "Perhaps it was from listening to all those pizza commercials while lying in the hospital bed. Without question, Ellen ordered the pizza and called Rich to join us for lunch."

Yes, his swallowing was back, but taste was another matter. When they got back home and the pizza arrived, the threesome of Brad, Rich, and Ellen hovered around the box for the unveiling of the pie. With great anticipation, Brad lifted open the box and let out the steam. For a moment, he beheld its magnificence. He was relearning a childlike appreciation of the small moments of life. It was like opening a Christmas present.

Brad slowly cut the tip off a single piece and placed it in his mouth. He chewed and chewed, waiting for the savory feeling as the Mona Lisa connected with taste buds.

But his taste buds had become inoperable.

"I couldn't taste the darn thing!" Brad said. "It was so disappointing."

Brad's perception of "taste" was now based on texture, and the PEG tube remained.

Brad was finally cleared to have the PEG tube removed, and a family friend, Dr. Rob Shaffer, the affectionate, world-is-my-oyster gastroenterologist in Birmingham, agreed to perform the removal. To set up the procedure, Brad phoned Cathy Phares, Dr. Shaffer's office manager and close friend of the Hawleys.

The day of the procedure, Bob drove down from Cullman to take Brad to the clinic. They arrived just after lunch. When Brad walked in, the waiting room was empty. He said hello to Cathy, who checked him in and escorted him back to a room.

Dr. Shaffer walked in shortly, to Brad's delight. Things seemed to be hunky-dory, copacetic, and as the pair of pals exchanged pleasantries, Shaffer cut an ivory-teethed grin at the recovering patient as if they were about to engage in a cavalcade of fun.

"We were literally shooting the bull," Brad said, "and in the middle of the conversation, Dr. Shaffer says, 'Well shit, Brad. There's no other way. *You ready?*'"

Shaffer clutched the PEG tube that was attached to Brad's stomach, gave it a one, two, three, and yanked with all his might.

"At that moment, I was thinking *Wait, what? Hold on. Let's talk about this.* At the count of three, he just pulled as hard as he could," Brad recalled. "And the pain that followed! I shot up and screamed, probably because it caught me off guard. He grabbed my shoulders and said, 'You're going to pass out!' He told me to breathe and tried to calm me down."

And with that, Shaffer tossed Brad Hawley's life-sustaining device in the garbage can and walked out like a boss.

Dumbfounded and humbled, Brad shuffled out of the room and down the hallway, using a wall for support. He was disoriented from what had just happened to him. Unsteady on his feet. He made a comment to the nurses that the procedure was "much worse" than he had thought it'd be. A cavalcade of fun it was not. Bob said that he had heard Brad scream from all the way in the waiting area.

In these little moments that are now scorched in his memory, Brad believes that he was being stripped of his dignity so he could be whittled into a finer specimen of a man. The humbling of Brad Hawley, once viewed as anathema, was a good thing.

Now that Brad could see and swallow, he had made a turn onto a straightaway. There would be challenges, yes. But those two essential functions—eyesight and swallowing—were major milestones in his recovery process. Brad found reason to celebrate, found great elation in those moments. Greater than, he would admit, performing well on a WOD or hoisting a heavier weight overhead. These were the moments of recovery that ushered in triumphal joy to the Hawley household.

And the most important thing. He made Thanksgiving dinner with his family, as he had hoped.

Thank You

November 2012
CaringBridge.org

Hello everyone. Brad here. I cannot begin to express my appreciation for the support and encouragement I have received. I know we all have our troubles, and the fact you have taken the time to care has meant the world. For those who have prayed for healing, I would like you to know that your diligence has worked. I am slowly on the mend, I am seeing one item in front of me, and I am swallowing food. The unsteadiness is the last remaining symptom, and I think I might need to get used to living with it. Regardless, any remaining prayers should be directed to one of two things: (1) get me stable or (2) my wife.

Many of you have mentioned what a rock I married. Well, if I didn't love and appreciate my wife before, now I certainly do. There is no way I would be at this point without her love. She has been amazing and has helped manage a chaotic family while nursing me back to health. I thank her for changing the dressing on my peg tube, for bringing me my first pizza, and for handing me a towel as I struggle through a shower.

As an update for those unaware, I am still somewhat on my back but am more than thankful to be breathing and spending time with my wonderful children and close friends. I am no longer suffering from double vision, and I have started eating solid foods. I have been humbled, and I feel quite blessed to be ahead of schedule. I was told to plan on a six-plus month recovery process, and today marks ten weeks. How amazing. This all on the tail end of life support and an uncertainty that I would ever recover. I can promise one thing: I am a new man and promise to be better at all aspects of my life. I have felt very unworthy of the caring you all have shown and for the grace God has given me.

I have had a number of emotional experiences over the last ten weeks. To name a few, the ribbons on mailboxes, hearing about the waiting room at the hospital, swallowing food for the first time, and visiting Steel Company Homewood. It has become an all-too-common occurrence that I cry. A signed flag from the Phoenix Club was another point that just about put me over the edge. I am just sorry that I cannot remember everyone at the hospital. In fact, I remember very little from the moment of the fall until week five.

In the end, I want one thing from all of this. I want every one of you to realize how precious life truly is. I was in the best shape of my life and took a short tumble that almost resulted in my death. I am thankful beyond measure for the moments that I get to spend with my family and friends. I took for granted simple things like breathing and eating the best pizza in town. I only hope that my journey inspires you to live in the moment and that you always take the time to be thankful for things such as walking to your car and sharing a meal with your friends. I guess I am a little more reflective than usual, but then again, what was I supposed to do with seven weeks in a hospital bed?

So upon reading this, I encourage you to take a moment and think about those close to you and the sheer fact you were able to get ready this morning. Life is good, and all of you have gotten me through this. I thank you for caring enough to read this site and taking an interest in my recovery. I look forward to once again being a thorough father, husband, friend, and an avid cross fitter. I have experienced a life-changing injury and only hope that you would also find humility and thankfulness in my journey. I cannot begin to offer enough appreciation. Here is to regaining all twenty-four pounds lost and for carrying my kids up the stairs. Let's make this happen.

The Armor

I used to think that in order to continue or progress as a man, I had to develop armor. I wore that armor. I shielded myself from the harshness of the world. When there were dark points in a relationship.

But the problem with that armor is that I kept things inside. Kept things from coming in AND out. The injury knocked the armor off. Everything I'd been keeping inside was let out. Once the armor was penetrated, that's when the healing started.

Intimacy is life's great risk. To allow another person to have the power to hurt you, to expose the most vulnerable territories of the heart. To let someone see the bruises, the scrapes and scars, the delicate zones. To step out on the ledge and dare to love.

Brad Hawley had a serious intimacy problem. It terrified him. By refusing to be vulnerable, to allow access to his emotion-prone inner sanctuary, his interactions remained trite and surface, relationships empty and hollow. Reckless in physical endeavors, he had walked on the emotional rim of life, like a child looking over the edge, refusing to dive in. There is great risk in diving. In diving, there is always a possibility of getting hurt, and men aren't supposed to be wounded. Men are supposed to be strong, impervious. Unemotional. At least, that was the world narrative to which Brad Hawley was listening.

Yes. Better to have never been intimate at all. Better to have kept things superficial than to experience the sting of failure or hurt. Better for love to have been kept shallow than to risk it all for something truly terrific. Intimacy is dangerous. For many men, scary dangerous. In ways, Brad felt that intimacy and romance had become "cheesy"—those old Casablanca-like notions of love now archaic, replaced with more modern forms of affection. His misguided sense of marital interaction would by no means inspire a Harlequin Romance.

Brad viewed manhood as a daily exercise of putting on armor. Every morning before he walked out into the world, he suited up in a proverbial chainmail of protection. Brad's was a world of fast-paced, dog-eat-dog businessmen. He had encircled himself with a society of superprofessionals, and in no way were they advertising the need for emotional help or Kumbaya. His world was telling him that the texture of men was supposed to be tough as pumice, with no soft or pliable element. Letting down walls of emotion was a discouraged. And, with overall cultural shifts in the general American male's view of sex, Brad's concept of intimacy was severely skewed.

"Sex was very lustful," Brad said. "A toned-down *Fifty Shades of Gray*. I thought like a very secular man."

After the Fall and as Brad was reduced to nothing, he had no libido. By October, he hadn't gotten aroused in two months. "I didn't feel like doing it, and I didn't even know if *it* worked," he recalled.

Brad says that in the past, he viewed sex as mainly "performance," echoing the mind-set that carried value in the rest of his life, whereas relationships, intimacy, and even kindness played second fiddle. Because he wanted to be a performer in the marital bed, he often stepped outside of himself and became a voyeur to the situation. An actor in his own play. At times, he was emotionally distant and not fully present with his wife because he feared intimacy and its extreme closeness.

Thinking his physical appearance would place him in greater demand in his wife's eyes, he thought that his wife would want him more if he sported six-pack abs and a ripped chest. Since he had objectified himself in such a way, he didn't see the entire value in himself, that there was much to offer Ellen outside of performance and physical appearance.

Furthermore, because he was too afraid to go to such an intimate address, Brad failed to find a complete marital connection with his wife. Like an unclaimed jackpot, Brad was wasting an available treasure. Ellen, knowing this was possible, pined for such. "I needed a man, someone who is spiritually and emotionally strong, not physically strong," Ellen said. "Men feel like physical strength is what we want. But we want to rely on somebody. That's the type of strength that is attractive to us."

In late October, Brad discovered that he could "perform" again. It had been quite a long furlough. Brad was worried whether Ellen would be receptive to his advances and if receptive that she would only be doing so out of concession or conciliation. He thought, *Ellen couldn't possibly want me right now. I'm 130 pounds.* Because Brad had placed his self-worth on his physical appearance and, now seeing himself as an unattractive, spindly shell of man—certainly not the physical specimen he once had been—he believed his wife would have no desire to make love to him. "Part of me wondered if she would be receptive due to sympathy," Brad said. "I had an 130-pound body with a tube running out of my stomach. I thought she felt an obligation to perform the marital act because I could again. That she was only doing this because she was my wife."

Which, of course, was true. What attracted her to Brad were more than just the characteristics of his personality and his physical appearance. It was the inherent covenantal intimacy of husband and wife. In Ellen's mind, the emotional and physical worked in symbiosis. She desired a partnership in all phases. It was true: she missed the physical connection. Indeed, she missed the closeness, the intertwined sanctity of marital love. Yet, even with respect to matters of sex, Ellen was concerned more about Brad than she was about herself. She worried that if Brad were not able to perform, it would be a blow to his self-confidence. So she sat back and allowed him to instigate the first move. "My thing was he's in a very bad place," Ellen said. "In October and November, we were terrible, and he was angry. He was verbally abusive, and I didn't know if he'd be able to, and I wasn't going to attempt to try. If he couldn't do it, all hell would break loose."

So Ellen waited. She wanted Brad to do things on "his time." That time arrived in late October.

"I felt very vulnerable," Brad remembered. "And it was the first indication that I needed to adopt a sense of vulnerability. That I needed to open up myself to the world, especially my wife."

This was an important moment in Brad's personal development. This was the moment Brad decided to let intimacy in. This turning point was the beginning of a magnificent unraveling. Over the next few months, the armor would come off, piece by piece. This is not to say Brad transformed easily or quickly. The residue of a hyperguarded life would take time to erase. Over time, Brad realized that if he could be vulnerable in one area, it might be OK to be vulnerable in others. He could be vulnerable with his friends. He could be vulnerable in his spiritual life. It was OK to relinquish control. It was a good thing that his grip was pried away. Good thing that he softened up.

It would seem natural to believe Brad's life was changed the moment he lost his grip on the pull-up bar. But that was not the case. When Brad began to lose his grip of emotional control, that's when he began to truly find himself. That's when he began to experience real freedom for the first time in his life.

There were other issues that needed the touch of Christ. Brad had developed a habit, when crossed, of bludgeoning the other person with harsh, cutting words, hurting the other person before he or she had the opportunity to hurt him. After these verbal clubbings, he'd simply shuck the perpetrator of the offense off like a worthless hull and elevate himself to a morally elite status. This occurred for two principle reasons: Brad's habit of self-preservation and perpetuation, and his obsession with having to win. When confrontation arose, Brad lacked the conflict resolution skills to remain calm. Instead, he pulled out everything in his verbal arsenal, marshaling anything that might give him an advantage. "Many times in the past, when I said something Brad didn't agree with, he would threaten to leave," Ellen said. "He would get freaked out."

The Fall of Brad Hawley

As he began to understand Christian intimacy and fruit-of-the-spirit loving-kindness, he realized he didn't have to pulverize everyone who crossed him into submission and cast them away before they had a chance to hurt him. He could approach difficult encounters, the subtle confrontations of his marriage, without having to win. As a result, he was able to forgive. He was able to give mercy and demonstrate grace. All these things occurred because the barrier to his heart was being removed. He began to let God in. He began to understand that Christ wanted more of him than mere head knowledge or recitation of creed, He wanted inside all of Brad's compartments, no matter how dark, ugly, austere. Brad began to understand that the Christian life was more than just things he believed *about* God, and that Christ was not a weekly box he checked. Now he was free to trust. Instead of the whole of his faith adjudged by the strict compliance to claustrophobic rules of religion and obligation, he discovered that instead Christ was inviting him to walk unabatedly down the streets of liberty through an abiding relationship. And here is the irony of all ironies: by descending, by lowering himself to that humble, eyes-heavenward posture, by letting go of the need for control, the need to have things firmly within his grip, he ascended into a greater plain in his walk with the Lord.

"When He put me on my head, God was saying, 'I will change this man. He doesn't know it, but I will,'" Brad said. "God, like a business-man, had a strategic plan for my life: 'I'm going to put him on his head and take him to the brink of death. I'm going to break him to every last fiber and then make him into the man I want him to be.' It's hard to imagine that someone has a strategic plan for *you.* But God allowed these things—generated these things—to happen. He gradually inserted more events in my life to show Himself to me."

Brad's erosion hadn't occurred abruptly, with flagrant markers. It was a slow and methodical, one-degree-at-a-time change through a series of small compromises, such that the man he was when he was thirty did not recognize the boy he was at fifteen. And the transformation from the man who was mostly secular with a little spirituality sprinkled in did not occur overnight either. Over time, Brad would gradually realize his need for God's presence in his life. How lost he had been.

Until the Fall, Brad operated in a Brad Hawley–centered cosmos, while the planets of faith, family, and friends orbited distantly. After the Fall and over a long recovery period, his faith would become more central to his life. This change fell somewhere on the spectrum between a nominal spiritual awakening and Brad becoming a titan of the faith. This is not a story of Brad becoming a preacher or evangelist. This is a story of a man—an every day person—who simply realized his frailty. His brokenness. His need for grace.

And that is perhaps the greatest conclusion of human life.

Brad had feared that a change in spiritual focus would require a change in personality. He didn't want to give himself up in that regard. What he found as he lost his grip and began to die to self was that his personality didn't have to change. He could still be the same person, but his attitude would need to shift to a Christ-lensed view.

"Before, I wanted to affect people's lives—physically, by being the workhorse, and in other ways," Brad said. "That was shallow, pre-Fall Brad. But the means to be effective, in my mind, have changed. Without a faith-based approach, that was hollow. My life was hollow. I was chasing the wrong things."

Brad had no problem whatsoever engaging in activities with physical risk. Bungee jumping, skydiving, triathlon, Steel Company. But was he willing to risk being emotionally wounded for the sake of intimacy? Was he willing to lay aside all fear to go after the deepest forms of love? Did he have the courage to chase a deep relationship with both God and Ellen?

"Making love again was almost, to me, symbolic that I could be a man again," Brad said. "I thought I had lost my masculinity. I was reduced to this dependent, childlike flesh. I could no longer protect and contribute. So it was one of the first indications that I could be a man again. And I can share this moment with my wife, and I had this internal conflict that was being resolved. I felt very vulnerable. When we've made love since, there have been many times when we've looked each other in the eyes and said, 'I love you.'"

Brad's forced descent, accomplished through the Fall, helped him to realize how much human beings desire relationship. He realized this bond, intended since the beginning of time and threading through the ages, is the necessary endeavor of human life. It's stamped in our DNA. Yet, like the tendency of modern man, Brad hailed independence and self-determination as the more cardinal virtue. Indeed, autonomy and self-sufficiency are the engines of many a red-blooded American male. Do it yourself. Get there without a map. Forget the manual. Don't ask questions. Grind it out. Suck it up. Don't cry. Don't be a baby. Whatever you do, don't *ever* ask for help or admit that you're lost. Whatever you do, don't let anyone see the chink in your armor. Instead of employing a leader/helper motif to his marriage, Brad's mania to be the Alpha Male became an obstacle to an efficient marital biosphere.

In the final analysis, perhaps what Brad feared the most was someone seeing his true self, that the people whom he cared about the most would look at him and reject the man that he was. He had to climb up on a pillar or mountain because he viewed manhood as an ascent. Brad was a pilgrim on the journey of life, climbing each mountain pass as he neared the summit. Once he was knocked off the mountain, like the prodigal son, he longed to fill his stomach with the pods the pigs were eating. He longed to perform even the basest activities of life. Like the prodigal son, he found himself a citizen of a foreign country of personhood, a wayward, listless sham who did not even recognize himself.

And he realized the only way to find himself was to go back.

LEARNING TO WALK

Since the fall of mankind, human beings have used a variety of pursuits to find Eden. There is an inherent longing within to carve out our own version of paradise on earth. Brad Hawley's version of paradise rested in the trappings of the American Dream. He drank mint juleps with socialites at a horse race. He reveled in the D.C. nightlife. He took expensive vacations all over the world. He had a closetful of designer clothes. He owned a series of pricey vehicles. He was a member of a posh country club. He was in phenomenal shape. He had a terrific family. Walling off his own world in the nicest section of Birmingham, Alabama, he had everything a man could desire.

But there, he did not find Eden.

To find Eden, Brad would have to walk through hell. It was every bit as much of an internal valley as it was a physical one. Along the way, he would learn that Eden was found, not in tangible things you could touch, but in the invisible things of this life. Eden was not a physical place, dressed with physical things. Eden was an internal place. The place of a contented soul.

For Brad, change was laggard. Before and after the Fall, Brad was the same person with the same personality, but it was his perspective, his focus, his intentions, and his motives, that changed in tiny shifts. As stated previously, Brad's demise and the whittling away of his true self—meaning the gentlemen fashioned by his Creator—did not occur overnight, nor would the death of his imposter *self* occur overnight. Veering off course for many years, his turning back had to be as profound as his turning away, for he had been down the road of the world for so long he had become lost in it. To embrace Christ, Brad had to realize that *self* had to die. He had to realize the identity he'd been projecting for years was a fake, and that his truest self was like the man who once walked through the fields of Eden: bare, real, and content.

Brad may have had enough money to afford a nice house and nice vehicles, but in many ways, he was spiritually bankrupt. He would have been considered "rich" by the definition of materialism, but his spiritual treasure remained buried. He may have been in great physical shape, but he was spiritually lethargic, limping. Now, even though Brad credited God for saving him both spiritually and physically, there was still no daily walk. His overall spiritual orientation was pointed in the direction of the flesh. After the Fall, all the bitterness and deep-seated pain Brad had internalized for so many years spilled out in an exquisite catharsis, and most deafening was anger's roar. It would take a long stretch of healing months for Brad to realize God's place in his life, for the hubris and the angst to dissipate. For his needle to turn toward Christ.

Though Brad could not attend church during his recovery process, he was a mainstay on the church prayer list. Hundreds, if not thousands, were praying for him and for Ellen. But Brad wasn't praying. He hadn't chucked more than a few short and uninspired prayers heavenward since his injury. He continued the pre-injury narrative of spiritual dormancy. True, he had concluded that the three-week period following his injury was "not his call" and that he was "in the hands of the Almighty," but Brad still had mental barriers to overcome before he could move forward in his walk with the Lord. In other words, his mind wasn't ready to accept what the Spirit was telling him because he was tormented by bitterness and rage stemming from his childhood—ungentle, worldly strongholds of which he was unable or unwilling to free himself.

Brad had not sought out grace. Grace came to him when God extended the initial invitation to salvation. His sanctification journey had been jagged, inharmonious. Now, screw-by-screw, God was loosening the armor. A friend's kindness here. A Bible verse there. A quote by Oswald Chambers affixed to his wheelchair that read, "Before God can use a man greatly he must wound him deeply." Not to mention the prayers. Ellen had displayed an unflagging faith through the stint in ICU, through Lakeshore, and through Brad's brimstone autumn, when every morning, she prayed for a change of heart. She would often wake up early for 5:00 a.m. quiet time. Although it may seem, to some, too convenient to attribute the changes to prayer, Ellen held fast to the concept that prayer was the main catalyst for change in Brad Hawley.

Before Brad could put on the full armor of God, however, he had to be stripped of the armor of man. It was a fierce, secular armor that he had built: the belt of worldly success, the breastplate of invulnerability, the helmet of pride, the shield of proving, and the sword of control. By concentrating on hardening his exterior, Brad had failed to realize how greatly he had hardened his interior. "For about a two-to-four-year period when I was in college, right after I had the fallout with my mom, I gradually became harder, more stone-like," Brad remembers. "I thought that's what I was meant to be. I wanted to be a being who stood out and protected my family from the incoming assault of the world. The Fall was the pivotal moment, the point that began my transition. For so long, I had tried to harden, harden, harden myself. I hardened myself as a father. I was a strict disciplinarian with no compassion. I think it filtered in big time in how I interacted with Christ."

In her letter to Brad on the plane, it was clear that Ellen wanted Brad to be the "spiritual leader" of the household, but it was not something Brad felt the need to seize on his own. "When I would talk about him being the spiritual head of the household, he'd get really angry. Sort of 'judgy' toward that. It made his blood boil," Ellen said.

Ellen would continue to intimate to Brad that she wanted him to "step up" and assume those duties, even though in the months of October, November, and December, the relationship was treacherous.

So Ellen prayed with the kids at night while Brad quietly recused himself. Ellen rose early to have prayer. Ellen shared Bible verses with Brad.

The Fall of Brad Hawley

It was true: Brad wanted the title of breadwinner. He wanted the role of protector. He wanted the role of "family workhorse." He wanted to provide the security of the white-picket-fence life. He wanted to project the image of stability and wealth. Yet the responsibility of "spiritual head of the household" was, at the time and in Brad's mind, a load too great to bear. With that noble badge came tremendous responsibility, a responsibility that Brad was not comfortable handling. But this would slowly change.

"I didn't want to assume the responsibilities," Brad said. "I went to Mass, but I didn't want to assume the image of a Christian. I was scared to. I was scared to be under a microscope. You know, I think individuals who claim to be Christians can be intimidated. Intimidated by openly being a Christian. I think they think you have to be a Bible scholar and always have to reference Scripture. They are scared to pray in front of people. They are scared of making a mistake as a Christian and someone else seeing them sin. I think that's why so many people fall away from the faith, and maybe that's why I had a lackluster faith before I fell."

The physical recovery was absolute. Brad's body was recovering at a faster pace than his spiritual life was growing. As his health improved, varying groups throughout Birmingham became interested in his story and requested him as a public speaker. The first such opportunity arrived when he was asked to address an organization with which he was already involved. With the help of Ellen, Brad addressed the Phoenix Club at a December gala held at Avondale Brewery, a massive indoor-outdoor pub located in an up-and-coming section of downtown Birmingham that lures young business professionals with music and craft beer. At the time of the Fall, Brad was the sitting president of the club, but, because of his incapacitation, several of the board members stepped up to manage the club in his absence.

The morning of the speech, Brad reached another physical landmark. He was finally able to put his pants on, one leg at a time. "I remember it well because it was momentous," Brad said. "I cried, alone in my bathroom. I had to hold on to the counter, but I was able to lift one leg at a time and put on my pants." Perhaps this vignette would fit nicely into his speech, Brad thought.

Getting to the party proved to be an ordeal. First, Brad had to get dressed in business casual attire. Sport coat and slacks. He was still getting used to his clothes, once tailored but now baggy from the atrophy of TBI. Then there was the impending question regarding use of the walker. Take it? Leave it at home? After a short discussion, Brad decided to skip it for this event.

Because of the painstaking exercise of getting ready, Brad and Ellen arrived at the event fashionably late. To get to the second floor of the facility, Brad had to negotiate a tall outside stairwell. Not an easy task for a TBI survivor of Brad's caliber. Already there were dozens of members and their dates partaking in cocktails, dancing, and chitchatting in the upstairs portion of the brewery. "Everyone was carefree and imbibing, and I was struggling to even get up there," Brad recalled. "Ellen had to help me a lot."

With Ellen holding Brad tightly by the arm, Brad toured the party, shaking hands and chin-wagging with several of his old buddies. It felt good to be back. Felt good to be the center of attention. Like someone might describe a famous football coach or Hollywood star, Brad's presence seemed to take all the oxygen out of the room.

After a period of socializing, executive vice president Clay Segrest walked to the front and, grabbing the microphone, calmed the crowd and the band. Segrest thanked everyone for coming, gave a few opening remarks, and asked if Brad wouldn't mind saying a few words. Silence took over the room as all eyes shot in Brad and Ellen's direction.

The crowd parted as Ellen helped Brad to the stage. It was a tense few seconds. Most everyone in the room knew about Brad's fall. For those who didn't, the phrase "He's the guy who fell and hit his head at the gym" was whispered into his or her ear. Brad hobbled up to the microphone with the respect and gait of an old man who had one last important thing to say before he went to glory. Seeing Brad being helped to the stage by his wife was indeed an emotional moment for the large crowd, as many found themselves choked up and misty eyed.

Brad clutched the microphone and told the crowd, now fiercely attentive, he was glad to be back and was glad to see that nothing had skipped a beat while he was away with injury. He did not do this in a patronizing manner. He was truly glad that the men had rallied to ensure the club perpetuated. Then he pivoted and went into an emotional spiel about how often people tend to take specific things in life for granted. He pointed out the ability to drive to the event, to laugh with friends, to put pants on, one leg at a time. He shared the story of that morning. The major victory of being able to dress himself.

When Brad finished speaking, silence gripped the audience as he scanned the room bashfully. Many of the women mopped tears from their eyes. The men swallowed hard, fighting off emotion. Then, after a momentary pause, the crowd erupted in thunderous applause. It was heartsease.

Dozens of the members and their dates wanted pictures afterward, and Brad gladly consented. To raise money for Brad's family during their time of crisis, the board sold Brad Hawley T-shirts with the Phoenix Club logo stretched out across the back. "Every board member went around the party with a sign-up sheet, and most everyone bought a shirt," Brad said. "It was emotional because it was what I considered an intimate group. A group of guys who obviously cared about me. It was my first taste of 'Wow. This story can be an inspiration to a lot of people.'"

January proved to be a big month in terms of physical progress. Brad would shed the walker, but a delicate hobble would be present for a great while before he achieved the milestone of a flawless walk.

He also bridged the ecclesiastical gulf that January when he returned to church for the first time in five months. "In January, I went back," Brad said. "I remember during Mass that they would always pray for the sick. I was on the Prayers for the Sick list for a long time, but I never heard my name because I didn't go to Mass. They used to say my name. My name used to be said in this parish. And then they'd pray for the dead.

"I never made that list. I will one day, but not yet," Brad says, wagging a finger.

By February, Brad was "running" and working out again. Not at Steel Company, but rather at the Lakeshore Foundation, a bustling, for-ty-five-acre rehabilitation venue cloistered on a tree-proud campus in the heart of Homewood. Lakeshore (not to be confused with Lakeshore Hospital) is a foundation whose mission is to assist "people with physi-cal disability and chronic health conditions," and campus landmarks included an aquatic center, climbing wall, marksmanship range, three basketball courts, and a massive six-thousand-square-foot fitness cen-ter. Lakeshore also boasts a two-hundred-meter Mondo surface track, where great-spirited senior citizens—wearing white Rockport tennies and creased trousers—circumnavigate the track.

Brad was still relying on Ellen for transport. Most of the time, she was the driver who dropped him off at Lakeshore. When she was un-able to take him home, Brad filled out a sign-up sheet for individuals to pick him up. This list included many of his fellow Steel Companyers, in-cluding Caine Hill, Clint DeShazo, Stephen Ogletree, and Clay Conner. Ellen's mom, Gail, often helped to coordinate the chauffeuring.

One day in February while working out at Lakeshore, Brad chal-lenged Webb to a race. Brad thought he had recovered to the extent that victory over his son was a mere formality. After all, he was once one of the top runners in the state.

"I thought there was no way I would lose," Brad said. "It was meant to be a confidence booster."

Webb won.

"And I tried," Brad said. "It made me feel inadequate. I thought, 'Holy Crap! I've got a long way to go.'"

Brad's weekly routine included lifting light weights in the weight room at Lakeshore and his three-day-a-week appointment at Eskridge & White, physical therapists. Brad quietly plotted to get back to Steel

Company and pushed himself with that lofty goal in mind. He was slowly gaining his weight back, his musculature, but he was nowhere near the bulging beefsteak that had strutted through the doors at Steel Company. Brad says he wanted to "jump right back on the mountain," and that was precisely what he tried to do in the weight room. "He would fall trying to lift weights," Ellen said, "and yell at anyone who tried to stop him. He has such intensity when he works out. It's like he can't do anything halfway. It's like he's always trying to prove something."

As weeks went by, vacations became possible again. Soon Brad, Ellen, and the kids took a trip to the happiest place on the planet: Walt Disney World. Ellen's dad had a work convention in Orlando at Disney World, and it was an event he was able to parlay into a family retreat. Ellen's sister and her family, along with Ellen's brother and his wife, were all invited on the trip. Webb loved his cousins, so a trip to Disney with them was a dream come true. Sharon and Tom were also invited to drive over from Tampa and join them.

On paper, it appeared to be a splendid family gathering, utopian in nature. One would have predicted that virtually nothing could disrupt the fun and cartoonish pageantry experienced with close family and a cluster of curious, Disney-besotted tykes. Ellen remembers the trip as a disaster, however. "It was terrible," she admits. "Brad was still a tightly wound ball of anger."

At first, it seemed as though the trip would work out fine. To make circulating the park a bit easier, Brad secured a handicap park pass that allowed them to go to the front of all the lines. It was a godsend, as Brad would not have been able to stand up for long periods of time. This was the one bright spot of the trip. Ellen describes the bleak atmosphere: "Brad was controlling and difficult during the entire trip. He didn't care what Webb wanted to do, only about himself. One morning, I planned to meet my sister and her family early so we could arrive at the park by nine o'clock to watch Mickey 'unlock' the gates. I got up early with Webb and packed the stroller with the supplies for the day—snacks, water, and jackets. Brad started yelling as I was leaving with Webb. He told me I couldn't go. I had to wait for him. I told him we had already made plans and reminded him that he had been on board with the plan the night before. Moments later he came downstairs and took the stroller from me as I was trying to go to the bus to meet my sister. I was furious. Webb and I went down to the bus with no supplies or stroller for the day."

Ellen fought back tears as she discussed the situation with her brother-in-law, John, who said, "It's hard to tell if that is just Brad being Brad or if it's the brain injury."

It's tough to ruin Disney, but somehow Brad managed to do just that.

Although there were lucid, joyful moments—the Phoenix Club gala, the swallow test, and the miracle of singular vision—a general narrative of misery occupied those first few months. *Will this ever cease?* Ellen thought. Could the malcontents ever fully repair their once-harmonious relationship, or would this stage continue in perpetuity? Brad was slowly letting his emotional guard down, but the outbursts were difficult to bear. As Ellen's patience continued to wear thin, she had to bear down in her prayer life just to get through each day. Many less committed individuals would have already checked out, but Ellen remained steadfast in her resolve to remain by Brad's side.

One option was increasing his prescription medication. But this was not the preferred option. Since ICU, Brad had been chewing a mixed bag of seventeen drugs. Ellen prepared cocktails every morning. That spring, Brad was re-prescribed Zoloft, an antidepressant administered during his stay in Lakeshore. Ellen says that Brad unilaterally decided to seek help when his anger bled over into public life. "Brad made the decision on his own," Ellen says. "Once he saw that it was affecting his reaction to people outside of his family, he realized it was an issue."

Brad had a chemical imbalance, and the medicine helped tremendously. "It helped him to better process things and, I think, recognize who he wanted to be," Ellen said. "Before he started taking medicine, he was angry but couldn't control the way he responded."

The Fall of Brad Hawley

By May, Ellen began to notice a small change. She attributes the "softening," in large part, to the medication. "May was when I saw that he was releasing anger. That was when I think the change started. That summer, he started to get better. And after about a year, he started slowly transforming."

But Zoloft didn't address the root of the issue. Zoloft was a temporary fix. A coping mechanism. Patchwork resolution wasn't enough for the long-term. Brad needed an eternal fix. The real transformative agents, the Hawley family believes, were small gestures wrapped in grace and the superior power of prayer. "The armor had not been completely stripped off by May, but by then I was accepting emotion," Brad reflects. "I was showing more compassion for Ellen. I started moving from Brad, Brad, Brad to *wow—this must be hard on Ellen.*"

One of the seemingly small things Brad did to appease the situation was to become a spiritual participant. No longer standing on the fringes, he inserted himself into family prayer time as the kids went to bed. Ellen took notice. "When the kids and I used to have prayer, Brad wouldn't be there," Ellen said. "After a while, sometimes he'd show up."

Webb and Marlen slept side by side in twin beds, in a toy-strewed room upstairs. As Ellen tucked them in every night, she would lead them in a now-I-lay-me-down-to-sleep-type prayer. Webb would often pray for the "whole world," while little Marlen offered prayers for such things as the ceiling fan and teddy bears. Over time, Brad's presence became more frequent at this beatific nightly phenomenon. He began to realize the importance of laying prayer as the bedrock for his children's lives and that he needed to be the superintendent of that project.

The simple act of praying with his family helped Brad to release many of the burdens that had been weighing him down for so long. Not only did it make an impact on his children and wife, it made an impact on him. It brought his family together more tightly. It seemed as though their souls were becoming intertwined, that the family was connected now in a sublime, cosmic way that transcended anything this lowly earth had to offer. Just a moment or two of spiritual activity every day had profound effects. "It was a big step when I started praying with my family," Brad said. "Generally, I came to the realization I needed to be the Christian leader of the household. I had been selfish and focused on nonspiritual things. I desired to have a profound spiritual moment, even for five minutes, with my family."

This was embryonic, mustard-seed faith at its purest. The slow transformation began with steps like these. Accepting intimacy. Valuing familial communiqués with the Almighty. Admitting grace when it knocked on the doors of his soul. If near strangers could pray with him, certainly he could pray with his own family.

Not only did the infrequency diminish but also over time Brad's bedtime prayers also slowly matured. As Brad gained more clout during prayer time, he insisted that he wanted the family prayer time to be more "substantive" and less childlike. "I could tell a difference in the way he was praying. And he wouldn't let the kids skip it," Ellen said.

Brad began to pray before meals too. As the family gathered around the dinner table, they joined hands and recited Catholic grace: "Bless us, O Lord, and these, Thy gifts, which we are about to receive from Thy bounty. Through Christ, our Lord. Amen."

Then he would lead the family in song:

God our Father,
God our Father,
We thank you.

One thing Brad had learned in the midst of his ordeal was to be thankful for life. Through this awareness, Brad gained a deep appreciation for the small, everyday blessings to which he had once been blind. "Even though the kids don't get it right now, I want them to understand as I understand. We need to thank God for the blessings we have. The physical ability to play, to attend a good church, that we have the resources to buy food, and that we have love among one another," Brad says.

The Fall of Brad Hawley

By being shoved onto the ledge of death, Brad's humanness and morality became palpable. Through this, he began to appreciate the precious commodity of time. "We pray for the time we have, however long that's meant to be."

Brad's mind sluggishly began to cede strength to God. But deprogramming from a two-decade mind-set in which the Church of Self ruled wouldn't be easy. The Fall would shift his mind-set from self-reliance to God-reliance. Through the injury, he realized his frailty. Through the recovery, he would eventually succumb to the understanding of his desperate need for God in his life. That he wasn't strong enough to walk through life's valleys alone. That his strength was limited. That there were situations he couldn't handle. That life throws us circumstances and trials for which we don't possess enough fortitude.

"He is constantly transforming as a person," Ellen allows. "He understands more who he is, what makes him tick, and that he needs something higher than himself. All you can do is continually try to better yourself. Before, he didn't even have that desire. He has the same personality, and he's still the same person. He's still driven and quick to anger. But he catches himself. He's more aware of his flaws and struggles. He began to change the way he responds to other people. He began to second-guess before he spouts off. He's the same person but with a different focus. His transformation took time, and it got worse before it got better."

Throughout his life, Brad had always been good at running. Running had become a habit in both his physical and personal life. Now, by being taken to the threshold of death, by losing his functional abilities, Brad was forced to learn to walk again. The irony in it all was that Brad was learning to walk both physically and spiritually.

In terms of the latter, the Fall exposed how truly out of shape he was. It simply took a long while for that thought to matter to him.

If I Would Have Died

*I*f I had died—it's actually a very weird thought. I would be pretty disappointed in my Christian leadership. Disappointed in my faith. What I should have been doing. I should have been leading my family. I had a tremendous responsibility as the head of the household.

I was not pointing my family in the direction of Christ.

I was into simple, worldly things. I didn't push to get ready to go to Mass. I would hesitate to pray. Aloud. At dinner. At night. I was a leader in everything else. At Auburn, I was a leader. On the surface. In the community, I stood above. But in the most important duty, I didn't do it.

I put too much importance on—"health" is too general a word. How we fed the kids. I made idols and gods of the wrong things.

If I had died, I'd have looked down on myself and thought, "How ridiculous. I had this opportunity to lead my family the way it should be led, but I didn't."

Through all of this, I had a hard perspective shift. Before the injury, I wasn't upset if we missed church, if we missed the tithe, and if we didn't pray. Really, Ellen was the catalyst. She'd get us all ready for eleven-o'clock Mass. I'd get ready and go. Sometimes, I'd make excuses that the kids weren't getting anything out of it, and having to deal with their unruliness was very hard. I would think, "What's the point? They don't understand it."

Now I realize that if Christ died on the cross for us, then I can deal with that stress for an hour. I have a very different way of thinking now. And even though they don't understand it, I think it is so important for them to grow up around the environment of the church. It just sets the proper foundation, and one day, they'll get it.

The Fall of Brad Hawley

You know, sometimes I hear people say, "God is good," and I always stop and think about that. I wonder sometimes if we just say that because it sounds good. People say, "I'm praying for you," and I wonder sometimes if we just say it because it sounds good. Sometimes I want to say, "Are you really praying for that person? Do you really think God is good?"

If I say that I'm going to pray for someone, I try to set a time that night and actually do it. Follow through with it. I don't want to just give it lip service.

I am so, so fortunate to end up with my wife and kids. To live in a beautiful place. I was so close to it not being this way because of my stupid errors. I dismissed a lot of what happened in my life. I was so casual. But then this intense, severe thing changed my life. I had to be broken. God let it go as far as He could and said, "I gotta do this to change this kid." But I also believe I was spared. I've got a sense of purpose now.

God really is good, and it goes much deeper than just saying this.

VEGAS

Las Vegas, Nevada. November 2014. Two years and two months after The Fall.

Pyrotechnics rocketed into the air in beautiful, angry columns as thousands of anxious contenders huddled below a purple banner that read THE ROCK 'N' ROLL VEGAS MARATHON. Branded as an opportunity to "Run the Las Vegas Strip at Night," the race is the only private event that has been granted authority to shut down the hallowed turf where millions of visitors descend yearly to drink, gamble, and participate in activities bound by geography—"What happens in Vegas *stays* in Vegas," the famed city advertises. Inside the mass of people scrunching toward the starting gate, there were some spectacular costumes: female runners clad in cute tutus, male outfits ranging from Elvis to Batman. And somewhere, in the horde of humanity, a speck among ten thousand specks, Brad Hawley waited nervously to begin the race and for the punishment that would be meted out over the next thirteen-plus miles.

For over two years, it had been a dream. A far-off world where his hopes were set. Even before Brad had scribbled "Vegas" on a piece of paper in ICU, he had dreamed of competing in the Vegas half marathon. And now, after a slow recovery process, Vegas had become more to him than just fantasy. Vegas was an end, a conclusion. In Vegas, Brad wanted to put a period at the end of the most onerous chapter of his life.

The Fall of Brad Hawley

Over two years had passed since that fateful event on August 27, and Brad had recovered to the extent that the only physical evidence of TBI was a finger-length scar on the back of his neck. He walked with an immaculate gait. He was working out again, full steam, in his driveway. He had gone back to work. But he needed more tangible confirmation that normalcy had been achieved.

Making the November trip to Vegas alongside Brad were friends Andrew Nix, Jamie Moncus, Joey Gomes and his wife, Lauren. And of course, Ellen. Nix, Gomes, and Ellen would compete in the race, as well as Brad, while Moncus and Lauren would cheer them on from the sidelines and provided aid when necessary.

They boarded a flight on a Saturday morning in Birmingham, the six of them studying the flyover stills as the plane nosed its way through the clouds to Vegas. The race would occur on Sunday, but Brad wanted time to "settle in" and get his bearings without having to rush.

Months of training had been required before Brad was ready to compete. In anticipation for the event, he and Ellen ran through their neighborhood four times a week, negotiating the slopes and hills, the straightaways, slowly and systematically increasing their stamina until they built up to a thirteen-mile standard of roadwork. "I trained pretty hard for it," Brad admits. "During the three to four months of hard training, Ellen was very good about not giving me slack on long runs."

In the driveway, Brad had graduated now from light weights to heavier weights, and on the streets from choppy run/jog/walks to distance running. He had even begun CrossFitting again—this time, with a partner, Ben. Together, Brad and Ben programmed the workouts. When it came down to it, Brad preferred the CrossFit model of exercise—quick, hard, and tiring—and began to tailor many of the exercises he had once learned to his own routine, using them as a foundation for his programming.

He would never return to Steel Company again.

Working out was not without issue. The initial point of concern was that Brad could not hit his head again, and it took a while for Ellen to convince him that he needed to use extra caution while working out. He omitted exercises he felt were inherently dangerous: snatch, rope climbs, and of course, toes to bar. Caution didn't always sink in. Brad could be as bullheaded as ever.

From a motor standpoint, the struggle for Brad was maneuvering his left leg. Every day as he ran, his leg dragged the ground. "I could not get my brain to work," Brad recalled, as if capable of some kind of mental sorcery. "I was extremely fit, but I could not get my brain to move that stupid leg." Therefore, on difficult training runs, Brad experienced emotion as he dragged his foot along the asphalt streets.

Still, he held out hope. Though he would never be the same again, Brad realized that physically, this was the end of the recuperation process. Brad might not be able to run a subminute quarter mile, clean 225 pounds, or perform toes to bar, but he wasn't incapacitated either. Brad felt that getting back to a place where he could enjoy physical activities as he once did was a victory in itself, but his competitive spirit continued to rage within. Brad's original goal was to run the Vegas half marathon in two hours. He felt that two hours was a plausible goal for the race, and if he could maintain an eight-minute clip, he'd have the 13.1 miles licked in under two hours.

For Brad, Vegas was more than just a race. Vegas was a symbol.

BRAD GOT OFF THE PLANE AND SMELLED DESERT. Arriving at the Mandalay Bay Hotel and Casino on Saturday, Brad and his pack checked in at the front desk and fanned out to their respective rooms. In the spacious suite, Brad tossed his bag aside, flung open the curtains, and for a moment, drank in the picturesque view. The reality of the moment began to set in as Brad scanned the skyline, his wife coming up behind him now and throwing her arms around him.

Since the race was Sunday night, the group had time to attend the Health and Fitness Expo that was a prelude to the event. Located at the Las Vegas Convention Center, the expo offered eighty exhibitors vending their wares: sample running gear, apparel, and other items related to the health and fitness genre. Runners were required to visit the expo to receive their bib number, T-shirt, and check bag. After touring the expo for several hours, the group decided to turn in early instead of catching dinner or a show. Vegas could be Vegas tomorrow.

On Sunday morning, the group enjoyed time at the hotel pool and played a few hands of blackjack before channeling their focus on the 4:30 p.m. event. Back in the hotel room, Brad unpacked his bag and pulled out his specifically chosen, symbolic running gear. In the year 2000, he participated in the New York City Marathon, and prior to the event, then-Auburn athletic director David Housel had given him an Auburn track jersey. He thought this outfit would add a bit of nostalgia to the race in Vegas, and as he packed his attire back in Birmingham, neatly folding it into his suitcase as though a treasure, he pondered these things.

Now in the hotel, Brad took the jersey out of his bag, laid it across his bed, and stared at it in a private moment of personal reflection. For just a moment, those old track memories came flooding back. He thought about the kid he had been and the man he'd become. He thought about the many things that had happened since his days in Cullman. He thought about Auburn. He thought about his kids. He thought about The Fall and how God had resurrected him from that hospital bed, allowed him to convalesce in his own home, gave him strength to fight for his physical survival, saved his family, taught him lessons he would hold the rest of his life, and demonstrated remarkable mercy, grace, and majesty throughout the past two years.

Then he looked across the room and saw his wife.

The race was to commence directly in front of the hotel, at the corner of Las Vegas Boulevard and Dewey Drive. The group met at three thirty, gathering downstairs in the opulent lobby. If Brad's friends had failed to understand the kind of emotional meaning this race had for Brad, they understood now. Brad and Ellen brought strands of two of the green bows that had been affixed to the neighborhood mailboxes when Brad was in ICU and tied them to their wrists as symbols and inspiration for the run.

The race began, and Brad took the first seven or eight miles in stride, reveling in the dramatic purple, blue, and green enticements of Las Vegas. He passed by the Luxor, the Excalibur, the Tropicana, the MGM Grand, the Bellagio, Harrah's, the Venetian, the Stardust on the Strip, and the Stratosphere Tower. The left leg was holding up, and he was maintaining an eight-minute mile.

About halfway through the race, Brad had to stop to go to the bathroom—"you can't drop your pants on the Strip"—and searched for the nearest port-o-potty to relieve himself. Emerging from that plastic latrine, Brad taxied back onto the street but realized his left leg had stiffened in the short time he'd been in the outhouse. "From getting cold," Brad said. "I was good up until I had to use the bathroom. Then my time went way down."

Feeling sorry for himself, Brad began to play the victim card like patrons playing the game of hearts nearby. "Oh God, I'm not going to make it in two hours!" he mumbled to himself. His time increasing dramatically, from an eight-minute-mile average to around a fourteen-minute average, Brad was crestfallen. He felt he had failed.

But then he believes God sent him a series of rapid messages in the form of people, making him rethink his overall attitude toward the race. "I'm not kidding; a hundred yards after I had that thought, I came up on a double amputee," Brad said, "and a hundred yards after that, I came up on somebody on a scooter with a broken leg. They were pushing that scooter through the whole half marathon. I thought, 'I'm not that bad. OK. I get it. Look at me; I'm on two feet. It might not be pretty, but I'm running it. And I am going to finish it.' It was almost like they were placed right in my path to pick my spirits up."

The goal shifting to simply finishing the race, Brad realized now how miraculous it was that he was even running it. "I went from 'run this thing fast' to 'just finish.' Before, I was only going to be happy if I did it in two hours. Now I would be happy if I just finished it."

Ellen and Joey had been trailing just behind Brad, and around the ten-mile mark, Ellen pulled up even. "Come on, B," Ellen said between hard breaths. Encouraged by Ellen, Brad began slapping his left leg like a jockey whipping a thoroughbred, yelling, "Go! Go!"

Sensing that Ellen was slowing down in sympathy, Brad said, "Don't you slow down and wait on me!" It was a conciliatory gesture, but Brad didn't really mean it. He didn't *really* want Ellen to pass. "So she takes off!" Brad, recalling the event, said incredulously, slapping his hands together to indicate the jolt in pace. "I mean, I was kidding! I might need help!"

Brad would need help. Two miles later, he tumbled into a guardrail, and a woman in the crowd helped him up. As Brad thanked her and dusted off the grit of the roadway, he was reminded once again of random acts of kindness during moments of peril. And he couldn't help but chuckle as he thought, *that should have been my wife!*

Perhaps the most emotional aspect of the race for Brad was Joey's bird-dogging of him throughout most of the race. Joey, as Brad describes, is a very serious and stoic individual, and took it upon himself to watch Brad throughout the entire race from the view of twenty yards to the rear. Joey had no aspirations in the race other than to make sure Brad was OK. "Joey is not an emotional or sappy guy, but he stayed behind, watching me, guarding me," Brad said. "Around mile sevenish, I realized that he'd been watching my back the whole time. It was touching."

The last mile, his leg still dragging, Brad grew anxious of the finish line. The crowd was gathering beside the road, and he could feel their cheers. Strangely, it was a different feeling than the unfettered elation he had felt in winning the high-school track meet in Hanceville when the boy dropped the baton. One hit off that drug was all it had taken for Brad to become an adrenaline junkie, and he had been chasing euphoria since that moment. He realized now that there was something better. He felt a peace, a joy wash over him. He felt a weight being lifted off his shoulders, a freedom that he no longer had to carry those burdens. Those emotions bore out into tears as he crossed the finish line, and Ellen was there waiting on him.

It was enough for Brad to be mobbed by an audience of one.

"You train for it and get to this certain level, and the whole time, there's doubt if you are going to get there. That was the weight," Brad said. "It was very much tied to the doubt, but the second, deeper component of the weight that I carried was that I was concerned that I would always be a shell of what I used to be. I'm not now. I did it."

Later that night, the group celebrated with a fine dinner. As a token of remembrance, Joey passed around an empty wine bottle; written on it was the word "RESURGENCE."

Everyone signed the bottle.

The next morning before going home, Brad tossed his right shoe in the trashcan and carried the left one home as a trophy. The toe of the shoe was threadbare from his foot dragging, and Brad had to shake out the rocks and grit before everyone signed it. "The shoe sits on my son's trophy shelf, and the wine bottle sits in my office as a daily reminder that God's messages come in many forms. In this case, it was a group of friends who showed me love. In Isaiah 41:13, God indicates, 'For I hold your right hand. Fear not, I am the one who helps you.'"

Reflectively, Brad realizes that he pushed too far. He understands that God created limits to life, not because He revels in controlling us or that He doesn't want us to have fun, but because there is danger in the extremes. We find our best selves by avoiding these calamities. God had been warning and warning Brad through minor injuries, but Brad had not been listening. It took a great fall for Brad to come to God, a rock-bottom moment. Applause was his drug.

"Why could I not have been at peace with just working out?" Brad reflects. "Hell, with toes to bar, why could I not just stop at thirty? That was better than a lot of folks. What made me push to do more? Was I trying to remold my outward identity to being something I really wasn't? I guess I was trying to become the number-one athlete at Steel Company. That was my checklist of identity. It's ridiculous to me now. I look back, and I want to be like 'Hey. Brad. Knucklehead. *Why?*'"

The Fall of Brad Hawley

Finding Brad Hawley would prove to be the toughest hurdle for Brad to overcome. Brad's struggle with answering the simple question, "Who am I?" led to years of consternation and the need to prove himself to others. Thus he elevated *self* and added plastic to his life. He realized he didn't have to control everything and everybody. That real strength is sometimes found by losing our grip. He tied his identity and self-worth to things, but God eventually led him to the understanding that he didn't need all of that to have peace in his life.

All he needed was the recognition that Brad Hawley was OK just the way he was: true, unencumbered, organic, and natural. He didn't need to be processed by worldly things or to add anything cosmetic to his life.

He simply needed to embrace the bright and great man whom God created and fall backward into the arms of the Almighty.

Epilogue

Confession

I have friends, though, who believe they are good men and good husbands because they have large muscles and keep their wives amply supplied with expensive clothes and vacations. I have friends who believe they are good because their wives are "allowed" to work outside the home. I have friends who believe they are good because they do not beat their wives as their fathers did. I have friends who believe they are good because they feel deep affection for their wives and spend quality time with them every day. I know one man who thinks he is a good man because he lets his wife take other men for lovers. Each of these men thinks himself good by some definition. Each has a system of belief that defines for him what it means to be a man. You see the problem? What definition of good and of manhood should we live by? I believe it ought to be God's definition as found in Scripture and the teachings of Jesus.

—STEPHEN MANSFIELD, *MANSFIELD'S BOOK OF MANLY MEN*

In June 2014, a tall, fidgety man sat in a hipster coffee shop in Birmingham, Alabama, legs crossed, sipping a dark roast sweetened with too much cream and Splenda, waiting for Brad Hawley. He thumped the keys of a freshly purchased MacBook Air and checked some e-mails to kill the time.

Where is this guy? he thought as he shook out the last drop of coffee, the warm beverage hitting the back of his throat. He scanned the room, where bespectacled, black-bearded, flannel-shirted men genuflected to computer screens. They were wearing headphones, and no one was talking.

He checked the parking lot. No movement.

Nine fifty-three.

It had been twenty-six minutes since the last text he had received from Brad: "Running a little behind. In a meeting. Sorry."

Brad had agreed to meet with him at nine o'clock that morning, but he was running almost an hour late. Customarily, the man would have left fifteen or so minutes after the appointment failed to arrive, but something told him to wait.

Around ten o'clock, Brad stumbled in and introduced himself. "Sorry I'm late," Brad said. "I got caught up in a meeting."

Always the fastidious dresser, Brad wore a tight, bicep-friendly golf shirt, khaki trousers, designer socks, and cap-toe oxfords. He was a good-looking guy. He was sharp, pleasant, well spoken, and ready to unload his story.

The man, typically annoyed by even the slightest truancy, deduced that Brad at least presented himself like someone who could be taken seriously. And because a mutual friend who felt that the two men "needed to talk had paired them" there was an undercurrent of obligation for the get-together. Not to mention that the man knew Brad had experienced a head injury, and there was no telling how that might have affected his overall sense of time, memory, or punctuality. So perhaps a bit of discretion and leeway was justified.

Almost two years earlier, Brad and the man had been invited to the same Christmas party at the home of a mutual friend. They did not meet that night, but the host mentioned Brad's fall to the man and how he had almost killed himself at the gym. Brad was still gimpy and it was clear that he was far from fully recovered. The other guests looked at Brad sympathetically, as did the man. He kept that image in the back of his mind as he waited for Brad in the coffee shop.

When the conversation started, any thoughts of exasperation over Brad's tardiness soon evaporated. The man was enrapt by Brad's tale.

Brad shared with him the bones of his story. He talked about the events surrounding the Fall. He talked about the subsequent recovery. He talked about Steel Company. Everything was superficial, but the man left the meeting with the impression that Brad was a walking miracle. As Brad walked away, the man caught a glimpse of the finger-length scar on the base of Brad's closely cropped head. He thought it unbelievable that Brad was walking expertly, without assistance. He stood amazed at how there was not a whit of evidence, save the scar, that Brad had even *had* an injury. He wanted to learn more. And Brad needed to tell more.

From the beginning, it was clear that this was Brad's story, that he was the protagonist, and that this story would be postured in terms of physical recovery. That, in itself, was enough, the man concluded. But after the meeting, as the story began to unravel, both the man and Brad understood that this was not Brad's story at all. This was God's story, as told through the life of Brad Hawley.

What started as a secular tale began to unspool into a story with intense spiritual conflict with God as the central figure. Had Brad not possessed enough spiritual underpinning, he could have easily viewed God as the villain. Brad might have posed the most challenging question in the universe: Why would a good God allow bad things to happen?

Although he didn't realize it at the time, Brad's confessions to this man both then and over the next two years would have an intense impact on Brad's spiritual life and would help him to overcome the obstacles that had been plaguing him since Sharon walked out the door so long ago.

At that initial meeting, the two men planned to link up once a week in order for Brad to get these things off his chest. So they met at local coffeehouses, and across the steam of warm beverages, talked about life. As they continued to meet, Brad began to understand that his problems ran much, much deeper than he realized. Every encounter was like peeling back the layers of an onion. Pain and hurt were buried underneath the surface and would require more than light drilling through crust and mantle. This was a core-level job. A job that would require piercing questions and, in turn, courageous transparency from Brad. Transparency he wasn't sure he wanted to offer.

After a level of trust was built, Brad soon invited the man into his home and introduced him to Ellen and the kids. After a while, the two men would often retire to the dining room or the back deck to open up and get serious, Brad's story beginning to unfurl. Brad slowly began to twist off the top of his life so that the built-up, potent vapor could escape. There were many long, heartfelt, gut-wrenching conversations between the two men. They were becoming close friends, and the man was able to see the real Brad, without pretense or having to prove himself. Brad stripped away all the guards, all the armor, all the worldly lies about men telling you not to be vulnerable.

One night while they were sitting outside at a coffee shop, the dark skies overhead and streetlights spraying their light, they decided to take a walk through the shadowy streets of Mountain Brook. As they talked and walked, it seemed that a force was magnetically pulling them in the direction of Steel Company. They walked over to the glass doors and pressed their faces close to the glass.

I once knew Brad Hawley.

On another occasion, they met at Trinity Medical Center and retraced Brad's steps through the ICU. They even talked to a couple of nurses who had taken care of Brad. Of course we remember him, they said.

Brad shared with him the very intimate details of his childhood, his college years, and his marriage. He let him into his interesting and happily twisted world, into the emotional spaces where no other man had previously had access. And perhaps, where no one else dared to go. What had started as simple storytelling evolved into full-blown catharsis.

That fall, Brad invited the man to a weekend getaway at Lake Martin, to Milton and Gail's lake home. Ellen, the kids, and two other families would arrive the next day, so this allowed Brad and the man some quality time to reflect on Brad's life and his story. The first night, Brad and the man dined at Willow Point, a local country club, and Brad allowed more of his tale to unravel underneath a black sky freckled with stars. The highlight of their trip, however, was taking the pontoon boat out for a chilly ride across the windswept lake that Saturday morning and Brad climbing a cliff and zooming into the water on a rope swing, no clumsier than Errol Flynn.

As the men shared life together, Brad continued to open up, allowing the man to probe deeper and deeper into the caverns of his mind. Shining truth into the dark places devoid of light. Brad became more transparent, reflective on his life. The man was able to share experiences he had had in his own life, oddly which mirrored Brad's. The two men began to feel a deep connection. It seemed as if they were walking and talking through all the muck. They felt that somehow, through divine appointment, their lives had converged at precisely the right moment.

As Brad continued to confess, he began to feel a sense of freedom and peace he had never experienced before. Just the simple act of talking and confessing had ramifications far beyond what he could have possibly envisioned. He began to release the heavy freight he had been hauling for many years. He became more introspective, more self-aware, and stronger. He looked inward for strength instead of outward, and it came, not through physical lifting, but rather his own admission of brokenness.

The man watched Brad transform into a more admirable father and husband. A stronger Christian. A gentleman. He jotted up notebooks with handwritten notes as he listened and continued to dig deeper as the months trudged on and their relationship grew closer. He noticed that the man Brad had become was walking further away, step by step, from the "old Brad" whom he vividly described and looked back upon with increasingly greater disgust. He watched Brad shed the unrelenting hubris and employ a God-first mentality to all of his affairs. He watched Brad embrace the mighty calling he had to impact others for Christ, where he would have previously shied away from such eternal feats. He watched Brad invite his mother back into his life and, finally, forgive her for walking out on him. He watched Brad attend fellowship groups at local churches. He watched Brad become more concerned with being fit for the cross instead of fit for a workout. He watched Brad start a small group with a friend. He watched Brad mute the lies of Satan, one by one, and choose the abundant life over his base self. He watched Brad celebrate life on Life Day—August 27—by performing the same WOD as he had the day of the Fall (minus toes to bar, of course). He watched Brad organize a water-balloon fight at his home. The teams were Brad and Marlen versus Ellen and Webb. He watched Brad clutch his children's hands and pray with them at the dinner table. He watched Brad drop his children off at school. He watched Brad put down alcohol because his body couldn't handle it. He watched Brad assemble a golf tournament for Webb's birthday. He watched Brad ingest a wide variety of books and become broader in the process. He watched Brad give an inspiring speech at the annual Anointing of the Sick Mass at his church. He watched Brad land his first job since the injury. He watched Brad coach his son's YMCA basketball team. He watched Brad complete the half marathon in Las Vegas in November of 2014. He watched as Brad and Ellen stole away for a four-night romantic getaway to sunny California. He watched an intact family, welded together like never before.

"He's a great dad now," Ellen says. "Before, he was a private person with his faith. But in the last few months, I've seen a transformation. We were just trying to survive and get through this thing. But as he began to deeply reflect on these three years, he began to think about what caused him to be the person who pushed so hard he almost killed himself and to analyze the person he was before the accident. He started changing his focus and putting God above himself. This process of talking it out has been therapeutic for him. It's helped him. It's helped our family."

In the summer of 2016, while sitting at a restaurant in Birmingham's English Village, the man asked Brad, "What is your testimony now?" Here is what Brad said:

I am consciously aware of opportunities that God gives me to impact people in my home and outside my home. I have submitted to the paths put down before me. I am aware, like most people, that I struggle with secular stimuli, the world and activities of the day. I'm consciously seeking God's Providence. I see things as providential, not happenstance. This includes big things like career opportunities and financial opportunities for the family. But it can happen with a person. Maybe it was providential that I ran into that person. I'm more aware now, much more conscious, very aware of how God impacts Ellen. Right now, Ellen is going through some health issues. I talk to God about that. When we pray at night, I pray that we are aware of opportunities to advance His kingdom. It doesn't always have to be this extremist, in-your-face Jesus moment, but moments that set the right example to advance His kingdom. You don't have to be a Bible banger; you can impact people by being who you are, being the man He created you to be. I absolutely believe it's real. Everything tells us to elevate self, beat our chest—our LinkedIn profiles and what can we post on FB to make us look successful and intelligent. But when I hit the ground, that was a breaking point. God has given me this gift, and I don't want to waste the second opportunity.

The man realized that he, too, was bettered by listening to Brad Hawley's story of death and redemption. Yes, there were many lessons to learn about the human condition through Brad's telling of his. The man was inspired by Brad's courage to face the most vulnerable details of his life.

He was deeply moved by Ellen's unflagging loyalty to her husband, her devotion to God, and Brad's Pilgrim's Progress journey back to embracing his true self.

Yes, he is a better man because Brad walked into his life in the summer of 2014. He is a better man for the three years he spent writing *The Fall of Brad Hawley*.

"I'm Al," I said as I greeted Brad at the coffee shop that first morning. "I'm glad you made it."

A Tribute

I t was the little things. Across several months, small-task servants assembled. Individuals led by the Holy Spirit to share the love of God with Brad Hawley. There was Peter Falkner, who said he was called to repave the Hawley's driveway. There was Andrew Nix: lawyer by day, champion foot rubber by night. There was Charlie Crabb, the Masked Medical Device Rep, who showed up at two o'clock in the morning on the second night after surgery. There was Ellen's sister Claire, who set up a meal calendar. There was Ashley Knight, who came to Lakeshore Rehab to offer prayer. Then there was the yard-raking Heath Buckner, who drove over from the outskirts of town when the Hawley's yard grew a beard of leaves that fall.

Brad, the recipient of such grace, witnessed these things in awe. For Brad, it was truly amazing how much the act of simply showing up affected him in such a profound way. "I remember Heath Buckner came to rake leaves, and we were sitting out back on the deck, and he said, 'Do you mind if I pray with you?' I was very moved by it," Brad reflects. "And then Ashley Knight. She showed up the day I was released from Lakeshore. We had a past working relationship, a couple of mutual connections, but very loose connections. She sat down, and we talked for a few minutes, and I said, 'So, are you here just visiting someone?' And she said, 'No. I came to see *you*.' Then she asked if she could pray with me. Ellen was in the room, and Ellen's mom. So Ashley knelt down beside my bed and grabbed my hand and prayed for me. It was almost like God was inserting these little moments into my life. He was chipping away at the armor."

When the injury occurred, friends and family were there round the clock, cobbling together many-tiered layers of support. When Ellen was low on energy, they offered prayers. When she needed a little wine—presto—they brought wine. When she was discouraged, they inserted kind words and comforting Bible verses into her life. They cleaned the house, babysat the kids, mowed the lawn, posted on CaringBridge, sent care packages, brought coffee, transported family members to and fro and everywhere in between, created thank-you lists, sent thank-you cards, listened, provided sounding boards, organized the ICU waiting room, brought blankets, got groceries, and prepared food.

Pride comes before the fall. But what happens after? In this case, friends rally. Love permeates.

Many stepped into roles previously unimaginable. Like water finding its channels, the current of friends ran to wherever there was need. None had minor roles. Every person who lifted a finger played a major part, and all were stars. In the case of Brad Hawley, it was small gestures that made all the difference. Small gifts wrapped in rapturous grace. Small things done with great love. Small prayers that touched the heavens and yoked his family in Christian harmony. Small but profound cleansing that purified the passageways of the vine of Christ.

The small things. Maybe it sounds cliché or even trite, but for Brad Hawley, there was nothing bigger.

After a while, of course, people go on with their lives. As many who have experienced tragedy will tell you, the initial deluge of support is eventually reduced to a slower stream, and then a drip. Regardless of the frequency or infrequency of the charitable actions of others, Brad was impacted nonetheless, and saw, for the first time perhaps, love without conditions.

A final thought

A lot can happen in seven feet.
In seven feet, you can break records. Or you could tumble into a white-hot romance.

Life can be profoundly changed in seven feet. You could lose your wife. Your kids.

Seven feet can paralyze. Seven feet can be deadly. Seven feet can kill you.

If you land on your head.

Brad Hawley's life was forever altered over the course of seven feet. Those seven feet from the bar to the floor. It was a mere seven-foot fall that killed him.

Does anything else matter when you fall? If you don't die, your only concerns are:

Did I break anything?
Am I hurt?
Have I lost something?
Did anyone see me?

Some falls are more severe than others. Harder. Some falls take months of hellish recovery. Some falls, you brush yourself off and you're on your merry way. Some falls are metaphorical and not literal.

Some are both.

Pride can lead us to a very dangerous place. It is a transgression so perilous that we often don't realize how close we are to falling, to losing everything. Of this, we are in constant danger.

The beauty of God is that, through the fall, we discover grace. God often brings us down in order to give us everything. To save us from our own self-destruction. God took Brad down to nothing to save his family. He stripped Brad of everything, wrung him out, and set him back on the hook so that Brad could realize his own desperate need for Christ. Brad was stripped of his dignity, his physical capabilities, and his coveted self-reliance. God exposed the frailty of the things Brad had put his faith in and the fleeting nature of idolatry.

Sometimes, all it takes is seven feet.

And sometimes, it's not how far the fall that really matters. It's what you fall into.

It is there, in these immortal events, that we rise, and walk, up from the craggy bottom surface, where we are free.

CPSIA information can be obtained
at www.ICGtesting.com
Printed in the USA
LVOW08s0725201217
560362LV00006B/1887/P

9 780692 790342